For Ann,
from i -
January 2012

Crime and Punishment

Crime and Punishment

A Concise Moral Critique

Hyman Gross

OXFORD
UNIVERSITY PRESS

OXFORD
UNIVERSITY PRESS

Great Clarendon Street, Oxford OX2 6DP

Oxford University Press is a department of the University of Oxford.
It furthers the University's objective of excellence in research, scholarship,
and education by publishing worldwide in

Oxford New York

Auckland Cape Town Dar es Salaam Hong Kong Karachi
Kuala Lumpur Madrid Melbourne Mexico City Nairobi
New Delhi Shanghai Taipei Toronto

With offices in

Argentina Austria Brazil Chile Czech Republic France Greece
Guatemala Hungary Italy Japan Poland Portugal Singapore
South Korea Switzerland Thailand Turkey Ukraine Vietnam

Oxford is a registered trade mark of Oxford University Press
in the UK and in certain other countries

Published in the United States
by Oxford University Press Inc., New York

British Library Cataloguing in Publication Data
Data available

Library of Congress Cataloging in Publication Data
Data available

Typeset by Newgen Imaging Systems (P) Ltd, Chennai, India
Printed and bound by
CPI Group (UK) Ltd, Croydon, CR0 4YY

ISBN 978-0-19-964471-1

10 9 8 7 6 5 4 3 2 1

For Joseph and Peter

Preface

In this book I revisit the fundamentals of criminal jurisprudence and suggest that, contrary to prevailing views, the criminal law and criminal justice are not enterprises to be carried on with moral enthusiasm in spite of the misery they produce. I also suggest that, while crimes may indeed be morally wrong, it is a source of mischief for theory and practice to deal with them as such under the law. Paradoxically, perhaps, only when free from moral infatuation can the criminal law and criminal justice appreciate and respect the very important restraints that an enlightened political morality places upon them.

The view I hope to encourage is one that is less smug, less self-righteous, less detached, and less chillingly vindictive about crime and punishment. There are numbers of villains, rogues, brutes, thugs, and sometimes even monsters in our prisons. But mainly our prisons are filled with socially battered, illiterate, drug-addicted, mentally deficient and mentally ill people whose unhappy condition is closely connected to the reason they have landed in prison. Recognizing the grim necessities of an awful business as the desperate expediency it is will check the ever-present tendencies we have to exploit crime and punishment for the satisfactions they provide to the least admirable side of our nature, and so will ease the way to enlightened reforms.

A composite of convenience that might be called the Anglo-American legal system is what I draw on for particular illustrations, though inevitably there will be elements in one place that are quite different from what are found in another. Moreover, though most points I make have a relevance in any society that deals with crime and punishment under a developed legal system, it would be foolish to suppose that in diverse political cultures and different legal systems these points will all have the same relevance. Particularly in Chapter 13, the discussion makes reference to issues and procedures that are familiar in the adversarial system of common law jurisdictions, but much less so, if at all, in the inquisitorial system of civil law countries.

At the outset I must confess uncertainty about the very concept of morality.★Whatever its distinguishing features may be, it seems to me that the only sure thing about morality is the ability it possesses to trump precepts and principles of any other kind whenever a conflict arises, though it is certainly true that in spite of its pre-eminence, morality often ends up taking a back seat when practical decisions must be made. In any case, it seems remarkable that while the concept of law has been a battlefield on which innumerable battles over countless issues have been fought, its complementary concept in jurisprudential wars—the concept of morality—has received scant attention. I am sorry to say my cursory requests for enlightenment among colleagues have not been fruitful, nor has my unsystematic rummaging in the literature been any more rewarding. And so I must rely throughout this book on what seem to me reliable intuitions about morality, consoled somewhat by Herbert Hart's reference to St Augustine's well-known dilemma about the notion of time when Hart embarked on his elucidation of the concept of law. "What then is time? If no one asks me I know: if I wish to explain it to one that asks I know not".*

I should mention one or two things that require the reader's indulgence.

The book is a critical essay, not a study. I try where possible to avoid those intriguing byways where alluring distractions would tend to weaken the effort to persuade on the main points. Many interesting opportunities for discussion of finer points have been passed over in order to avoid such distraction and to allow a picture to be sketched more swiftly with broader and simpler strokes. There are, however, some places where attention to more exacting detail was necessary to make clear some points of crucial importance. Throughout I have tried to adhere to Albert Einstein's rule that things should be made as simple as possible, but not any simpler than that.

To maintain a steady focus in the text I avoid explicit engagement with other authors. Only a very few names appear in the text, and reference to other work appears in the Notes and in Some Further References at the back of the book. This less prominent positioning should not be taken to indicate any lack of importance of such work for the development of my own views, and I cheerfully acknowledge that my efforts have benefited most from a consideration of those ideas with which I disagree most strongly.

Cambridge
June 2011

Contents

Introduction

Like the weather, crime and punishment is ever present and a topic of universal interest. Everyone is intrigued by crimes that make the news, and still more by those artful renditions of crime and its consequences that supply the publishing and entertainment industries with many of their best products. No one is immune to the fascination produced by serious departures from the straight and narrow, while truly bizarre excursions are likely to cast a magic spell. There are, as well, crimes of ingenuity and daring to seduce an envious audience that secretly longs for release from the safe and tedious life of good people who abide by the law.

When crimes are no more than recreational material, paying attention to the rights and wrongs that lie beneath the surface would spoil the fun. The imagination has been let off the leash, and a tiresome and tendentious lesson in morality is the last thing it wants. But when real crimes are still fresh, something more than passive interest is in evidence. Bringing whoever did it to justice is part of the story, but so is the audience's insistence that this must be done. Getting hold of whoever is guilty is the first order of business, and punishing him for what he has done must follow. The fun and the fascination have not entirely disappeared, but a darker mood creeps in, putting a more serious and more urgent complexion on what has happened and what must now be done.

When the wheels of criminal justice begin to turn, a new set of concerns emerge from the shadows. Guilt or innocence poses questions that go beyond whodunit. Crimes do not come ready-made for purposes of law enforcement, and in deciding what crime, if any, might have been committed, police and prosecutors must pay close attention to exactly what was done, in what circumstances, and with what outcome. In court, judges and juries examine the evidence not only to judge its reliability, but to consider just what its significance might be for the ultimate question of guilt or innocence. And for those who are found guilty, there is the question of what sort of sentence to pass, what its extent should be, and how it is to be served. Questions that seem to have something of a moral element in them now dominate crime and punishment. And while the public retains an interest in the highlights—apprehension, conviction, and punishment—it is bored, and often irritated, by the niceties that now must occupy the system.

How are these questions with a moral tinge to be dealt with? Mainly by resort to intuitions that we all share, but now guided by the conventions of the criminal process. It is the ability to make everyday assessments of those items of right and wrong conduct that transcend everyday matters of right and wrong, but with those assessments harnessed to a procedural system that does not permit arbitrary or idiosyncratic decisions to go unchallenged. The vast discretion at the heart of criminal justice depends on this arrangement to allow it the latitude it needs, while at the same time keeping its decisions in harmony with the conclusions that any reasonable person might be expected to reach.

However, far removed from the practical demands of police stations, courts, and prisons, more detached and more critical projects are carried on in universities, where ideas are valued mainly for their own sake and theories aim above all else to achieve the sort of intellectual merit that attracts recognition in the academic community. Fundamental questions that need never bother those who make and enforce the law are pursued, not for any practical benefit, but because they are regarded as important in their own right. It is not that influencing affairs in the great world is in any way despised. On the contrary, any suggestion of such a possibility is most welcome, and media opportunities do provide a kind of consolation for the meager influence that this sort of work exerts in the outside world. In the hermetic world of the academy, the principal vocational concern is development of theories that please the restive intellect, and so it is no surprise that they exert so little influence in meeting the practical needs of lawmakers and law enforcers. In academic work of this sort actual cases are much in evidence, though seldom to tie down and test theories in any rigorous way. And especially in America, there is the complementary phenomenon of distinguished academic works being cited in judicial opinions to provide intellectual ornamentation.

Law reviews now devote a great deal of space to articles by philosophers or lawyers with philosophical inclinations who discuss various issues of criminal jurisprudence that otherwise lie quietly at the foundations of a system of criminal law. At the same time, many articles of the same sort, though shorter and without voluminous footnotes, appear in philosophy journals. Part of the attraction for philosophers is the wealth of opportunities for conceptual analysis in contexts that seem

truly momentous. Traditional philosophical concerns about responsibility and punishment can be discussed in a more concrete form by reference to the goings-on in a legal system. In America work of this sort is
encouraged by the presence of philosophers on law faculties, where they
add intellectual scope to conventional legal education by discussing policy issues and conceptual problems in a less parochial way. Crime and
punishment appears in much of this work as a moral concern, with an
assumption that many of the difficulties at the roots of criminal justice
are to be resolved by a better understanding of the correct moral position. As I hope to make clear, this results in fundamental misconceptions
about crime and punishment, and has the unfortunate effect of giving
support to regressive tendencies in the public domain by encouraging
the belief that criminal justice is some sort of exercise in righteousness.

What I propose to undertake in the pages that follow is a voyage of
discovery, or perhaps more accurately, of rediscovery. It is *the obvious* that I
endeavor to rediscover. With the field of crime and punishment more accurately charted, so that fictive moral elements are eliminated and genuine moral elements are given the prominence they deserve, the morally
important issues in criminal jurisprudence can be dealt with in a way that
is genuinely enlightened from a moral point of view. It is a matter of freeing theory from the constraints of the moral mindset to allow a more
civilized political morality to exert its influence over the business of crime
and punishment.

In the first three chapters I consider again the most widely and most
thoroughly discussed issue in criminal jurisprudence, viz the justification of
punishment. I am unhappy about the easy ride that theorists of various
stripes give themselves in their attempts at justification, and especially their
disregard of the violation of basic human rights that serious criminal punishment inevitably involves. My conclusion about what is justified and why
is a kind of *practical* existential imperative, a theory with a distinctly conservative complexion and a thoroughly unambitious outlook.

In the two chapters that follow I consider other positions that seek to
justify the institution of punishment. All of them fail to satisfy the requirement of indispensability that I argue for in the preceding chapters. Moreover, all of these theories—retributive as well as utilitarian—turn out to be
consequentialist, or forward-looking theories in which punishment seeks
either to improve or to remedy some state of affairs. This is in contrast to the
theory I argue for, in which punishment seeks to do neither.

The next chapter is devoted to the basic principles of injustice that must be guarded against in the criminal process. In opposition to the moralistic approach, I argue that a claim that punishment is deserved does not have the positive spin that it is thought to have, and that just desert is also only a protective principle that seeks to ensure respect for innocence. Proportionality between crime and punishment is another favorite of the moralist, but again its importance lies not in striving to match to moral perfection but rather in avoidance of the kind of gross mismatch that is easily recognizable as injustice. Disparity of sentences is the next moral hazard. It is universally recognized as a form of serious injustice, but its moral failing lies in its arbitrary or idiosyncratic treatment of cases, not in failing to follow some morally endorsed formula for assessing and matching the criminal conduct in two cases that are said to be candidates for similar treatment. And finally, there is a minimalist principle that seeks to limit punishment to what is necessary to keep the law credible, even when there is a good case that more than that is deserved.

In the next chapter I consider what a crime is, and particularly with reference to the harm that seems always to hover in the vicinity and often to occupy the limelight. The notion that there is always a moral wrong at the heart of the matter turns out to be very misleading. There are, in fact, five different categories of crimes whose difference lies in their different relationships to the harm that gives them their criminal character. And there are three different reasons why crimes may be morally wrong, all of them related to harm. Although many crimes are morally wrong, it is never the case that there is, or ought to be, criminal liability for them because they are morally wrong. Moreover, there are many crimes that are simply not morally wrong, though since there are good and sufficient reasons for having them on the books, imposing criminal liability for committing them is not wrong from a moral point of view.

The next three chapters go to the heart of the crime: the conduct that constitutes the crime, and the culpability that on the moralist's account is the essence of the conduct's criminality. But culpable conduct turns out not to be activity masterminded by a malign or morally indifferent inner self, and in itself culpability tells us nothing about the person whose conduct it is. Criminal culpability has an altogether different role to play, and it is a role that gives no support to the moralist.

Not surprisingly, some theorists, especially those with a moralist bent, would like to give persons and their character, rather than their conduct, the more intense scrutiny. After all, the crime is committed by a person, and it is punishing the person for his crime that is the point of criminal justice. In this next chapter I examine that idea and point out what is wrong with making the person the star attraction. I also look more closely at the troubling notion of a choice, troubling because the moralist wants to attach moral weight to the fact that what the actor did was a matter of choice.

In the next chapter I examine four consoling fictions which make it easier for people of moral sensibility to accept the awful business of crime and punishment. The first of these seeks to soften the idea of punishment and make it easier to evade what is really going on. Then there is the consoling ideal of punishment that fits the crime, a perfect match that comforts us by ensuring that justice is done. After that I consider the difficulty of cases in which what seems wrong now quite understandably seemed right at the time, and the fiction the law must employ in order to punish what is morally innocent. Finally, there is the dilemma of sympathetic or even empathetic engagement with those who commit a crime and the antidote to such moral engagements provided by the notion of evil.

In the last two chapters I consider two great issues of political morality that overshadow criminal justice. The first concerns the radical moral deficiency that permeates the way the law is enforced. The second queries the institution of criminal punishment when seen in historical perspective as one among several social institutions with which it shares certain morally reprehensible features, as well as a certain respectability. Viewed in this perspective, progress toward a more civilized response to crime appears to be a moral imperative.

I like to think that in some small measure the book will help create a new moral environment for crime and punishment, an environment in which incidents of human failing that are public business are seen for what they truly are, and are dealt with in ways that avoid as much as possible compounding the quantum of injury that must be suffered. Morality as the guardian of genuine well-being needs our whole-hearted support, while morality as the crusader against evil needs to be eased into retirement. Nowhere is this more important than in criminal justice.

A new heart I will give you, and a new spirit I will put within you; and I will take out of your flesh the heart of stone and give you a heart of flesh.

Ezekiel 36: 26

1

Crime and Impunity

My point of departure is a feeling of abhorrence that is shared by everyone who is capable of normal human sympathies. It is the feeling of horror and revulsion that we experience through books and films about prison, and the terror that the very thought of our serving a prison sentence strikes in our hearts. It is a feeling that drives unrelentingly the need to justify punishment in spite of our abhorrence of it, or more to the point, because of our abhorrence. The feeling is so strong that only powerful countervailing emotions can keep us from deploring the very existence of prisons and taking steps to do away with them. These emotions are, of course, produced by accounts of crimes, and especially those that make us feel most vulnerable, those that are most frightening, most revolting, most heart-rending, and those that most clearly illustrate the immense human capacity for cruelty and depravity.

Since punishment for any serious crime is an awful business, we are reassured by thinking of the worst sorts of crimes by the worst sorts of people as the true paradigms of serious crime, and our response to any serious crime draws its strength from those paradigms. We can always choose to dwell on the harm that occurred, or that might have occurred. We feel certain then that it would be as wrong as anything could be to turn our backs on the dreadful things people do to one another, and frightening to think of people who do such things being left at large.

When the crime is the sort that provides no victim and no opportunity for outrage, we resort to indignation. We imagine the serious injustice to the rest of us that would occur if we allowed the person who commits such a crime to get away with it while we deprive ourselves of attractive opportunities and continue to live in fear of the law and of the awful consequences to be suffered if we break it.

But overwhelming our feelings of compassion and common humanity with even stronger feelings of outrage, fear, and indignation is not good enough. Making ourselves feel better about the suffering we cause is important, but it is cold comfort unless behind those feelings there are very good reasons for engaging in practices that damage and destroy lives. We need to know with certainty that crime without punishment—impunity—would be, or would produce, an intolerable state of affairs. Only then can we punish crime with a clear conscience.

But what is impunity? Most people who commit crimes get away with them. Many crimes are never even detected, and the perpetrators of many crimes that we do know about are never identified. Many who we rightly believe to be the perpetrator of a particular crime are sought but never caught. Others are never prosecuted because the case against them is not strong enough, or because they cooperate with the authorities as informers or witnesses, or because their lawbreaking is judged insufficiently serious in the competition for limited prosecutorial resources. And of course there are prosecutions that fail even though the defendant did in fact commit the crime. But among this great army of those who are never punished for their crimes there is not a single instance of impunity. For impunity, more is required than crime that has not been punished.

If someone has been allowed to commit a crime without being called to account, and without a reason for that dispensation that is recognized as legitimate in the legal system, there is an instance of impunity. When hollow formalities leading to acquittal are substituted for true law enforcement and genuine administration of justice, there is also an instance of impunity. But the most dramatic form that impunity can take is universal impunity, which exists when there is the total absence of any effective law enforcement. There is then not only an absence of punishment for crimes, but an absence of any credible threat of it. Impunity on such a grand scale means that life as we know it in civilized society cannot exist, or so we have very good reason to believe.*

For one thing, strong feelings produced by those crimes that are most feared would remain unassuaged. Revenge would be the only source of the indispensable comfort now provided by criminal justice, and acts of revenge would be a commonplace feature of social life. But the spontaneous, passionate, and disordered character of such a response to crime would ensure that large numbers of innocent people were made victims of barbaric vengeance, and that only those who either were themselves stronger or were able to muster stronger forces could hope to protect themselves against this desire for vengeance. Crime with impunity would leave us no choice but to take the law into our own hands by whatever means we could, to retaliate and even to strike pre-emptively, with the prevailing state of violence making life together as we now know it impossible.

There is another more obvious and more immediate reason why impunity as a general state of affairs would be intolerable. The punitive system of law enforcement that we have makes the policeman the threat that he is and gives the laws on the books the influence they have. Without punishment for breaking the law as a credible prospect even the policeman at one's elbow would be a much diminished force in keeping even those who are normally law-abiding from doing what the law prohibits when there is a tempting advantage to be gained by disregarding the law and no obvious harm caused to anyone in particular. It becomes easy to turn one's back on the law when others who are respectable members of the community are doing it, and in a world in which there is no need to fear punishment one can easily find a pretext for quarrelling with the law when it stands in the way of temptation. Though the effect of universal impunity would be most dramatic among those people who now respect the law, a world in which even an immediate police presence is largely meaningless would also encourage those who now seek out criminal opportunities to enlarge by a quantum leap the scope of their activities.

A picture now begins to emerge in which exacting punishment is no longer the purpose of enforcing the law. Punishment is simply a necessary condition if the process of law enforcement is to be effective in preventing the evils of impunity. Law enforcement that is taken seriously is the indispensable prophylactic device, and the availability of punishment as part of law enforcement is necessary if law enforcement *is* to be taken seriously. Without punishment we may still have arrest and prosecution resulting in a conviction that is a matter of public record. This may well provide an ordeal of shame and immense inconvenience that lasts for a very long time, but it does not provide sufficient comfort for the victim, nor can it be relied on to help stay the hand of those who see a distinct advantage for themselves in breaking the law.

This leaves punishment with only a supporting role. No longer is it the star attraction it usually is taken to be, and there is no point in trying to find in it qualities that make it inherently worthwhile. It plays its modest, though indispensable, part in a process that prevents impunity, but it has no part to play beyond that. Indeed, since criminal punishment as an undesirable fate is second only to death itself, it *must* do no more than what is needed to prevent impunity.

This modest role for punishment is bound to produce disappointment for its many enthusiasts. It will also be a source of consternation for those who have responsibility for legislative prescriptions of punishment and sentences passed under them. The effects of those threats that are on the books and the effect of carrying out those threats are both largely unknown. We are equally in the dark about how to measure victim satisfaction and how to set its proper boundaries. But accepting that punishment's *raison d'être* is limited to its role in preventing the consequences of impunity, we can at least abandon widespread, but futile, attempts to punish away crime by punishing more swiftly, more severely, and more extensively.

We now have a strange picture of crime and punishment. Contrary to what is usually supposed, putting teeth in the criminal law is necessary mainly to preserve a system that allows those who now are law-abiding to remain so. Against those who are not now law-abiding there is little the threat of law enforcement can do other than to divert them from opportunities where apprehension appears more likely to opportunities that seem safer. Even among the law-abiding there are a great many crimes that a system of enforceable laws cannot prevent, as for instance, when people are affected by momentary feelings that overwhelm their settled habits, or when they find themselves in the grip of an obsessional scheme that they relentlessly pursue regardless of the consequences. Domestic homicide, by far the largest class of killings, provides abundant examples of normally law-abiding people who pay no attention to the law, and the same is true in many other kinds of crime in which perpetrator and victim have well-established personal relationships. Still, most of us can and do, most of the time, abide by the law, and this depends on our maintaining a system that protects us from ourselves as we would have to be without such a system.

This view of criminal justice is profoundly conservative. On this view its aims are what many may regard as excessively modest, since keeping the law-abiding from changing their ways will not reduce the number of crimes that are committed, nor will preventing those who commit crimes from committing even more make us safer than we are. It follows that on this view judging the success of the criminal justice system by reference to crime rates is a mistake. Crime control is certainly the aim of the system, but not by reducing the incidents of crime that threaten us in our daily lives. It is the kind of crime control that allows the general conditions of life that we enjoy to continue, allowing us to live in a generally peaceable way, and allowing us to enjoy the benefits of social cooperation in spite of the threats of crime that continue to exist around us. For more than that we must attend as best we can to the causes of crime, including both those things that make crime an activity of choice for those who commit crimes, and those matters that enhance the opportunities for crime.

Because criminal punishment is a terrible source of human misery, its reduction represents moral progress, and it should be carried on generally at the lowest level at which it can still be effective in playing its part in preventing the evils of impunity. It does seem unthinkable that we should ever find ourselves able to tolerate universal impunity and do away altogether with punishment for crime. Imagine, for example, a scheme of social insurance that would compensate victims so handsomely that in most cases they are far better off than they were before the crime. If satisfying an insurance claim were our only response to crime, we would still feel that something important that must be done had been left undone. And no matter how well we came to understand the person who committed the crime in ways that explained why it occurred, we could not simply console ourselves with our understanding and treat a serious crime as no more than a profoundly shocking and deeply regrettable incident. What does seem reasonable is a continuing enlargement of our understanding of crimes to reduce the distance we maintain between ourselves and those who commit them, with the hope that in this way we may reduce the sense of alienation that invigorates the punitive response.

There is also the need to maintain the dread that allows the law-abiding to remain that way, and that ensures that a police presence does have an inhibiting effect. Obedience to the unenforceable is a mark of a truly civilized community, but surely even among the most civilized in a punishment-free society, some particularly inviting criminal opportunity will always seem more important than keeping to the paths of the law and avoiding the stigmata of the lawbreaker, especially when breaking the law does no palpable harm.

For these reasons the total abolition of punishment is neither a prospect to be feared nor a cause to be devoted to.* But punishment striking terror in the hearts of would-be offenders must be recognized as the nonsense it is and abandoned, along with appetites for revenge and expressions of moral superiority advanced in the name of justice.

2

Sufficiently Good Reason

Criminal punishment is by far the worst thing the law allows. But more than simply allowing it, the law is an enthusiastic practitioner and has even endowed itself with exclusive rights. Notwithstanding this august patronage, oceans of ink have been consumed in attempts to justify the institution of criminal punishment, though curiously it is almost never concluded that such a social practice is simply not justifiable. It is generally believed that punishment is the right response to crime. But what makes it right is a question that is opened ever wider as the answers to it multiply. Two sorts of strategies are employed to reconcile decent people to a practice that is inherently repugnant.

One of these purports to show that beyond the degradation and misery there are benefits, not only for the person being punished, but for the rest of us as well. He is being improved by being made to learn that crime does not pay and that it is in any case wrong. At the same time we are spared the crimes of people who might otherwise engage in criminal pursuits but are deterred by the example of what happens to those who are caught. We are also spared the further crimes that might be committed if someone who has committed a crime were left at large.

The other line of argument is radically different. Punishing crime is not deemed to be right because it is expedient. Punishing crime is taken to be wholly praiseworthy in itself, like acts of charity or of heroic rescue. Crime is seen as an evil, like poverty or some catastrophic natural disaster, and the great display of enthusiasm for dealing with crime by punishing it suggests that for those who take this line punishment is a moral imperative of the greatest importance, perhaps even greater than helping victims of catastrophic misfortune.*

In its more extreme forms, the retributive *élan* appears not to offer any opportunity for justification since our immediate experience tells us incontrovertibly that crime and punishment for it are morally, metaphysically, or logically inseparable, like two sides of the same coin; hence there is no possible need for justification. In its less extreme forms the retributive spirit recognizes the evils of suffering and deprivation at the heart of punishment, but they are made right according to some governing principle which they are meant to serve, such as paying the debt that was incurred by committing a crime, providing the satisfaction to which a victim is entitled, righting a wrong that otherwise remains a shameful stain on the social fabric, or undergoing what fairness to others demands in a community based on universal self-restraint.★

But criminal punishment is not merely great harm allowed by the law. It is the most powerful and the most widely used device that the law has at its disposal, as well as the crudest and the most frightening. Unrelenting efforts to make it respectable are explained by that fact alone, though more is at stake than simply the enjoyment of a clear conscience in enforcing the law. The justification of punishment *tout court* is surrounded by satellite issues of justification that are of great importance in their own right, and these issues cannot be dealt with properly unless we know why it is right to make things punishable in the first place.

We need to know that we are justified in making some particular item of conduct punishable when it is suggested that it ought to be against the law. Surely punishing anything in particular must not be inconsistent with those reasons that pass muster as justification for punishment in general.

Then there is the question of what sentences to prescribe for those crimes that do belong on the books, and this leads us again to consider why we are licensed to punish at all. Even more obvious is the need to revert to basics when confronted by the difficult job of passing sentence so that sentences will not be influenced by wrong ideas about punishment. What punishment may consist of, and under what conditions it may be carried on, must also be influenced by those considerations that give punishment its legitimacy.

Furthermore, we take it for granted that if anyone may punish crime it is the state only. But the reason for that goes to the very heart of what justifies punishment at all, and it is in the light of such justification that we must address questions of contested or conflicting jurisdiction when crimes committed in one place are sought to be punished in another, as well as questions of when, if ever, the state may delegate to private interests its right to carry on the activities of law enforcement and punishment.

There are many intriguing issues bearing on responsibility that are embedded in defenses claiming dispensation from criminal liability, and the way they are dealt with can miss the point unless there is an understanding of the context in which these issues arise, particularly with reference to what it is that justifies the attempt to punish in the first place. Moreover, there are dispensations from liability that are based on cooperation with the authorities—in the form of plea bargains or by acting as informers or witnesses for the prosecution—and these practices raise questions about what openings in the net can and should be tolerated, questions that cannot be managed properly unless in the background there is a sound appreciation of why we are justified in treating those who are criminally liable as we do.

Though many other important issues are involved in resolving these satellite questions of justification, a settled view of what makes punishment right is essential. There is in fact hardly any issue of importance in criminal justice that does not query, at least implicitly, the reason we engage in the notoriously brutal practice of criminal punishment, and hardly any issue whose resolution does not reflect a view of why punishment is justifiable. In view of the momentous importance of getting it right, and in view of the dreadfulness of what is being justified, there are compelling reasons why the standard for the justification of criminal punishment must be very demanding and must be rigorously applied to exclude proposals that do not make punishment a matter of strict necessity.

The most basic requirement for liability to criminal punishment is proof beyond a reasonable doubt of all of the elements that are necessary for the commission of the crime. In a case before the US Supreme Court, Justice Brennan stated the reason for such a requirement.

The accused during a criminal prosecution has at stake interests of immense importance, both because of the possibility he may lose his liberty upon conviction and because of the certainty that he would be stigmatized by conviction. Accordingly, a society that values the good name and freedom of every individual should not condemn a man for commission of a crime when there is reasonable doubt about his guilt.*

It seems plain enough that for the very same reason it would be wrong to condemn anyone to criminal punishment unless criminal punishment itself were *justifiable beyond a reasonable doubt*. It would be perverse in the extreme to insist on the greatest possible protection against unjustifiable liability to punishment, while at the same time licensing through punishment the destruction of the lives of those who are found guilty even though there is room for doubt about the justifiability of punishment. Beyond moral inconsistency, it is politically barbaric to ensure as well as we can against the possibility of unjustified liability to punishment, while at the same time leaving the justification of punishment itself in a state where reasonable people may disagree. "We are sure beyond a reasonable doubt that you are liable to punishment", says the jury, but the legal system must add, "Though we are not nearly as certain that what you are liable to is justifiable". In fact such uncertainty is precisely the state in which we are left by the great debates about the justification of punishment, which leave retribution, deterrence, incapacitation, and all the rest of the "here's a good idea why" arguments deep in controversies of the most intractable sort. Justification beyond a reasonable doubt, like proof beyond a reasonable doubt, does not allow for the possibility of plausible conclusions to the contrary, and certainly the panoply of reasons that are usually offered in justification leave room for abundant doubt.

Still, being certain that one is right about guilt, while being uncertain that one is right in visiting punishment on the guilty, might be glossed in the following way. Proof beyond a reasonable doubt is necessary to ensure that the awful fate of the guilty befalls only those who we are sure truly deserve it, and indeed we must be as careful as we can be to avoid error not only because the fate of the guilty is so awful, but also because we are not as sure as we would like to be that this fate is really justified.

Such an argument is, however, either perverse or internally defective. Our purpose in seeking to justify punishment is to be able to carry on a very worrying practice with a clear conscience. It is perverse to claim that a scrupulous determination of guilt is all that is necessary for an easy conscience when we think of the consequences for those found guilty, since such a claim deliberately ignores the troubling source of our conscientious concern and pays attention only to the procedures of proof that precede it. If, however, the argument accepts as a premise that once guilt has been properly determined then punishment is deserved, the argument is defective in failing to come to grips with the question that needs to be answered in order to relieve our conscience, and instead simply assumes without more and for reasons unknown that the apparent barbarism we practice on the guilty need not trouble us.

The conclusion we are left with, then, is that uncertainty about punishment has a claim on our conscience that is no less urgent than uncertainty about guilt.

There is a different sort of argument for rigorous standards of justification that rests on political principle. Criminal punishment is the severest deprivation of rights—some would say violation or abrogation of rights—allowed by the law. It is the state exercising its authority to curtail those basic human rights whose protection it otherwise regards as its most pressing obligation, and in effect the state becomes the perpetrator of acts that otherwise it punishes through the criminal law. Nothing in government takes precedence over its duty to protect those within its jurisdiction from serious harm at the hands of others. Yet criminal punishment consists of the state deliberately inflicting many serious harms, as well as being responsible for many others by imposing conditions of life that inevitably increase the likelihood of serious harm in prison at the hands of others. The burden of justification that the state must meet in doing this is obviously great.

American constitutional law has developed a doctrine that provides guidance in political principle to meet this challenge. When there is legislation (or other acts of government) that gives rise to suspicions of unfair or discriminatory treatment against, or in favor of, members of some group, the courts are bound to scrutinize the legislation with special rigor to make sure that the guarantee of equal protection of the law is not being flouted. Groups to be protected with the strictest scrutiny are those that are in positions of disadvantage generally, and particularly those that are in a relatively weak position in the political process or are victims of prejudice, stigma, historical antipathy, or animus in the community at large. Measures that have the effect of depriving members of such groups of the enjoyment of rights that are enjoyed in the community generally are subject to strict scrutiny by the courts. Similarly, if legislation deprives those subject to it of basic rights, no matter how broad the class affected, such legislation is subject to strict scrutiny by the courts. It is not good enough simply to show that there is some rational basis in public policy, so that the law is shown not to be a naked abuse of political power. Nor is it enough to show that in fact some important governmental interest is advanced by the legislation. When truly strict scrutiny is called for, to justify the legislation there must be a *compelling* governmental interest that cannot be dealt with satisfactorily by less drastic alternatives.★

The institution of criminal punishment has been adopted by the law as its most widely used legislative device. Those who are convicted of serious crime and are subject to punishment form a group clearly recognized by prisoners' rights law. Members of this group are in a position of the greatest disadvantage in every way, in society and in the body politic. They suffer the severest stigmatization and are objects of the strongest feelings of antipathy. The legislation that authorizes their punishment licenses a violation of rights that normally the law punishes with great severity. It is therefore obvious that unless criminal punishment is a matter of *compelling necessity*, it is not justifiable. It is not good enough simply to argue that it is a good idea to punish crime, that it improves those who are punished, takes people who commit crimes out of circulation, by its example keeps others on the right side of the law, and makes us all feel a lot better than we would be simply by forgiving and forgetting. The standard of compelling necessity requires us to show that the consequences of not punishing crime would be intolerable, or at least requires us to make a convincing case for that proposition even though we are incapable of gaining confirmation by social experiment.

I have said that the doctrine of strict scrutiny is a guide to proper political principles in seeking to justify punishment by the state, but without any suggestion that American constitutional law now requires that all penal laws be subject to strict scrutiny. In fact, in a number of cases that themselves illustrate the especially despised status of prisoners, the federal courts have held that only a rational basis review is appropriate in connection with Congressional legislation curtailing such a basic right as a prisoner's access to the courts, and to the same general effect the US Supreme Court has endorsed a lower standard of equal protection for prisoners.★ But constitutional law is a living organism with discernible tendencies to change in certain ways, and throughout its history elevated moral consciousness has overwhelmed precedent on many occasions. There is already evidence that an increasingly strict standard for the justification of punishment may be required by the cruel and unusual punishment clause of the Eighth Amendment.

To begin with, there is the frequently cited statement of Chief Justice Warren that the Eighth Amendment "must draw its meaning from the evolving standards of decency that mark the progress of a maturing society".★ It is not only gratuitously punitive practices that have been challenged successfully in the name of higher standards of decency. The conditions under which a sentence is served have been subject to judicial review, with the ultimate question "Is that really necessary?" whenever what would not be tolerated in the outside world is imposed on someone in prison. This minimalist attitude militates against good works to be achieved by punishing crime and supports an ambitionless view of punishment, a view of punishment as a social necessity whose single aim is to do no more harm than is unavoidable. So conditions of confinement that result in needless suffering are unacceptable, and even nothing more serious than ignoring the health risks of passive smoking are now prohibited under the Eighth Amendment.* Obviously, decent living conditions, personal security, good food, recreation, satisfying work, and educational opportunities are essential parts of a regime that seeks to do no more harm than is unavoidable. But the point of general importance here is the recognition that anything objectionable that is imposed upon those who are being punished is illicit unless it is strictly necessary, just as the practice of punishment itself would be.

Under the rubric of the Eighth Amendment courts have also taken seriously the issue of marked disparity between the seriousness of a crime and the severity of the punishment for it. When the punishment has been found to be disproportionately great, the principal objection has been that gratuitous suffering is being inflicted. From this recognition that a sentence may be no greater than what is needed to serve as proper punishment for the crime there follows the largely neglected point that any punishment at all is justified only if it is truly needed.*

The fate of capital punishment is also instructive. Its history in the United States was marked by a spectacular event in 1972 when the Supreme Court decided that the death penalty in every jurisdiction of the land was unconstitutional as cruel and unusual punishment. Different reasons were offered in the five opinions supporting the judgment of the Court, some emphasizing the arbitrary and discriminatory way in which the death sentence was imposed, some the inhumanity of such a practice, and others the fact that such a practice was simply unnecessary. Though the death penalty was subsequently resurrected in new laws that had the support of a majority of the Court, the momentary abolition of capital punishment was an instant of enlightenment for punishment in general.*

Justice Brennan spoke of all extreme methods of punishment as condemned not only because of the pain involved, but because

they treat members of the human race as nonhumans, as objects to be toyed with and discarded. They are thus inconsistent with the fundamental premise of the [Cruel and Unusual Punishments] Clause that even the vilest criminal remains a human being possessed of common human dignity.

Any punishment that is not strictly necessary likewise represents a failure to respect common human dignity, though admittedly the lack of respect when we kill is more pronounced than when we imprison. The opinions of Justices Marshall and White both emphasized that the death penalty was not needed and for that reason was unconstitutional (Justice Marshall arguing that life imprisonment appeared to be an adequate alternative, and Justice White arguing that the infrequency of the death penalty deprived it of its supposed deterrent effect). And Justices Brennan and Marshall consistently dissented in subsequent capital punishment cases, essentially on the ground that the death penalty is an unnecessary cruelty. All of these views again stress necessity as the only possible basis of justification, and though capital punishment is the more barbaric institution, imprisonment is surely troubling enough to require an equally demanding standard of justification. Indeed, it is useful to think of capital punishment, like torture, as an institutional practice in its own right, and not simply as one among a number of methods of punishing crime. When viewed in this way, the moral progress toward its abolition that can be seen throughout the world will surely suggest that punishment itself can progress along the same paths, even if the goal is more modest in aiming at reduction rather than abolition.

If punishment is to be justified, I have argued that we must invoke a strict standard of justification that requires a convincing demonstration of the indispensability of punishment. In support of such a standard I have pointed to proof beyond a reasonable doubt, to the doctrine of strict scrutiny in constitutional law, and to important features of the constitutional prohibition of cruel and unusual punishment. Strong support for such a standard is also provided by the substantive criminal law itself.

When a person is attacked or is otherwise put in a position of immediate danger to life and limb, the law allows him to protect himself even at the cost of the life of his attacker, and perhaps when such a sacrifice is unavoidable, even at the cost of the life of an innocent person. Not only must the harm threatened be truly serious, but it must be imminent, and the threat of it inescapable except by the use of force that may prove deadly. There are, of course, issues of whose reckoning of the situation is the right one to use in deciding whether these conditions have been met, for what we know when dispassionately considering all the facts that are available at a later time may well be very different from how things seemed, or should have seemed, at the time it was happening. But on whatever account we proceed, there is always great stringency in the requirements for the defense of self-defense or (to the extent the law allows harming an innocent person) the defense of necessity.★

Punishment, viewed as a measure of social self-defense, is in much the same position. The tremendously injurious effects of punishment can be justified only if the consequences of impunity would be intolerable. If social survival depends upon the existence of the institution of punishment, then punishment is justifiable. But if we are less than certain about the consequences of impunity, or if we know that other measures will do the job without the devastating effects of punishment, then we have no right to continue to inflict unnecessary harm on those who have committed crimes.

The compelling need to take extreme measures to defend ourselves in extreme situations seems clear enough, and simply pointing to the consequences that otherwise are quite certain to follow seems itself to clinch the case. But naked self-interest in preserving oneself is not a view that pleases everyone. Why should one be privileged to place a greater value on one's own life than on the life of someone who threatens it? This transcendental view of the matter requires that we provide something better than a demonstration of how desperate our predicament was. It requires a denigration of our victim so that his life turns out to be worth less than ours. The preferred method of accomplishing this is by claiming that he has forfeited his right to life (or whatever else he happens to have lost) by his act of aggression. Becoming an aggressor may itself work the forfeiture, or else it may be simply his breaking of the law that does the job. In either case he has lost his innocence and the harmful act that befalls him is justified because he has lost his right to be free of that harm.★

In the same way, it might be argued that punishment is justified as harm that is visited on those who have by their unlawful conduct forfeited their right to be free of such harm. Under such a theory, it is no longer necessary to show that punishment is a matter of compelling necessity, since the criminal conduct itself radically changes the status of the perpetrator and leaves him bereft of the rights that are enjoyed by those who abide by the law. He is then fair game for the harm the law might choose to inflict on him as punishment for his crime.

The mistake here lies in supposing that such rights are ever subject to forfeit, either by the state or by the person who possesses them. A person may choose to expose himself to serious harm, as an aggressor facing others who are prepared to defend themselves to the death, or by committing a crime that merits serious punishment. Having chosen to expose himself to such harm, he may be estopped from claiming that his right to be free of such harm has been violated. In such a case the right has not been forfeited, though by choosing to expose himself to harm its possessor has compromised his right to assert it on that occasion. Similarly, the state may not deprive a person of his right to be free of serious harm, though it may invoke a person's choice to expose himself to punishment by committing a crime as a good reason for not vindicating his right to be protected by the state from such harm on that occasion.

The rights in question are basic human rights. For that reason they are inalienable and so not subject to forfeiture. Though there is no more important obligation of the state than protection of these rights, the state does not confer these rights and the state cannot withdraw them. They are not entitlements that are creatures of the state, like tax deductions or unemployment benefits. They are not human rights that are simply derivative from basic rights, like rights not to be discriminated against or the right to travel abroad. Since rights to be free of serious harm belong to all humans simply by virtue of being human, they cannot be cancelled through the commission of a crime. And since serious criminal punishment inevitably consists of the state harming the person punished through confinement, degradation, and other violations of basic human rights, its justification must consist of sufficiently good reasons not only for failing to protect these rights, but also for failing to respect them.

Justifying a disregard of basic human rights is not a matter to be undertaken lightly, and no matter how good an idea it might be to punish crime, punishment cannot be justified simply because it is a good idea. What encourages us to think otherwise is the insidious notion that those who have lost their innocence under the criminal law are, for the time being at least, no longer fully fledged members of the human community. In dealing with them we think we may disregard certain basic rights that we cherish for ourselves in order to achieve certain benefits for them and for ourselves. Proceeding from such a premise, we regard ourselves as licensed to punish in order to implement some policy of crime reduction or moral correction. But if we respect those basic human rights that endure regardless of criminal conduct, we are free to inflict only such harm as may be strictly necessary to protect ourselves, for it is that harm only that is justifiable and so that harm only that the perpetrator has exposed himself to in committing the crime.

3

Taking Human Rights Seriously

The last two chapters placed stress on the fact that criminal punishment by its very nature must be an experience that is deeply harmful, and that looked at in isolation the harm is a violation of basic human rights. This prima-facie case against the right to punish was challenged by what appears to be an inescapable necessity. Punishment, it seems, must be maintained as part of a system upon which our very survival depends, both personally and socially. But the part that punishment plays in this system is a modest one, even though it is indispensable in preventing what otherwise would very likely be a descent into hell.

Other accounts of punishment do not appeal simply to self-preservation but seek instead to portray punishment as necessary or desirable to make things better than they are. Some of these accounts need no crime to create the need for improvement, but they do require a crime to warrant acting on that need. Other accounts of punishment make its warrant depend entirely on a need for improvement that exists just because a crime has been committed.

Accounts of the first sort all suggest that the commission of a crime provides a special sort of opportunity for improving public safety or for improving those people who threaten it. Punishment of those found guilty is seen as a cautionary and sobering example for those who may be tempted to stray from the paths of the law. It is also thought to provide a painful experience for the person who has committed the crime, something he will not wish to risk undergoing again. Even more certainly, through imprisonment in the name of punishment, a person who is thought to have shown himself to be a criminal danger is removed from our midst and kept in a place where he cannot harm us again.

There are thought to be many ways of improving people while they are serving their sentences. Some of these programs are based on assumptions about the reason the crime was committed, others are based on more general notions about what a person who commits a crime is in need of. Some even spring from the enlightened recognition that there is a lot of time to fill and it is no bad thing to put a more friendly face on punishment by providing those who are serving time with genuine opportunities to improve themselves and their prospects for a better life.

The other view of punishment looks at the unsatisfactory situation that exists because a crime has been committed and sees a need for punitive measures to make things better. Some who favor this view point to a presumed harmony or tranquility in the community that has been disturbed and that can be restored only by punishment. Others stress a need for a truly emphatic condemnation of the crime through punishment to make it clear to one and all that impermissible conduct will not be tolerated. There are others who think an undertaking of self-restraint has been violated, and the unfair advantage gained by the violator must be nullified by punishment. Still others are keen to make the moral universe a happier place than it would be with an unpunished crime and an unpunished criminal sheltering in it. And some aim at nothing more grand than making victims and their many sympathizers feel better by making the guilty suffer.

But neither the preservationist view that I have advocated nor any of the many meliorist views proposed by others can avoid the challenge that is presented by basic human rights. It is a challenge in two parts. First, there is a general objection to the sacrifice of basic human rights in the cause of punishment. It poses the question of what, if anything, can license treating people who are convicted of crimes in ways that are otherwise regarded as so seriously wrong that we do not even need any criminal law to tell us they constitute crimes. The second objection addresses the question of whether *my* basic human rights need to be transgressed when I commit a crime. Even if a general practice that sacrifices basic human rights is justified, might not some occasions of the practice be dispensed with in order to reduce the aggregate amount of human rights violations and so avoid needless suffering if such dispensation does not make the practice less efficacious? Responding to both these objections requires a closer look at basic human rights. And so does my claim that only the requirements of self-preservation can withstand the objections posed by basic human rights.

Basic human rights are being ignored when there is serious criminal punishment. These are the same rights that are violated by a variety of serious crimes against the person. They are what might be called *natural* human rights because they belong to every person simply by virtue of being a person, and because they are enjoyed against the whole world regardless of what any legal or political authority might say for or against them. Their origin and their persistence can be fully explained by reference to human needs and the universal elements of human experience. They are not the creatures of government, nor is their origin to be found in any broad consensus among governments, and though their existence does not depend upon governments in any way, it is the first duty of any government to recognize and protect them. Nor is it possible for any person to give up his basic human rights, by word or by deed, since these rights are as much a part of being human as anything else that makes a person human, and so these rights endure as long as the person exists.

What is done to someone who is sent to prison is often more terrible than what is done to someone who is the victim of a rape, a kidnapping, or a brutal physical assault. If one had a choice one would be foolish to choose a significant term of imprisonment over any but the most dreadful and enduring experiences that befall a victim of crime. In prison a person no longer fully owns his life, and the rest of the world says that it serves him right. Guilt has an almost magical effect in hardening our hearts to the plight of those being punished. Having so completely degraded them as fellow human beings, we do not wish to face the consequences of what we have done. But imagine that the person in prison is innocent, or even better, that he is known to be innocent. Of course there is then a special sympathy for the harm he suffers by virtue of the injustice itself. But moving beyond the injustice we can see more clearly just through his experience what it is that makes us dread being in prison ourselves, regardless of guilt or innocence. As victims of serious crime our rights are violated in spite of the law's efforts to protect them. Perpetrators being punished for their crimes have those same rights ignored by the law and so are made into victims by the law.

This equality of crime and punishment in overriding natural human rights has an interesting consequence. Hardly ever does anyone bother to ask if there really is a right to punish, even though that question is an obvious, even compelling, preliminary question in the unrelenting quest for that holy grail of criminal jurisprudence, the truly incontrovertible reason why we ought to punish crime. In fact, "There is a right to punish" appears to be a truism as uncontroversial as "On a clear day the sky is blue", and in both cases the only question worth pursuing is the question "*Why?*". The right to punish remains uncontroversial as long as its moral foundation is the tit-for-tat of elementary fairness. But if we move on from elementary fairness to a more developed stage of moral consciousness, we recognize that two wrongs do not make a right, and that disregard of natural human rights, no matter by whom and on what occasion, constitutes a case to be answered.

The existence of natural human rights is independent of anything that governments may say for or against their existence, but there is no suggestion that in general governments are not deeply involved in the protection of these rights. In fact, it is the first obligation of government not only to protect but to respect natural human rights. Governments that violate the right to life by murder perpetrate wrongs as great as any murders committed by those who are governed, and a government that does not exercise its powers to protect against murder is bound to bring into question its very legitimacy. Imagine a society in which there are no laws prohibiting those common crimes that need no legal recognition to be recognized as crimes. It is doubtful that such a society would even be regarded as a functioning political society. Any other laws and any other acts of government would simply not be credible as an exercise of genuine authority, and almost certainly would be met with a contempt and defiance that would make effective government impossible.

Natural human rights are too fundamental to appear as explicit elements in those items of legislation that aim at protecting them, and so the law of homicide, for example, may vary in detail from one jurisdiction to another without any compromise of the underlying human right. These rights are, however, given clear expression in the kinds of overarching documents that are meant to make governments behave with proper self-restraint and to enact laws that both respect and protect these rights. The American Declaration of Independence refers to "certain Unalienable Rights" with which all men are endowed by their Creator, and then goes on to say "that among these are Life, Liberty and the pursuit of Happiness", and that "to secure these rights, Governments are instituted among Men". The Universal Declaration of Human Rights adopted by the General Assembly of the United Nations in 1948 speaks in its preamble of "the inherent dignity and of the equal and inalienable rights of all members of the human family". Article 3 states that "Everyone has a right to life, liberty and security of person", and Article 5 declares that "No one shall be subjected to torture or cruel, inhuman or degrading treatment or punishment". The European Convention on Human Rights was signed in Rome in 1950. Its first substantive provision is that "Everyone's right to life shall be protected by law", and the next Article declares that "No one shall be subjected to torture or to inhuman or degrading treatment or punishment". Article 4 provides that "No one shall be required to perform forced or compulsory labour".*

I cite these passages as examples of an official awareness of what I am calling natural human rights, and particularly of those that are implicated in criminal punishment. But whatever official recognition these rights may receive adds nothing to the fact of their existence, even though their enforcement will depend entirely on such recognition. It is true that, without an eyebrow raised, punishment of crime is universally accepted in official circles as consistent with respect for basic human rights. But this need not be an embarrassment for the claim that punishment is prima facie a transgression of such rights. Human rights at the official level incorporates a political consensus that can be unresponsive to fundamental moral concerns. Moreover, the acceptance of punishment for crime as an allowable practice by advocates of basic human rights need not be a retreat in principle to be explained by the pressures of practical politics since without any compromise in principle basic human rights can accommodate criminal punishment when criminal punishment is truly a matter of dire necessity.

A neat list of natural human rights is not possible since there is no neat formulation of what it is that every human being is entitled to simply by virtue of being human. The touchstones of what I call a natural human right are those indispensable conditions of human life that we believe must be valued for their own sake by everyone who is part of the human community, or so nearly everyone that possible exceptions need not worry us. As with many other rights, those who enjoy these rights might not think of themselves as possessed of them, but this lack of awareness does not in any way diminish the possession of them. It cannot be far wrong to suggest that life, liberty, security of person, and the essential dignities of human aspiration and self-respect mark out the principal territory of natural human rights, and that they are rights to be *enjoyed* rather than rights to be exercised. They mark out a personal sphere of inviolability for each person which the rest of the world must respect.

The right to protect that inviolability remains non-exclusively with each person who enjoys the right, though it is the aim of any proper government to minimize the need for self-protection. At this most basic level of human concern, self-protection is itself an auxiliary right of the sort that is *exercised* rather than simply enjoyed, and its exercise is limited to occasions when the mechanism of collective protection under government is not available.

It must be added that all natural human rights as we recognize them are in fact not valued for their own sake in every political society and under the cultural norms of every community. But in deciding what we must recognize and what we must respect, it is only *our* beliefs that matter, for we must live our moral lives according to our own moral lights. Trying to persuade others is inevitably part of that enterprise, but appraisal of our own practices does not depend in any way on how successful we may be in our attempts to persuade others. The existence of societies that countenance torture, slavery, and an assortment of other brutalities and indignities that violate natural human rights is not an argument against the universal existence of such rights, though plainly it is an argument against their now being recognized and respected universally.

Is the purported right to punish to be viewed as a right that is *exercised* in the name of self-preservation, and so able to trump the natural human rights that are enjoyed by those who are to be punished for their crimes? Its analogue in the criminal law can be understood in this way, so that the right of self-defense turns out to be a trump card that prevails over the right to life that the assailant enjoys.

But neither natural human rights nor rights of self-preservation lend themselves to such a suggestion. Natural human rights do not provide immunity from harm to oneself no matter what one does to bring it about, and the collective right of self-preservation does not confer a license to sacrifice the most basic rights of some for the common good. In the earlier discussion of self-defense, it was suggested that an aggressor who chose to put himself in harm's way could not claim the benefit of inviolable natural human rights when the harm that might be expected befell him. It is tempting to take the same line and say that, when a crime is committed, the perpetrator puts himself in harm's way and therefore cannot complain when harm is visited upon him in the form of punishment. But though the prospect of life in a world of impunity makes protective measures imperative, the prospective harm does not have the immediacy that is at the heart of justifiable self-defense.

The claim that punishment in the interest of collective self-preservation demands that natural human rights be sacrificed for the higher good is for this reason a morally dubious claim. There is a less problematic analysis of the right to punish that does not involve any sacrifice of these basic rights, though it does not confer a right to punish crimes of every sort.

Those crimes that need no law to make them crimes—murder, rape, any serious acts of violence, to begin the list—are all violations of natural human rights. If we do not do enough to vindicate these rights when they are violated these rights are weakened and their protective power dissipated. What constitutes a sufficient vindication is not a settled matter, and it is not inconceivable that at some time, and perhaps even somewhere now, a mixture of confession, apology, and compensation might be enough, without punishment, to vindicate those rights that are violated, even for the most serious crimes. Programs of truth and reconciliation, schemes that bring together victims and those responsible for the harm they suffered, and public insurance for criminal injuries, do at least provide a hint of such a possibility. But as things are now, punishment remains indispensable most of the time for the vindication of fundamental rights when they are violated by the most serious crimes. Allowing the weakening of these rights through impunity does not affect the existence or possession of these rights, but it does transform them from the foundation that makes life in society possible to ineffectual claims whose enforcement is an ideal yet to be achieved. Rights, after all, are what we make of them. We qualify natural human rights to permit the punishment of serious crimes *that violate natural human rights*, even though such punishment would otherwise itself be a violation of natural human rights, and we do this because as things now stand, without punishment for violations of natural human rights they would soon become little more than unaffordable moral ornaments in a world preoccupied with survival.

This account of punishment leaves most crimes on the books in limbo. If we put aside the most serious crimes that need no legal credentials to qualify as crimes, we are left with a vast array of crimes, some of them extremely serious, that are made punishable in the same way as the indispensable crimes even though they do not violate natural human rights. Can we justify the apparent violation of natural human rights involved in punishing these crimes? In Chapter 7 these crimes are discussed in more detail, but some examples here will be helpful in arriving at an answer.

Though the harm in certain crimes is plain enough and not to be treated lightly, it does sometimes fall short of what we can insist the law must protect us against. Breaking into my home at night is an act that needs no law to mark it as a crime, and violation of natural human rights seems without question to be implicated. But breaking into my factory is another matter. *Let the owner beware* might be the policy in a society that favors measures of self-protection when only property interests are involved, and, even in societies that regard a factory as entitled to the law's protection a claim that natural human rights are violated by a break-in would have very dim prospects of success.

For a great many other crimes, though the punishments are sometimes draconian, the harm may not be at all obvious until the law is enacted, and even then for many of these crimes the harm is more a matter of speculation than of fact. These crimes are products of the political process rather than instinctive reactions to harms that are experienced without any help from politicians. Some of these crimes, like those associated with narcotics, are based on genuine harms that needed to be discovered or that have been brought into political prominence only through the workings of government. Other crimes, like many of those associated with sex, are on the books to protect certain moral orthodoxies, and are based on supposititious harms that are intended to give credibility to the criminalization of things that are disapproved of with a passion by people who have attained a politically persuasive consensus. Still others, like tax evasion or refusing to perform military service, are creatures of penal legislation designed to ensure that a policy of government is not rendered ineffective by non-compliance.

Punishing any crime that does not violate natural human rights is an act of political immorality unless, once again, as with self-evident crimes, there is very good reason to believe that impunity for these crimes produces an intolerable state of affairs that cannot be avoided by less drastic measures.

It is plainly the case that policies promoting the general welfare at the expense of some individual interests cannot be implemented without the coercive force of penal provisions to back them up. Self-evident crimes at least have the moral force of their self-evident harming to restrain most of the people most of the time, but measures mounted by the political process cannot expect to have the same claim on conscience and would often be disregarded when self-interest prevailed over habits of obedience unless the penal consequences of disobedience made such cavalier behavior seem unacceptably dangerous.

With the exception of crimes that merely enforce morals, many politically created crimes are indispensable for effective government, which in turn is necessary for the general welfare in any political society. The welfare at stake is not simply a matter of increasing general prosperity, making the world a safer and healthier place, and promoting the happiness of citizens in the many different departments of their lives. The general welfare that is at stake is nothing less than survival as a political society in conditions that are better than a state of nature would allow. Consider the consequences of a general disregard of laws requiring taxes to be paid and military service to be performed. Since government could then no longer do anything at all, and the country would in any case be at the mercy of whoever had the power to exploit its impotence, life in society as we now know it would be at an end, and any other laws on the books would be dead letters. It is safe to say more generally that no government can survive if those laws that purport to promote the general welfare can be freely disregarded.

This does not, however, confer a blanket moral endorsement on all such penal legislation. If there are practical alternatives to achieve compliance, the penal route is not justifiable. If the policy to be enforced by penal legislation is frivolous, arbitrary, or is in some way morally objectionable, punishing those who do not comply is unjustifiable. And if the policy being implemented is manifestly unsound as a means of achieving its avowed aims, once again the provisions making non-compliance a crime are unjustifiable. In all of these cases, impunity would not contribute to the creation of an intolerable state of affairs, and so preventing impunity by measures that are a violation of natural human rights cannot be right.

What I am suggesting here amounts to strict scrutiny of all measures that create, rather than recognize, serious crimes. This would ensure that all crimes that are merely creatures of government pass muster as genuinely necessary to promote the general welfare, which is the only proper business of government in any case. It would expose penal promiscuity and ensure that punishability would be adopted by politicians only as a last resort.

The enforcement of moral orthodoxy and the punishment of practices that represent moral heresy can never justify a violation of natural human rights since impunity for such offenses can never promote an intolerable state of affairs, either by frustrating government as the indispensable agency of general welfare, or in any other way. These offenses do produce extreme displeasure, even outrage, although there is no experience of harm. But it is not the business of government to gratify whatever strong feelings public opinion might confront it with. The business of government is containment of such feelings, which it does very well when crimes of the worst sort come to light and are dealt with in a civilized manner. The history of any random sample of recent morals offenses—obscenity, contraception, sexual preferences and practices, attempted suicide, flag desecration—makes clear their evanescence, and the embarrassment produced by an even longer historical review of these sorts of offenses marks these misadventures in criminalization as an abuse of public power.

There is finally the question of why each crime must be punished. Since punishment is the infliction of serious harm in derogation of natural human rights, and since only the minimum needed for self-preservation is justifiable, should we not amend the system so that dispensations are granted to reduce the overall harm that is done?

The reason we cannot do this is that another obligation of government would be ignored by such a pattern of arbitrary dispensation, an obligation hardly less important than the duty of government to protect and preserve natural human rights. It is the obligation to avoid inequality of treatment in the exercise of its powers and so respect equally the natural human rights of each person over whom its powers may be exercised. A regime that leaves its citizens unprotected is intolerable, but no more so than a regime that favors certain people by arbitrary exemption from the terrible demands that must be made in the interest of self-preservation.

Viewing punishment in this way may suggest some important similarities to military service in time of war. Both punishment and military service to some degree suspend respect for natural human rights, though of course one far outdoes the other, not least in punishment's deliberate infliction of harm, while in military service the harm is both unintended and far less serious. Compulsory military service is justifiable only because of what may reasonably be presumed to be the consequences of leaving the country unable to defend itself against an aggressor. Punishment is justified by similarly stark conclusions about what would happen if it did not exist. And just as those positive attitudes that stress the virtues of military service and the glories of war are no longer accepted to justify conscription, so those views that stress the benefits of punishment cannot withstand the claims of basic human rights.

4

Crimes as Pretexts for Improvement

Every attempt to confer proper credentials on punishment, or just to prove that none are needed, has been dominated by the idea that punishment makes things better. In contrast to the preservationist view of punishment that I am advocating, all of these other theories adopt a meliorist position, stressing what are thought to be the improving effects of punishment. This applies to theories that take punishment to be retribution for crime no less than theories that view it as a way of making people better and the world we live in safer. The main difference between the so-called retributivist and the so-called consequentialist or utilitarian points of view is the significance that each attaches to the commission of a crime. The retributivists concern themselves with the unsatisfactory state of affairs created by the crime and the remedial measures required to put things right. The consequentialists treat the crime simply as a necessary pretext for remedial measures intended to reduce the number of crimes committed in the future. The difference between them lies in what each thinks needs remedying by punishment. Since both stress the beneficial consequences of punishment, it seems that *consequentialist* or *utilitarian* are not really the best labels to identify distinctively those who are not retributivists and who view the crime as a necessary pretext for doing good through punishment in a more general way. I would suggest calling views of this sort *pretextual*, a term that highlights their main distinguishing feature.

In this chapter I want to look at those accounts of punishment that take the commission of a crime as warranting a response intended to prevent crimes in the future, and in the next chapter I want to look at the positions taken by those who are concerned about the untoward state of affairs *that a crime creates,* and especially at their view of the remedy that punishment is said to provide for this. My aim is to make clear the fact that none of these theories gives a convincing account of punishment as truly indispensable.

Deterrence must lead the list of notions providing comfort to those who are troubled by the need to punish. Not unreasonably, it is supposed that without punishment to back up its threats, the law would become a paper tiger that could safely be ignored. But that simple truth is not enough for most people, and especially not for those in government or the media who wish to exploit the fear of crime for their own political or commercial advantage. It is often suggested that crime can be punished away by increasing the severity of what is threatened and by making its certainty greater. Twin myths support this assumption. One is that in general crimes are committed by people who pay attention to what they risk if they are caught and then decide to commit the crime only if what they are risking does not frighten them off. In fact it is only the immediate risks of getting caught that normally occupy those who contemplate committing a crime. Moreover, many crimes, and especially crimes of violence, are committed by people who have not thought about committing them at all, but are acting on the spur of the moment in response to what is happening. The other myth is that rational consideration of the consequences would likely lead to abandonment of any criminal designs. In fact a rational appraisal of the statistical chances of being caught and convicted would encourage rather than deter, and to that may surely be added the further encouragement that follows from the belief normally entertained by anyone with a criminal project that he or she is smarter than those unlucky few who do get caught and convicted.

The literature on deterrence can fairly be described as a few tightly circumscribed islands of hope in a great sea of doubt, with abundant evidence that no reliable connection can be established between lower rates of crime and more severe regimes of punishment. It is this great uncertainty that at the outset disqualifies deterrence in general as a sufficiently good reason for inflicting the harm that we do in administering criminal punishment.*

The conventional objection, most notably associated with Kant, is of a different sort, and its prominence warrants a brief digression. On this view, someone who commits a crime has apparently lost certain basic human rights, and so harm may be inflicted for the crime within limits that do not "make an abomination of the humanity residing in the person suffering it", as Kant put it, which undoubtedly still leaves ample room for a regime of punishment that on its face makes a mockery of natural human rights.★ What Kant cannot abide is something else—*using* someone convicted of crime simply as a means to bring about something desirable, like, for example, a more law-abiding community. Such use of a person amounts to a denial of his autonomy, which is apparently among the gravest of moral derelictions. Discernment of the fine line between illicit exploitation and permitted use remains a very difficult exercise, but it is one that need not occupy us here since it is glaringly obvious that the harm suffered by a person made to serve a prison sentence is itself a far more serious harm than the purported offense to his autonomy that occurs when someone who has committed a crime is put in prison to serve as an example to others.★

But punishment may deter by the experience of it and not simply by the threat of it. It is widely assumed that the unpleasant experience of punishment tends to make those who have experienced it unwilling to undergo it again, and so makes them more disposed in the future to avoid activities that are punishable. No doubt many who experience criminal punishment are strengthened in their resolve to avoid it again, but since having been in prison makes it more difficult for them to live a life that avoids criminal activities, their resolve is most often not to get caught again. A criminal record is a devastating handicap for anyone who wishes to have normal prospects as a law-abiding citizen, and without decent prospects, the motivation upon which a law-abiding life depends will be absent. Moreover, the loss of self-respect that a prison sentence—or just a conviction—entails for a normal person is itself a hugely debilitating psychological trauma. And for many in prison, the need to find a way of life that provides much-needed protection and basic human gratification leads to new and stronger associations within the criminal community that prison has created, associations that often are the foundation of a life outside once a sentence is served. True enough, a certain portion of the prison population consists of people who are hardened and so less affected in the ways I describe. But they are unlikely in any case to be deterred by their experience of prison since they no longer have either inclination or opportunity to consider the possibility of a law-abiding life. What we have, then, is an effect of punishment that on the whole is precisely the opposite of deterrence for those who are in principle deterrable, and the absence of any effect upon many others for whom the prison sentence is simply a piece of bad luck. In short, not only is specific deterrence through punishment a needless pursuit, it is useless and worse than useless since in many cases the punishment tends to produce exactly the opposite of what it professes to be aiming at.

Imprisoning people who commit crimes takes them out of circulation and leaves them unable to commit further crimes in the community at large, and so incapacitation is asserted as another point in favor of punishment for crime. But only if people who commit crimes have a tendency to commit them does incapacitation serve the intended purpose. Conventional wisdom reassuringly tells us that crimes committed are evidence of a tendency to commit crimes, for in view of the terrible consequences, who would commit a crime if he were free of tendencies to commit it?

But in fact many crimes—many murders, for example—are committed by people whose lives have been lived as law-abiding citizens, and in most cases there is no reason to believe that the special circumstances that led them to commit their crime would ever again be present. Some people who commit crimes are undoubtedly more likely than others to commit crimes again. But criminal liability does not depend upon there being a likelihood of reoffending, and for that reason alone it is clear that incapacitation is not the reason why in general we imprison the guilty.

If we really wanted to find out more about criminal tendencies and the likelihood of future crimes, we would have procedures very different from those that are required by our criminal jurisprudence. Evidence regarding dangerousness is generally excluded from determinations of criminal liability because such evidence would shift attention from the question of whether *this* crime was committed by the accused to the question whether the accused *might well have committed a crime of this sort*. Our criminal jurisprudence guards against any substitution of the second question for the first because of the great attraction of *might well have* to juries, an attraction that question has for everyone who fears crime or is able in some way to profit from exploitation of that fear. This includes not only politicians and the media, but also the police when they target unsavory characters in the not unreasonable expectation that achievement of their main aim—getting a result and closing the case—will be made easier by such tactics. In view of the limits imposed by our criminal jurisprudence in arriving at determinations of criminal liability, conclusions about dangerousness can at best be only speculative, and incapacitation as a reason for punishment must therefore stand on very shaky ground.*

It is also worth noting the strenuous opposition that confronts every suggestion that determinations of criminal dangerousness be made among the population at large without regard to whether or not there is a criminal record. Quite understandably, basic human rights are invoked to sink any such suggestion, even when the proposed target population is to be carefully defined to include only those persons whose age, race, and other statistically relevant biographical facts indicate a very high probability of criminal convictions in the future. Basic human rights ensure that each person, so long as he is deemed accountable for what he does, is accountable only for what he does and not for what he may do. Incarceration for the sake of incapacitation is objectionable on the same general principle.*

Two further points about incapacitation are worth noting.

Those people who commit crimes and are most clearly dangerous are the people least likely to be punished. These are the people who either are manifestly unable to exercise self-control or are so deluded or wanton in their behavior that conventional avoidance of harm to others cannot be expected of them. In short, they are deemed not to be responsible for what they do because of serious abnormality. It is true that we take such people into custody with the aim of incapacitation, and plainly restraint of their liberty is no more offensive to basic human rights than is violent resistance to an assailant. In neither case does a basic human right provide a cloak of immunity for those who endanger others, whether by actual attack or by having shown oneself to be a human bomb that might explode again at any moment. This presents a considerable embarrassment for those who think that punishment for the sake of incapacitation is punishment vindicated, since they must recognize that we refuse on principle to incapacitate by means of punishment those who are most certainly dangerous, yet they wish to claim a right to punish for the sake of incapacitation those who are less certainly dangerous, or, as far as we can tell, not dangerous at all. Only when we are as certain as we can be about dangerousness can we incapacitate in derogation of basic human rights, and incapacitation simply in the name of punishment clearly defies this restriction.

The other point is this. Prisons are normally very dangerous places in which to live. If we say we are sending those who commit crimes to prison because they are dangerous, we are acknowledging the fact that we are contributing to, and not simply tolerating, the very dangerous environment which we force people to endure when we send them to prison. We have quite deliberately created a community of dangerous people if the incapacitation rationale is correct, and the affront to the rights of all those whom we force to live in it is therefore even greater.

The next rationale is of a very different sort. There are certain purposes suggested for punishment that cast it in an expressive, indeed a declarative, role. Apparently when a crime is committed it is necessary to tell the perpetrator in no uncertain terms that what he did was wrong, and perhaps necessary, as well, to remind the rest of us lest we forget. Those who hold such views see punishment as the only method of expressing with sufficient emphasis the disapproval that is felt. Most versions turn out to be something of a hybrid, combining retributivist and pretextual thinking, seeing punishment as both doing what needs to be done because of the crime that was committed, as well as acting on the opportunity this presents to improve things for the future. On balance, concern for future improvement predominates, and so this view of punishment is included among those views that take the crime to be a pretext for improving the perpetrator and the social environment.

Some of these views of punishment stress the need for public condemnation of a crime in a suitably unequivocal fashion, which a spell in prison will achieve quite nicely. Mere reprobation will not do as a response to crime without the hard treatment that is punishment plain and simple, for the unfortunate truth is that telling how we feel about things—no matter how emphatically—is not the same as showing how we feel. Others welcome a criminal conviction as a public occasion for reaffirmation of the shared values that the criminal law embodies by punishing those who have shown a disregard, even a contempt, for these values. All of these views of punishment share a certain high-minded attitude that takes punishment to be something more than the grim necessity of a *pis aller*. Crimes are of course not welcome events, but punishments are a kind of silver lining.*

Transforming the horrors of punishment into a worthwhile message gladdens the hearts of decent people who are forced to sanction an indecent practice. But really this is self-deception. That it is wrong, and how wrong it is, is either plain on the face of a crime or else can be made plain enough by the same sorts of explanation that make clear the wrongness of things other than crimes. Social cohesion may indeed be adversely affected by the absence of punishment for crime, and the widespread disaffection generated by such impunity could well be catastrophic, but this could not be attributed to a failure to criticize crime and reaffirm the fact that we think it is wrong. If a crime is punished in a way that makes it clear that the perpetrator is not getting away with his crime, that is enough. Nothing so awful as criminal punishment could possibly be justified by the moral criticism it entails since that criticism is not necessary to preserve us from the apocalyptic effects of impunity.

It is said more generally that improving people who commit crimes is a good reason for punishing them. Such views have a long philanthropic history. They have a long misanthropic history as well. Caring about people who have problems and not treating them in an unfeeling way is always the right thing to do, and when the problems they have are intimately associated with the crimes they commit, the decent thing to do is to consider the crime in the light of the problems. Passionate concern about the crime and indifference to what brought it about can never be right. But neither can it be right to be concerned about the crime only as evidence of some personal or social pathology.*

The unhappy history of attempts to change people who have been marked as criminals embraces attempts at reformation, as well as more modern efforts carried on in the name of rehabilitation. Reformation assumed that crime was a defection from the proper order of things, and that inducing an abiding acceptance of that order and a steady conformity to its requirements was an important aim in punishing crime. Rehabilitation rests on quite different assumptions about criminals and places emphasis on deficiencies, anomalies, and abnormalities which need to be treated therapeutically or require correction in some other way. In its most benign forms, rehabilitation includes programs of education and therapeutic intervention that are no more intrusive or manipulative than what is on offer to the population at large—opportunities to achieve the kind of improvements that should make it easier to live a law-abiding life. In its more malign forms, rehabilitation can include programs of training and discipline whose self-righteous, sadistic, and authoritarian origins are much more in evidence than any good results that they might be supposed to produce. Among its more exuberant excesses are such things as castration and psychosurgery, practiced in the smug belief that nothing could be worse than yet another crime.

But no matter how enlightened or how debased the improving program might be, it cannot be a sufficiently good reason for the punishment under whose auspices it is carried on. If an enlightened program of education or therapy were ordered by a court, without the harrowing experience of imprisonment, that would not be punishment, and it would not be a violation of natural human rights. If, however, rehabilitation consisted of the same enlightened program carried on in prison, the prison experience would still be a violation of natural human rights and could not be justified by the program, for the simple reason that the program, unlike the punishment, is not an institutional practice that is necessary to prevent an intolerable state of affairs from developing. Genuine programs of personal improvement that respect the basic human rights of prisoners: by all means. But only with a recognition that they do nothing to justify the imprisonment.

The conclusion regarding improvement of the person is the same whether carried on in the name of reformation or rehabilitation. As an incident of punishment, it is unnecessary to preserve us from an intolerable state of affairs and therefore cannot serve as a justification of punishment. If it is simply an incidental consequence of criminal liability, it cannot be counted as punishment at all.

Theories of punishment do not all place the same importance on the need to justify the existence of the institution of punishment, and some seem quite happy to assume that justification is simply not needed. This seems to be the case when economic theorists of law turn their attention to crime and punishment. Crime prevention is self-evidently a good thing, but just as economic behavior is supposedly determined in part by disincentives that influence the choices made by rational actors, so the disincentive of punishment will tend to deter criminal behavior. On this view, it is no more important to consider whether punishing people for their crimes is right than it is to consider whether imposing a cost upon a transaction is right. Both are to be regarded simply as inevitable expediencies in pursuing a desired objective. From the viewpoint of the economic theorist, human rights could have a significance only in terms of a cost to be paid, either by respecting human rights and allowing more crimes, or disregarding them and preventing more crimes—a cost in crimes or a cost in rights. As elsewhere in the economic analysis of moral issues in the law, what is left out of account is what seems most important. Striking a balance between costs and benefits is not a satisfactory resolution of concerns about crime and punishment. If the rights in question have any importance at all, respect for them is not negotiable, no matter how attractive the bargain that might be struck by giving them up. Allowing crime to flourish as a matter of expediency is unacceptable, and so is allowing, as a matter of expediency, violation of basic human rights, whether through punishment or otherwise. Economic theorists appear to have entered a demurrer regarding the question of justification, and so really they have no theory of punishment to offer as a possible foundation for the *right* to punish.★

5

Crimes as Demands for a Remedy

Punishment is seen quite differently by those who believe there is an urgent need for remedial action when a crime is committed. Unlike the views surveyed in the previous chapter, those positions that can be thought of as retributivist treat punishment as a required remedy for some unsatisfactory state of affairs that the crime itself has created. It is not a matter of seizing an opportunity to improve public safety or to render those who threaten it harmless, but rather a matter of not allowing a deeply disturbing situation to go uncorrected. Both approaches aim at making things better, but with a marked difference in concerns, perhaps not unlike the difference between a public health expert and a practicing physician in dealing with the challenges of an epidemic.

There are various views of what it is exactly that crime creates and punishment remedies. Six different sorts of theories cover the ground quite comprehensively, though it is not always possible to tell exactly where one ends and another begins. In fact, none of them makes a convincing case that punishment is a dire necessity, and so none of them makes a satisfactory case for its justification.

The first of these theories stresses those communal values and moral precepts which are said to be transgressed by a crime. This constitutes collateral damage to the community that is especially serious since only with the moral fabric of society intact is it possible for individuals with sharply conflicting interests to live together peaceably and engage in those projects of social cooperation that are required for the common good. Unpunished crimes sap the vitality of these common values and endorse their selfish disregard in the community at large. Punishment is also seen by some as a device for correcting the moral defect of the lawbreaker, evidenced by his breaking of the law, and a way of reconnecting such a person with "correct values".★

Criminal punishment as a moral nostrum can be faulted on many grounds. The criminal law is not, and is not meant to be, a repository of the values and moral principles we live by and owe an allegiance to. It is part of a scheme designed to protect against various sorts of harms and threats of harm—some deeply personal, others remote in the regions of public policy, and many somewhere in between. Murder may be morally wrong, but surely that is not the reason there are enforceable laws on the books to deal with it. Fear, inhibition, aversion are what the criminal law may be expected to produce, but not an appreciation of what is right and wrong. But even if one were to accept such a morally intoxicated view of criminal justice it is plain enough that the brutality inherent in serious criminal punishment could never be justified as some sort of moral correction for the simple reason that life without such moral correction is not intolerable, and because the preventive and pacifying effects of enforcement of the law, which *are* indispensable, are not impaired by the absence of moral correction. Furthermore, to the extent that upholding moral values is deemed a matter of vital interest, there is little reason to believe that embodiment in the criminal law is the only way, or the best way, of achieving that goal. Education in its many normal forms is far more likely to bring about an awareness of what is right and wrong and a commitment to avoiding any serious deviation in one's behavior. Better living conditions and better economic opportunities are also more likely to preserve and advance worthy moral ideals than are criminal prescriptions and the sanctions that back them up.

But vindication of moral precepts as a reason for criminal punishment has an even more serious flaw. Social cohesion through moral affiliation sounds like a cause worth supporting until one looks at test cases. What characterizes the society we live in is moral diversity and a pragmatic social cohesion that derives from practical matters connected with maintaining one's own and others' well-being. Other societies—and there are many in the modern world—need to maintain social cohesion through aggressive affirmation of certain core values, and sanctions against those who defect is an important feature of that social cohesion. Societies based on religious extremism come to mind, but there have been many societies in the twentieth century that insist on a conformity to dubious moral principles and call for a massive sacrifice of its members' individual freedom of choice in the interest of achieving certain collective benefits, or even worse, in the interest of bringing about the destruction of other people or other ways of life. No doubt the most spectacular example of social cohesion through punishment under law in recent times is the twelve-year history of Nazi Germany, and it illustrates well the political society's urgent need to enforce its morality through law when that morality is relied on as social cement, and especially when the moral ideals of that political society do not reflect the natural moral inclinations that endure among the people in spite of the supervening political will that seeks to change them.

There is another sort of objection to thinking of all, or even most, crimes as morally wrong. Those who conspired and attempted to kill Hitler committed serious crimes that are recognized in the criminal laws of any country, yet who would be disposed to say that what they did was morally wrong? The larger context in which we view their crime puts it in a different light. But any crime can similarly be viewed in a larger context than is allowed by the procedural limitations of a legal system designed simply to determine issues of criminal liability. Moral assessment of conduct is a matter quite different from its legal assessment, and in many cases of criminal liability, even though within the law there is no license to commit the crime, the moral case in favor of the defendant is stronger than the moral case against him. The business of the criminal law is dealing with the harm that has allegedly been produced or threatened by the defendant's conduct. But there is other business that is brought to light by novelists, historians, playwrights, film makers, biographers, journalists, and even (though much less often) by philosophers concerned with law and morality. Literature and history abound with examples of indisputable legal guilt and equally indisputable moral innocence welded together, and even in the humble everyday workings of criminal justice, the truth of *tout comprendre, c'est tout pardonner* resides in the very different moral assessment that the fuller context produces. And then, of course, there are numbers of crimes—like escaping from prison—that on their face concede the moral high ground to the perpetrator, no matter how ingenious a contrivance the embarrassed theorist may wish to wheel in to uphold such a law. Consider also perpetrators of drug-related crimes, who happen to make up a very large part of the prison population in many countries. There is little doubt that for most of them the case for moral exoneration would be stronger than the case for moral condemnation if all of the morally relevant elements bearing on their criminal conduct were given due consideration. It is not that the legal system means to be morally parsimonious or morally perverse, only that its role as protector and enforcer would be fatally compromised if what seemed the best case to be made morally, with everything of moral relevance admissible, were allowed to prevail in a court of law.

Moral wrongdoing, therefore, cannot be the touchstone that justifies criminal punishment for the astonishingly simple reason that the moral case in favor of exoneration may well be stronger than the moral case against it.

Punishment as the payment of a debt is a second principal theme of retributivism. No one imagines that this sheds much light on why we punish crimes, but everyone seems to agree that in serving his sentence a criminal is paying his debt to society. As John Mackie has pointed out, if there is any paying back going on it is society paying back the criminal for his crime, and not vice versa. But that point aside, the criminal paying a debt can hardly be given a literal interpretation for the simple reason that punishment in any plausible form debilitates the criminal and makes him unable to make any significant reparation for whatever harm he may have done. A different interpretation conceives the debt as a debt of suffering owed for the suffering caused by the crime. However, many crimes do not cause any significant suffering and so simply do not create the sort of debt that this interpretation contemplates. When there are victims that suffer as a result of a crime, recompense through suffering does have a strong primitive appeal. But surely it cannot be taken seriously as the principle underlying the law's most controversial institution in any society that has advanced far enough morally to discredit tit-for-tat and replace it with two-wrongs-don't-make-a-right. Since the metaphor of debt payment makes no sense either factually or morally it is not unreasonable to conclude that its popularity is attributable to a reassuring message. Having squared oneself, one's dignity is restored and one can walk once again with head held high. But what a starry-eyed message that is. There is, in fact, the continuing stigma of a criminal record and the enduring disgrace of having lived in prison as part of a community of criminals, which ensures that one is regarded far more poorly for the rest of one's life than if one were never punished at all.*

Victim satisfaction, and by extension public satisfaction, is the third item on the retributivist's remedial agenda. Crimes frighten people, anger them, and make them vengeful. Punishment makes them feel better. Victims of crimes that produce great personal trauma often have more complicated feelings that are not always helped by punishing the perpetrator, though failing to bring him to justice can be counted on to add the kind of insult to injury that impunity always produces. Even when no particular person can be identified as a victim, the very fact of a crime having been committed will produce a measure of indignation and resentment if it is allowed to go unpunished.*

Certainly the effects of impunity are a fact of life that arguably does justify punishment, and among those effects, the consequences of unassuaged feelings are of great importance. But there is a great difference between maintaining a system of punishment to protect against the baleful effects of impunity, and using punishment to gratify those appetites that crimes produce. The first seems a dire necessity, the second not at all necessary and a source of public mischief. It is the duty of enlightened government to curb vengeful appetites by enlarging the context in which the crime and its consequences are considered, providing in this way the moral ventilation that criminal proceedings cannot afford to let in. JF Stephen famously compared the relation of criminal punishment and feelings of revenge to the relation of marriage and the sexual appetite, a comparison that might be given a contemporary gloss. Just as the idea of gratifying the sexual appetite in a respectable way through marriage belongs to a past moral age, so the idea of satisfying vengeful (and other) feelings through punishment belongs to an earlier stage in our moral development.

A fourth grievance to be remedied concerns fair play. A popular theme among retributivists evokes the unfairness of allowing some members of the community to get away with breaking the rules while the rest exercise self-restraint and remain law-abiding. If crimes went unpunished, so the argument goes, those who broke the law would gain an unfair advantage over those who respected the law, and punishment is therefore justified as a means of redressing the unfairness that is created each time a crime is committed.*

Some crimes, though certainly not all, are crimes of gain—pecuniary or otherwise—and it appears that such illicit gains do confer an unfair advantage. A person who steals money enjoys an unfair advantage over someone who has to work for it. This is because the person who steals has given nothing for what he gets, while the other person has had to give his labor for it. The unfairness resides in the thief getting something for nothing, which is something we would all like, but which the law does not permit us to have. But is that really correct? Everyone, including the person who steals, is deprived by the law of the same opportunities, though the person who steals has not been stopped by the lack of such opportunity. It is open to all of us to follow in his footsteps and run the risks that breaking the law entails. All of us have an equal opportunity to break the law and gain an advantage over those who abide by the law. The advantage is not *unfair* because everyone is in an equal position under the law to gain such an advantage. It is true, of course, that stolen property should be restored to the rightful owner because it is his, but not because it is unfair to the rest of us for the thief to be allowed to keep it. Depriving the thief of what he stole is in any case not part of his punishment, and the question remains: what does punishment have to do with remedying unfairness?

Since we are all free to commit crimes and run the risk of being punished if caught and convicted, there would be unfairness if, having chosen to abide by the law—with its threats of dire punishment for violation—we find that those who do break the law are allowed to commit their crimes with impunity. In that case, however, our grievance is against the political authority responsible for such radical maladministration of the law. It is perfectly true that punishing crimes according to the law must be carried on as a general institutional practice in the legal system to prevent unfairness to those who might wish to commit crimes but choose not to because they believe quite reasonably that they might be punished. The principle to be observed is one of equal deprivation of opportunity, and punishment must play a crucial part in upholding it. Punishment does not, however, have anything to do with depriving the person who commits a crime of some illicit gain or some unfair advantage that he would otherwise enjoy over the rest of us.

It should be noted that only a relatively small number of crimes are crimes that result in the perpetrator having gained any advantage at all. Many more consist simply of harmful or otherwise unacceptable conduct, prompted perhaps by errant impulses or by any of the numberless moments of profitless malice that are part of the human condition, and that provide no benefit for anyone. There are, however, two other versions of the unfair advantage thesis that do not depend upon the crime itself conferring any advantage.

The first of these abstracts the rules of law as such from the crimes they prohibit. We then have a model community governed by rules whose authority all of the members are expected to recognize and whose prescriptions they are expected to follow. In such a community anyone who does not abide by the rules has behaved badly just because he has broken a rule, quite apart from whatever else he has done in breaking the rule. So if I display business papers in some part of the Club where this is not permitted, I am subject to censure just for breaking the rule, and it is plainly the case that if I am allowed to break the rules while other members are not, I am in effect in an unjustifiably privileged position and enjoy an unfair advantage over them. Viewing the criminal law in this way, as a set of rules with communal obligations implicit in them, does indeed allow claims of unfair advantage to pass muster.

But one must question how apt a model this model of rules is. The law conceived as a system of rules is a commonplace of modern jurisprudence, but it strains credibility to claim that the concerns of the criminal process are mainly concerns about the observance of legal rules rather than concerns about the crimes themselves. If one were to take the model of rules seriously, the first question to be asked is why is it necessary to impose calamitous punishment for serious crimes when it is after all only the unfairness entailed in violating a rule that is the reason for punishment. True enough, someone who breaks the law could be said to be a bounder and a cad who is willing enough to enjoy the safety and security conferred by the law-abiding habits of others, while at the same time acting in a way that threatens their well-being. Severe censure and even ostracism might well be appropriate. But how can the measures we take to punish serious crimes ever be justified on those grounds, especially since the retributivists who take this position adhere scrupulously to the principle of proportionality between crime and punishment?

Another account of unfairness puts freedom in the spotlight. The criminal law imposes "moral restraint" on everyone within the ambit of its jurisdiction. A person who commits a crime has enjoyed the moral restraint of others, but now by committing a crime he enjoys a release from his own moral restraint, which represents a measure of freedom that others do not enjoy. It is this supposed illicit benefit that puts the law-breaker in the position of unfair advantage which punishment remedies.

But is there really unfair advantage here? Most people who are careful to abide by the law and do not commit crimes do not feel they are suffering any loss of freedom, and it is unlikely that any attempts at philosophical consciousness-raising on this point would meet with success. Even if these people could be convinced that they are suffering some theoretical loss of freedom, if they do not care about it they could hardly be heard to complain that they are being deprived of something of value to them. No doubt there are some people who are anxious to commit crimes if only their conscience did not make such a nuisance of itself, and of them it can indeed be said that the moral restraint they exercise is a kind of sacrifice of freedom. "I would very much like to kill someone too, but my conscience won't let me, and it's damn unfair that someone like you, without such scruples, exercises his freedom in a way that I cannot." Is there here a legitimate complaint of unfairness that needs to be redressed by punishing the criminal for the extra freedom he has enjoyed? If there is a legitimate complaint of unequal freedom it is the same general complaint that could be made against the more unrestrained acts of anyone who is indifferent to the inhibitions that keep others from doing the same thing themselves. Why should the law seek to remedy such inequality of freedom, and in any case what could possibly justify the horrific medicine of criminal punishment to remedy such a relatively mild complaint?

Next among the suggested remedial powers of criminal punishment is the curious view that punishment somehow restores the lost dignity of the criminal. The point has already been discussed in connection with paying one's debt to society, but belief in the restorative powers of punishment appears in many different guises. A very special idea of human dignity is required, one that selectively excludes the terrible stigma that marks for life anyone convicted of a serious crime and disfigures permanently the reputation of those who serve time in prison. It relies on a conception of human dignity that ignores the steady diet of indignities heaped on prisoners as part of their daily life, and focuses simply on the fact that punishment can purge a person who commits a crime of his guilty conscience and the many anxieties that such feelings of guilt produce when a normally law-abiding person commits a crime, meanwhile ignoring the fact that merely confessing and repenting will almost certainly accomplish the same thing much more economically. Furthermore, restoring lost dignity has no relevance for people who live lives of crime and have made the psychological adjustments that are necessary to live as they do, since they have found dignity in lives of crime. In short, punishment to restore dignity is unfaithful to both the realities of criminal punishment and the facts of human dignity, and therefore cannot be taken seriously in the contest to justify punishment.

Finally, there is punishment as annulment, which is surely the least coherent of all remedial accounts of crime and punishment. Hegel certainly, and quite possibly Kant before him, stressed a supposed nullification of the crime, conceived as a wrong, through punishment of the one who committed it. The concern appears to be with unpunished crimes as still alive and kicking, and the remedy of punishment putting an end to this unhappy state of affairs. But surely the only thing that punishment can annul is impunity. The crime remains just as it always has been and always will be, an event like all events to be judged and explained in shifting perspectives and with evolving consequences, regardless of whether someone is punished for it or not. The annulment of a crime through punishment is no more coherent than the annulment of an injury that has been suffered by the infliction of another injury in return. Crime annulment to justify punishment therefore remains a starkly incomprehensible proposal.★

More than one writer has attempted to grow a theory of *lèse majesté* on the back of the nullification theory. Crimes are viewed as an arrogant presumption, an overriding of "the equal moral rights of others", and so in effect an arrogation by the criminal of an authority to which he has no right. According to this anti-chutzpah theory, punishment is a repudiation of this arrogant claim of privilege, and the hard treatment that it regularly entails is necessary to bring home this repudiation.★

The recurrent image of the calculating criminal who has decided to act in disregard of the law again asserts itself here, though in fact most crimes do not lend themselves to such a description. But even imagining that most crimes could be described in this way, it is hard to see what could possibly justify the destruction of lives that hard treatment entails in order to remedy the arrogant presumption that is alleged. Equally arrogant presumptions abound all around us, and though they may provide grounds for searching criticism that leads to avoidance and social ostracism, they are not normally taken to be proper occasions for punishment at all. We are left, then, with an account of punishment that starts in the obscure regions of Hegelian metaphysics and ends up with criminal punishment for the sort of socially unacceptable behavior that loses friends, antagonizes voters, and puts business deals in jeopardy.

In the depths of frustration and despair, there have been suggestions that any and all attempts to justify punishment be pressed into service. One writer puts the matter this way:

> The criminal law (even when its responses are non-punitive) habitually wreaks such havoc in people's lives, and its punitive side is such an extraordinary abomination, that it patently needs all the justificatory help it can get. If we believe it should remain a fixture in our legal and political system, we cannot afford to dispense with or disdain any of the various things, however modest and localized, which can be said in its favour. Each must be called upon to make whatever justificatory contribution it is capable of making.★

Do the various theories, aims, purposes, rationale, or whatever else that we might propose in support of punishment somehow constitute a grand scheme that provides collectively the justification that none could provide by itself? Is the cumulative effect of worthy objectives and good reasons acting in combination great enough to overcome our scruples?

It seems rather a strange suggestion that "such an extraordinary abomination", which surely it is, should be weighed in a balance against all the respectable purposes that it is said to serve. Once it is admitted that human rights of the most basic sort are at stake, it is hard to see how anything short of absolute necessity could possibly license their transgression. In that case, we are not weighing up the pros and cons, but only recognizing that in the most extreme circumstances there is a limited exception to what otherwise are unexceptionable rights. Failing to recognize such an exception would make a self-destructive tyranny of these basic rights, since measures that are absolutely necessary to preserve them would be barred by them.

There is another point. If, as we said in Chapter 2, justification of punishment means justification beyond a reasonable doubt, it is hard to see how this reason and that could ever in combination overcome the doubts that make each reason alone unsatisfactory. When the reasons are considered in combination the doubts are multiplied, not reduced, and certainly they are not eliminated.

6

Punishment and Injustice

Finding criminal punishment to be a morally acceptable social institution is only the first step in certifying its legitimacy. Beyond that, its practice must be carried on in a way that does not produce injustice in individual cases.

Clemenceau famously observed that military justice is to justice as military music is to music. He was commenting on the court martial of Alfred Dreyfus, which took place many years before Clemenceau became the French Prime Minister toward the end of the First World War. Whatever failings there were in the system of military justice that allowed Dreyfus to be convicted, they were hugely exceeded during the war (and not only by the French) when the rudiments of justice were discarded to serve the needs of a savage military discipline. Even the slaughter of innocents before a firing squad was accepted as a grim necessity in the midst of an unspeakable carnage whose message was kill-or-be-killed. Refusal to face death was punished summarily as cowardice or mutiny or desertion, and the penalty of death was imposed without hesitation in a setting in which life itself had become hardly more than chance survival. The killing of innocent soldiers arbitrarily selected *pour encourager les autres* was a sacrifice that passed muster as part of the great depravity of war.

We are shocked now by these stories, shocked even more than we are by the stories of immense slaughter in the midst of which these events took place. But why should the terrible fate of a handful of soldiers have a claim on our moral imagination more powerful than the fate of vastly greater numbers who lost their lives in combat? I suggest it is mainly the immense power that injustice possesses, its fundamental principles combined in these tragic episodes to give what happened a truly barbarous aspect.

Killing as punishment is gratuitous killing, which is to say it is inhumane, and when practiced under the authority of the state it violates a basic political right. Punishment in spite of innocence is always unconscionable, whether it is brought about by finding the wrong person guilty, or by treating a person as guilty when in the circumstances he is entitled to exoneration. It is deeply disturbing when punishment seeks to be monumental rather than measured, when it is selective or arbitrary rather than even-handed, or when it is simply unnecessary. In all of these respects military justice *in extremis* proved to be fundamentally unjust.

I want now to look more carefully at each of these forms of injustice to help understand what is required in administering punishment for crime in a manner that avoids injustice. Along the way I want to note some twists that are commonly given to concerns about injustice by those who want to make sure that a punitive response to crime is not interfered with.

First, there is injustice in the form of inhumanity, which is something that the enterprise of punishment naturally encourages. Serious criminal punishment has taken forms that represent the worst the human imagination is capable of. Learning gradually to restrain ourselves, we have managed over time to accept a quick death as a substitute for a slow and agonizing death, degradation as a substitute for torture and mutilation, confinement within sociable areas as a substitute for caging, workshops instead of galleys, or mines, or chain gangs; though certainly there has not been any steady progress from darkness into light. Concern about exactly what punishment should consist of has generally been regarded by theorists as a matter of detail that is beneath their professional dignity. Accounts of what people are actually subjected to in the name of justice are not part of their usual fare. Instead, conceptual subtleties are brought to light and arguments about basic principles are examined with great care, almost as though rigorous intellectual exercise will ensure that whatever is done in the name of justice need trouble us no further if only it is free of incoherence and irrationality.

This triumph of ideas over experience seems remarkable. What, one would suppose, should be of greater moral concern than what is actually being done when we punish? The experience of suffering, the lasting effects on those who experience it, the devastating consequences for others in a shattered and disgraced family that must share in the punishment—surely these are matters that deserve great attention from a moral point of view.

But the moral theorist finds it easier to deal with inherently abstract concerns like the nature of proportionality between crime and punishment, what really do we mean by like treatment and like cases, and is it really the same person who committed the crime that we are punishing throughout the entire period of the prison sentence. For the theorist, the savagery inherent in serious criminal punishment is an embarrassment easily avoided by a flight to abstraction. But this evasion can be costly. Moral revelation takes place in the immediacy of experience. In the realm of ideas, where critical assessment of that revelation must take place, the unpalatable truths that have been revealed have to be kept in mind with their concreteness and vitality undiminished if moral progress is to be made.

But moral concern about what is done in the name of justice is more than a compassionate concern that insists on humane treatment for fellow human beings. Criminal punishment is an invasion by the state that overwhelms basic human rights, and the way that invasion is carried on is important. The state must be held to strict account in not abusing its exceptional license. The incursion into the rights of those convicted of crime must be strictly limited to serving those purposes that justify the incursion. Anything that would violate the rights of people who have not been convicted of crime cannot be tolerated in the treatment of those who have been convicted if such treatment is not strictly necessary to prevent the consequences of impunity.

Next, injustice may consist of a failure to respect innocence. Credible threats of punishment in one form or another are indispensable in every area of life. Obedience, conformity, compliance, and cooperation, in whatever setting, depend heavily on what those who are subject to the will of others believe will happen to them if they do not do what is expected of them. Childhood, the military, and crime are the times and places where the idea of punishment is most at home, since being subject to naked coercive authority is not thought to be out of place there. Though *punishment* is not a favored term for the way control is exercised in normal adult settings, there are disciplinary measures, sanctions, penalties, and disincentives in every organization to help keep people doing only what they are supposed to do. The ubiquity of threats of undesirable consequences is, however, a menace to innocence. People are falsely accused or unjustly blamed for things that were not their fault—sometimes deliberately, but more often by mistake or with an indifference to the truth when that seems the most expedient course. To protect innocence we recognize a principle of desert and say that only those who deserve to be punished (in whatever form and by whatever name) may be punished. This principle of desert is no more and no less than the indispensable articulation of the rights of innocence in a world fraught with the dangers of false accusation and unjust blame.

Unfortunately, the punitive spirit is restless and will not leave the matter there. It seeks to infuse the principle of desert with a positive moral force, a mission far more ambitious than protection of the innocent. Those who are guilty and cannot claim that punishment is undeserved may indeed be said to deserve punishment. But beyond that first step, the punitive spirit seeks at least a license, and preferably a mandate, to punish those who are unable to claim that their punishment would be undeserved. In its less fierce aspect, the positive face of desert declares that those who deserve to be punished should be punished whenever there are not good reasons for not punishing. Dispensations may indeed be granted, perhaps for cooperating with the authorities, or because of old age or illness. These are cases in which punishment is thought to be deserved and therefore should be imposed were it not for the supervening reasons that are grounds of forbearance. But there is a more robust version of desert that insists that once it is determined that punishment is deserved, it is a failure of justice not to impose it. Considerations of mercy or expediency may still moderate its imposition, sometimes even cause its suspension, but never its nullification. On this view, whatever is deserved for wrongdoing *must* in principle always be exacted even if occasionally there are obstacles that stand in the way of exacting it in practice.

Protecting innocents by showing that for them punishment would be undeserved is a cause that compels universal allegiance, though the concern shown is not equally great everywhere. By contrast, punishing the guilty *in order to give them what they deserve* is a proposition that enjoys widespread and passionate, though by no means universal, support. For those who are especially concerned to see the guilty punished, the zealous protection of innocence is likely to be regarded as overzealousness and a hindrance to doing justice. The protection of innocence is seen by these people as important mainly to prevent punishment being brought into disrepute. On the other side, those whose main concern is protecting the innocent worry that suspicion rather than proof is most often the basis of accusation, that accusations are often made by people who have their own agenda, and that the case against the accused is often likely to be an exercise in plausible inferences rather than direct evidence to support the accusation. But regardless of where the balance of concern might lie, for everyone there remains a great mystery concerning punishment that is not undeserved. Once claims of innocence have been vanquished and liability to punishment has been established, what exactly is wrong in deciding arbitrarily not to inflict it? In such circumstances is there something more to doing justice than simply producing feelings of punitive satisfaction? If there is, what is it, and why is it so important? If there isn't, why should doing justice by punishing command our respect as a moral constraint?

Unjust deserts threatens innocence in a different way, and a principle of *just deserts* protects innocence against that threat. Lost innocence, like a lost umbrella, is an unqualified loss and not, like a loss of reputation, simply a diminution. But innocence is lost only with regard to the particular crime that has been committed. There is not the sort of transformation that takes place when through some special experience—having sex or being in combat, for example—a person is once and for all deprived of a certain innocence. Innocence remains intact regarding any crime for which guilt has not been determined, and that innocence is protected by a principle of just deserts limiting punishment to the crime for which guilt has been determined. Since all crimes are not regarded as equally serious, and since punishments are meant to reflect the seriousness of the crime, punishments are not all equally severe. The principle of just deserts imposes a limit on the severity of punishment to ensure that there is no infringement of surrounding innocence when a particular crime is punished. It has an important part to play in restraining the wish to punish the criminal *qua* criminal, rather than simply punishing him for the crime for which he has been convicted.

But once again the punitive spirit is restless, this time wanting to make sure that there is a good match between the severity of punishment and the seriousness of the crime, but doing so in a way that misconceives the seriousness of the crime. Concern about the seriousness of the crime derives ultimately from concern about the effect of the crime upon victims—actual or prospective. Just deserts in its aggressive aspect therefore appears as a principle meant to provide adequate satisfaction to victims. In this aspect, doing justice no longer is the dedicated but dispassionate service of an ideal. It is an instrument employed to assuage feelings, and the measure of its use is the strength of the feelings that must be assuaged. These feelings may derive from the experience or anticipation of harm, or they may be more obliquely related to harm as moral sentiments in the face of wrongdoing. In either case appetites are to be appeased, and just deserts then represents misery inflicted in sufficient measure to satisfy a victim's appetite, even when that appetite exceeds what an objective appraisal of the crime would indicate.

A sense of proportion between crime and punishment must be maintained if injustice is not to overwhelm the proceedings. This gives rise to a fourth cautionary principle, and one that goes beyond the protection of innocence. The harm or wrongfulness that a particular crime represents may be great or small in relation to any other crime. The urge to punish the crime is determined by these untoward elements, and the urge is measured by how harmful or how wrong that crime is seen to be. It is simply a matter of feeling more strongly about one crime than another, more fearful, more angry, more indignant, or whatever else it is that will leave us unsatisfied if we feel a crime has not been properly punished. Those who have the power to prescribe or impose punishments are expected to share this sense of proportion and to exercise their authority accordingly. If they do not and we find that shoplifting and rape are punished in much the same way, there is then an abuse of power since either suffering greater than is necessary to obtain satisfaction is being inflicted, or there is a deficiency in meeting the demand for satisfaction. Excessive punishment seems the more egregious abuse of power and the greater injustice. Throwing away the key is, however, politically popular, and to mask the injustice it will often be carried on under the familiar slogans of incapacitating the dangerous, making a forbidding example of (and for) the wicked, and reforming the wanton. But community service for a murderer or a life sentence for a three-time shoplifter is in either case injustice in the form of abuse of power.

The requirement of proportionality has universal intuitive appeal as a negative principle that protects against injustice. But as a positive principle its practical application appears hopeless. It is unclear whether the seriousness of the crime should be measured by the harm associated with a crime, or by the wrongfulness of the conduct that constitutes the crime, or by some combination of the two. Though it is beyond controversy that murder is more serious than shoplifting, it is by no means uncontroversial when or whether armed robbery is more serious than arson, and it is indeed a vexed question generally how we are to arrange crimes in order of seriousness, and with what intervals between them on the scale of seriousness. Difficult as those questions are to resolve, there is the no less difficult question of how to devise a matching scale of punishments, and how to tell when a correct match is made between seriousness and severity. With regard to the scale of punishments itself, a sentence of eight years is not twice the punishment of a sentence of four years, since the quantum of punishment relates essentially to the effect upon the life of the person being punished as he experiences it, and eight years may well transform a person as he comes to see himself in ways that would not occur if the sentence were half as long. There is also the very challenging point that the experience of criminal punishment varies enormously with the person who is punished and with his circumstances.

Proportionality does, however, serve as a bulwark against injustice if it *appears* to be pursued, even though the pursuit is carried on through legislation embellished by a mechanical scholasticism and driven by shifting political winds, with implementation from case to case according to the idiosyncratic sentences of judges whose exercise of discretion depends very much upon their own very different personalities, backgrounds, and views about crime and punishment. It serves as a bulwark in spite of these eminent defects because it ensures that concerns about seriousness and severity are not altogether disregarded, as they well might be if some political expediency were being relentlessly pursued, or if the emotions of the moment were allowed to carry the day.*

At this point another principle emerges. Great efforts have been made to achieve a sentencing process whose decisions are as free as possible of idiosyncratic judgment. These efforts are prompted mainly by concern about another source of injustice—unwarranted disparity. Unwarranted disparity in sentencing occurs when there is no *relevant* difference between two cases, yet the sentences are not the same. Unequal treatment of those whose criminal liability is the same is on the face of it second only to punishment of the innocent as an occasion of injustice, even when the unequal treatment does not result from any kind of discrimination against a convicted person and is simply a matter of how and by whom the pre-sentence report was prepared, or who the sentencing judge happens to be and how he is feeling that morning.*

But what is *relevant* in distinguishing two cases is a question so vexed that the idea of a scheme of mandatory "guidelines" is eagerly embraced as an escape, even though in many cases it constrains the judge to impose a sentence that in good conscience he would never otherwise impose. Ignoring the person and paying attention only to the crime reduces opportunities for judicial prejudice to make itself felt in deciding on a sentence, and so reduces the amount of variation in sentences for crimes that in themselves seem equally serious. But at what cost? Disregarding the likely effects of a sentence on the one who must serve it is wanton indifference to suffering, while disregard of the personal background that makes sense of the crime avoids the moral issues that transcend the crime but should influence the punishment. The injustice of treating like crimes differently and producing disparate sentences may be outweighed by the injustice of treating like crimes alike if that means disregarding matters of moral importance that are different in each case.

There is one further prophylactic principle that needs greater recognition than it generally receives. We have seen that the institution of punishment serves a very modest purpose that requires that sentences be passed when there is a conviction. But the sentence need be no more than is necessary to keep faith with the institution of punishment with regard to the limited preservationist purposes that justify its existence, and any sentence that is more than that is excessive. Such a sentence would be no less unjust than any other sentence that is excessive.

This minimalist principle can only hope to have an influence on sentencing by providing a background which enables the sentencer to reflect on his reaction to the crime. This background is where the haunting questions arise for every thoughtful lawmaker and every conscientious judge when they see that such an awful business needs to rest on principles that are truly sound. Otherwise popular passions will be exploited for the political capital they can produce and politicians will perform a charade of solemn public duty to justify the systematic production of unnecessary human misery.

7

Crime, Harm, and Moral Wrong

So far we have developed a deeply unsettling view of crime and punishment. Crime without punishment would be intolerable, yet punishment is a morally debased practice that we would wish to abandon if only we could.

But there is another possibility to be considered. Perhaps if we understood exactly what a crime is we might take a more tolerant view of punishment for it. We might see crime in a light that makes punishment look better. In this chapter and in the three that follow, we look more closely at the essential elements of crime with this in mind.

We might begin by considering the banal observation that all crimes are wrong. It is widely assumed that this can be taken to mean that all crimes are *morally* wrong, and that in so far as they *must* be punished, crimes must be punished for that reason. Admittedly, when looked at in isolation punishment is itself an object of moral opprobrium. But if the wrong for which the law prescribes criminal liability is a *moral* wrong, then punishing it justly will dissipate that opprobrium, and punishment will appear to be a good thing after all; exactly what serious moral wrongs require, especially when they are serious enough to be treated as crimes.

But in order to know whether punishment can be viewed more positively in this way, we need to know more about why crimes are wrong, and in particular we need to investigate the claim that they are morally wrong.

There are two elements that in combination determine that conduct is criminally wrong, and that serve to measure how wrong it is. One of these is *harm*, which is the untoward feature of what normally happens when a crime is committed and prompts us to make certain conduct criminal in the first place. The other element is the *culpability* of the conduct associated with the harm. Culpability reflects the relationship between a person's conduct and the harm that occurred or was threatened.

First we turn to harm, and start with some preliminary points.

All crimes are endowed with harms of one sort or another. Sometimes the very conduct that constitutes the crime also constitutes the harm. Crimes of physical violence are generally of this kind. But harm is sometimes the consequence of the criminal conduct, as when willful neglect has fatal consequences, or indeed when any criminal act may be expected to have injurious consequences. Sometimes the harm is to be found in a collateral state of affairs that is promoted by the criminal conduct—stealing promoted by the receiving of stolen goods, for example—one of many crimes in which what is done is free of harm itself, but at the same time serves to promote harm elsewhere.

The relationship between conduct and the harm associated with it is of the greatest importance. Criminal conduct may simply *threaten* harm but not produce it, as it does in crimes of attempt and other inchoate crimes like conspiracy and solicitation which also aim to produce some criminal harm, though at a greater distance. In fact, it is the threatening character of *all* criminal conduct that makes it criminal. Harm is important in defining what is threatened, and it is harm that gives the threatening conduct its criminal significance. The seriousness of the harm weighs heavily in assessing how serious is the threat posed by the conduct. And so does the magnitude of the threat, which is measured by the imminence of the harm that may result from the conduct. Together they tell us a great deal about how wrong the criminal act is.

Although all crimes have their associated harms, not all of the harms come ready-made, and it is useful to distinguish those crimes that leave us in no doubt about the existence of harm from other crimes that require the invention of harm to make the interdicted conduct convincingly criminal. Five different classes of crimes can be distinguished. Crimes in the first three have their harms ready-made, while in the other two the harms must be contrived to make the criminalization convincing.

The first class comprises those core crimes that violate natural human rights. Murder, rape, and robbery need no recognition in a legal system to enjoy their status as crimes. They are crimes in which not only the harm and the victim come ready-made, but so does the crime. Their legal credentials will include definitions that are helpful in resolving those disputes that inevitably arise at the boundaries of any crime, but no credentials are necessary to identify them as crimes.

A second class consists of crimes that come similarly equipped with harm and victim already provided before the law confers its recognition, but the crime itself needs legal recognition to enjoy the status of a crime. Embezzlement, for example, needs its legal credentials to be a crime. It is easy enough to imagine a legal system that is different from ours and sees no reason to make punishable the spending of another's money as one pleases if one has been given temporary custody of it by the owner, just as one might imagine a legal system different from ours in which people who are able to pay their debts are punished if they refuse to pay. Victims there certainly are in both cases, and the harm is perfectly apparent, yet only if the legal system has made it a crime is it a crime.

Crimes comprising a third class are concerned with conduct that we discover to be harmful, rather than conduct in which the harm is obvious. These harms are either unknown until we become aware of them as we learn more about the world, or else they are brought from relative obscurity to a prominence that mandates penal legislation. Crimes of this sort are found in every area of activity in which there is government regulation. The environment, the economy, transportation, and national security signal the beginning of a long list of governmental concerns about dangerous or harmful activities that are brought to public attention by experts, by journalists, by people who discover they are victims, or by politicians who think public awareness would be a feather in their cap. The crime that goes on the books is created to provide appropriate protection, and activities that previously were innocent become criminal with a stroke of the pen.

This brings us to crimes in need of a harm. There are two different groups.

The first of these consists of crimes that produce intense displeasure rather than harm. Paradoxically, the offending activities are most often engaged in simply for pleasure or some other variety of selfish indulgence. Many of these offenses are nothing more than jumped-up taboos, an excursion by the law into the land of the forbidden. We do, after all, cherish our taboos, and will not see them violated with impunity. Still, there is a certain uneasiness when the public force is brought to bear on what is harmless, even though it is widely perceived as dissolute or even depraved. "It displeases us in the extreme, therefore you may not do it" is the voice of naked tyranny, whether spoken by an overwhelming majority of the community or by an autocratic custodian of public morals. "You will be punished for doing what displeases us" is the ultimate political insult, and so to exercise political power in a respectable way, harms are invented.

It is no surprise that these made-to-order harms tend to be remote and speculative, or that they are usually more, rather than less, dreadful. If the harm were a hovering presence and quite certain to occur under certain circumstances, there would be no need to contrive its existence and the crime would belong in different company. But since there is no such constraint, those who wish to see these activities as harmful are free to exercise their imagination as they will, with suppositious harms contrived to shock the rest of us out of our complacency and justify the inordinately severe punishments that are prescribed. Obscenity destroys the moral fabric of society, pornography turns the excited male into a potential rapist, marijuana is the port of entry for the evils of heroin addiction, sodomy and bestiality the subversion of the natural order—the list is limited only by the number of taboos that are felt to need protection from aggressive irreverence. Speculative products of the scientific imagination, especially when bolstered by statistical conjectures, are especially prized as items of harm because of their pseudoscientific authority. And when the prospect of harm is particularly remote, there is always the slippery slope and the thin end of the wedge to confirm our apprehensiveness.

Not all crimes in this class are violations of taboos. Some are simply an offense to sensibility in the form of a disturbance or an insult, an embarrassment, or something disgusting. In these cases a harm is easily provided by requiring a suitable setting for the crime—in a public place, so that the need to avoid the unpleasant experience will constitute a limitation on free access by the public, or so the experience itself is likely to produce public disorder. In this way genuine harms can be made to spring forth from the circumstances with only minor definitional contrivance. Offenses to sensibility then have increased credibility as crimes and they can be prohibited by law for a better reason than that they displease others.

In an especially thoughtful and thorough work on the subject by Joel Feinberg, offenses have been distinguished from harms, and when sufficiently worrying are allowed to serve in their own right as a warrant for making conduct criminal.★ The issue is whether some harm is required to justify criminalization, or whether certain things that offend without harming may be prohibited. At the outset it is necessary to decide how to draw the boundary between harm and those experiences that are intensely unpleasant but leave a person unable to say he was harmed in any obvious way. There is disgust and revulsion; shock to moral, religious, or patriotic sensibilities; shame, embarrassment, and anxiety; fear, resentment, humiliation, anger. In extreme forms, these are the kinds of experiences that seem to provide grounds for criminal liability regardless of harm.

But Feinberg's examples depend upon the setting in which the offensive conduct takes place. Remove it to a place where it is easily avoided without inconvenience to those who are otherwise forced to endure the experience and criminal prohibition becomes problematic. It is not the offense to sensibilities, then, that supports criminalization, but rather the fact that as a practical matter the victim *is forced to endure it*. That does constitute a harm, just as *being forced to endure* physical pain or psychological trauma constitutes a harm. By contrast, if the same offensive conduct is easily avoided, neither the intensely displeasing idea that it is going on, nor the experience of it that one has chosen not to avoid, can lend support for criminal liability since in neither case is there any harm done. It might still be the case that some intensely offensive conduct that is easily avoided is nevertheless likely to provoke violence or create unacceptable public disorder. In that case, the threat of harm is ready-made, and no invention is required. Collisions do of course occur when rights of free expression meet countervailing rights relating to security and public order, and claims of harm are by no means dispositive of the deeper issues that are then presented. My interests here bypass the great questions of political liberty, and are limited to looking into the harms, authentic or notional, that are produced to give certain conduct its color as criminally wrong, and so give support to its criminalization.

The fifth class of crimes consists of crimes that also require the contrivance of harm, though in contrast to the high public morals profile of the last group, the conduct in these crimes is best described as morally inert.

Many policies of government are formulated to achieve objectives entirely indifferent to considerations of harm. Both the policies and the ways of implementing them are part of a process of change driven by the winds of political expediency, and rules that allow certain activities one year may be changed to prohibit them the next. When compliance is important, as almost always it is, penal sanctions are introduced to keep on the straight and narrow those on whose activities the success of a policy depends. The crimes created for this purpose bear some resemblance to those crimes that are created to deal with conduct that we *discover* to be harmful, since both varieties exist only to implement policies of government. But there the similarity ends, for in the first case certain conduct is found to be harmful and appropriate action is taken, while in the second case harms are contrived to make a law more acceptable when it is deemed desirable in the public interest to make otherwise harmless conduct punishable. The tax code, for example, is a constellation of ever-changing rules reflecting a myriad of fiscal policies. To effect compliance, blanket penal provisions are enacted. And to make the crime of tax evasion seem appropriately criminal, fanciful harms are invented which portray as victims all those who depend on tax revenues, meaning everyone, as well as all who must share the burden of producing those revenues by paying taxes, meaning almost everyone.

There is a universal harm suggested by all lawbreaking, and to the extent that such a harm is given recognition, there is a further class of crimes that is a universal class encompassing all crimes. Membership in such a class is an especially welcome prospect for all of the crimes that require the contrivance of some harm to infuse them with criminality. This purported universal harm is the harm done just by violating the law. The very act of breaking the law is imagined to be some sort of harm to society. It threatens, perhaps disrupts, social solidarity and undermines the bonds of community and good citizenship—there are many rhetorical embellishments used to convey the message.

It is something of a paradox that the suggested harm might well be construed as a beneficial harm if the law that is broken is bad. Solidarity in support of a bad law is something to be opposed, and even if breaking the law is not an acceptable way of opposing those who support it, the harm being done to such solidarity is itself no bad thing. It is also worth noting that in this scenario the harm constituted by every incident of serious lawbreaking is the same. Presumably, then, all lawbreaking as such is equally wrong no matter how serious the harm being dealt with by one law or another. For that reason the wrong that is constituted by the very act of lawbreaking is of no use for purposes of determining how wrong a particular crime is. It can be of use only if it is collapsed back into a crime of a particular sort which affects social solidarity more or less according to the seriousness of the crime. But that is to say no more than that included among the harms emanating from each crime is a blow to social solidarity, more or less mighty depending upon the seriousness of the crime.

What we have then is a medley of harms, some suppositious and no more than notional contrivances, some as real as can be and manifestly criminal when associated with appropriately harmful conduct, some real enough but needing to be made criminal by the law through the political process. Not all crimes, and not all criminal harms, fit neatly into a single category, and many can be seen as belonging to more than one. It is not easy to say, for example, just how far natural human rights extend and exactly which crimes are a violation of those rights; or when it is that the law is only giving official recognition to some harm that is already notorious rather than recognizing some newly discovered harm that needs to be dealt with through penal prohibition. Allowing crimes to be members of more than one class is the most convenient answer. But however we choose to classify particular crimes, membership in one class or another has interesting consequences for the question of why, exactly, a crime is wrong, and the question of how wrong is it.

It is generally thought that crimes are *morally* wrong, and that the harms that are associated with them play an important part in explaining why they are morally wrong. There are three different theses that can be advanced to support this view. Many versions have appeared during the long history of the moralization of crime, and though they differ in detail, they can be distinguished along certain paradigm lines. I shall call these theses the rights thesis, the social obligation thesis, and the infliction of suffering thesis. They can be summarized in the following way.

In the straightforward cases of serious crime that readily spring to mind, someone is seriously harming an innocent victim without any element of excuse or justification. Such an act is a violation of the most important personal right the victim has—a right to be safe and secure as one lives one's life and goes about one's business peaceably among one's fellows. If violating such a right is not morally wrong, it is hard to imagine what could be.

Another view of the matter takes social obligation to be the crucial element. In the interest of each individual's well-being, as well as the common good, each member of society is presumed to be bound by a solemn undertaking to obey those laws that protect each member from being harmed by other members and that otherwise promote the common good. So long as the law is the outcome of a process that accords with the reason for submission to this rule of law, each member has a moral duty to abide by his undertaking of obedience. Violating the law is morally wrong as a breach of that duty.

The third thesis has the most powerful intuitive appeal since it relates to the victim's suffering. Crimes are morally wrong because of the consequences for victims. In whatever context, the occurrence of avoidable suffering is necessarily a matter of moral concern. Nothing in our moral life is more indispensable than compassion, and an indifference to suffering marks the end of all moral capacity. Since those crimes that concern us most are commonly a source of great suffering, the harming to which that suffering is attributable must surely be morally wrong.

The questions that we need to pursue are: which crimes are morally wrong; why are they morally wrong; and to what extent, if any, is the criminal law concerned about them as moral wrongs?

First, there are those core crimes that have independent standing as crimes regardless of legal recognition. Understandably, the harms associated with these crimes produce the strongest feelings since they are the most serious harms, with death surely in first place, since nothing is more important than life itself. For all of these crimes, violation of a natural human right can be cited when the crime is committed. The harm done normally entails a great deal of suffering by those who may be accounted as victims. And whatever undertakings there might be to abide by the law surely they are breached by the commission of these crimes. These crimes are therefore most certainly moral wrongs according to all three theses that support a view of crimes as moral wrongs.

But the important question is not whether these crimes are morally wrong, which they surely are, but whether the harm they represent is being dealt with by the criminal law because that harm is morally wrong. This question is important because our expectations would be quite different if it were moral wrongs that were meant to be protected against and redressed. It would not be mainly a matter of dealing with harm and threats of it among people who are naturally made fearful and vengeful by such events, but instead the criminal process would be occupied with what had happened against a background of rights, duties, and sufferings that make moral investigation the important human activity it is.

Though the criminal law is not in the business of dealing with moral wrongs as such, there are indeed important moral concerns that weigh heavily in the criminal process. If basic rights are not recognized and protected by our criminal law, we may rightly argue on moral grounds against this political failure. If there are exemptions from criminal liability for those in privileged positions, so that the obligations of the good citizen are not universal, again there are moral grounds for demanding an end to such a state of affairs. Similarly, if the law fails to take note of the suffering inflicted by some on others, the complaint against that failure is grounded in moral argument. But in all of these cases it is the morality of the criminal law that is being criticized, not the morality of criminal conduct.

There are a number of other points to be made against the view that the criminal law has as its mission the punishment of egregious moral wrongs. The first of these is a general point about the social obligation thesis, which (unlike the other two theses) purports to have an application to all crimes that are put on the books.

In its benign versions the social obligation thesis posits an obligation to abide by the law that is binding upon each member of society in the interest of protecting everyone. This seems unobjectionable enough, though perhaps naive in its oversimplification of social facts in order to achieve a certain grandeur in principle. One thinks first of Anatole France's observation that the law applies equally to rich and poor in making it unlawful to steal bread, to beg in the street, or sleep under bridges. But there is a more insidious feature to the social obligation thesis. In many regimes there is a premium placed on the obligation to obey the law in order to eliminate whatever it is that the government opposes, all in the name of protection of the common good against what has been designated as socially harmful. The government may have seized power, or like Hitler's, may have come to power by democratic election and be representative of the will of the people. Hitler's great program of German resurrection and purification was based on a program of social cohesion under law that had as a principal objective purging the country of Jews and other undesirables who were said to be the source of the country's most serious evils. But it is important to remember that it was not because the Jews were not in reality a social menace that laws against them in Nazi Germany were a bad thing and entailed no moral obligation of obedience. The objection is more general. Obligations to abide by laws that deal with alleged harms are no better morally than the outcomes they produce, and those outcomes comprehend a great deal more than success or failure in dealing with harm. What price in freedom, justice, humanity, and dignity is exacted to provide a safer, healthier, more prosperous, and more secure community is a question that can easily result in very depressing answers anywhere. For this reason one must treat as suspect the unadorned social obligation paradigm that is meant to make the criminal law *tout court* seem an exercise in public morality.

Other difficulties that undermine the moral view of the criminal law are encountered while still in that heartland of self-evident crimes where harms are unmistakably criminal. It is a basic tenet of the moral position that how wrong a crime is will depend, in part, on how great the harm is. A vengeful murder of one's partner is more wrong than a vengeful burning down of his house, and this is because of the difference in harm. But if how wrong a crime is depends, in part, on how great the harm is, we must know what harm is in fact attributable to it, with reference to the extent of the harm as well as the kind of harm.

Looking first at the question of extent, we are confronted with a deeply entrenched tendency to view everything bad that occurred as a result of a crime as part of the harm attributable to it. But sometimes these things are matters of pure chance and not foreseeable, or they are injuries waiting to happen because of conditions the perpetrator could not possibly know about. Such objections, however, will normally be brushed aside even though they clearly have great moral weight bearing on questions of responsibility. When a crime is committed no harmful occurrence is excluded in assessing how wrong it is so long as the harm would not have occurred except for the crime, and this is true no matter how unexpectable such a harmful occurrence might be so long as there is not a more immediate independent cause of the harm. This represents a triumph of feelings over moral sophistication and allows one to disregard the question of how wrong the crime really was in favor of how strong are the feelings it produces. The restraining principles that limit responsibility are overwhelmed by the will to exact punishment.

When the same general problem arises in tort law, there is the same tendency toward amplification of the wrong to include whatever harm occurred, though there are limits imposed with regard to circumstances that are well removed from what was done. It seems right that when the object of the exercise is compensation for what was suffered, the victim should not end up uncompensated for any part of his injury even though it is not reasonable to expect the wrongdoer to have anticipated some elements of it. The question then is one of fairness in determining who should suffer the loss, and at the outer limits the innocence of the victim prevails over the innocence of the wrongdoer because we feel in fairness that those who act assume risks that are not assumed by those who have not acted. But when a crime is committed and the perpetrator is brought to justice, there is no loss to be adjusted. The disposition to include whatever harm has occurred in judging how serious the crime was defeats an assessment of its moral wrongfulness and in its place substitutes a decision based on what is best suited to gratifying the victim's feelings.

Immoderate concern about harm is currently much in evidence. The cause of victims' rights quite remarkably reached the stage of a proposed amendment to the United States Constitution that was approved by the Senate Judiciary Committee in 1999, aimed at ensuring that the voice of the victim would be heard in deciding what sentence to impose. Victims' rights is, in essence, a movement inspired by the conviction that the punishment should fit the harm, whatever it might be. Its most prominent feature in the United States has been the emergence almost everywhere of victim impact statements, which in effect allow what was formerly excluded as a source of passion and prejudice to be introduced to measure the extent of liability. Gratification of passions, rather than containment, is the uncivilized message that is unashamedly declared by this movement.

The difficulties encountered in placing limits on the harm attributable to a crime are compounded by difficulties in identifying the kinds of harm that matter in determining how wrong a crime is. The difficulty lies partly in the protean character of harm, and is also due in part to the diversity and the complexity of the victims who suffer it, all of them persons and so very complex beings indeed.

Rape is a much discussed crime, and serves as a good example.* Something called sexual autonomy is generally regarded as the interest whose violation constitutes the harm of rape. In stark legal terms, rape is intercourse without the woman's consent. Certainly a woman's right to choose whether or not to have sexual intercourse needs robust legal protection, and a violation of that right is a very serious business. But typical instances of rape involve things considerably more serious than a failure to respect the victim's right to decide whether or not to have sex. There is the physical and psychological harm suffered through force or intimidation. There is degradation and humiliation of a very special kind in not being able to escape the experience of unwanted sexual intimacy. There is even the notion, now no longer fashionable in most Western cultures, of grave harm to the respectability of the victim and the victim's family. These harms and others suggested by them come to light in any sensitive account of the details of a particular case of rape. But the law provides no mechanism for assessing the wrongfulness of what happened in each case by weighing the multiplicity of harms of various sorts. If it were simply sexual autonomy that mattered morally, rape would be no different than other serious crimes of coercion in which a person is made to do something disagreeable against one's will. But to get it right *morally*, there must be an assessment of all the various harms in order to come to a conclusion about just how wrong is the violation of each of the personal rights constituted by each of the harms, and how great the suffering that was inflicted. In determining liability for rape, however, the criminal law is concerned only with the harm inherent in the conduct constituting rape. Such an account is morally impoverished. Beyond the issue of consent, the stories of different cases of rape have very different moral complexions depending in large part on exactly what took place, with whom, in exactly what circumstances, and with exactly what results. Criminal liability itself, however, has no need for such extended considerations and treats them as irrelevant. It is only lack of consent that matters.

The next set of difficulties is presented by that second class of crimes where harms and victims come ready-made, but where the wrong needs suitable legal recognition to enjoy the status of a crime. The reason why such recognition is required is quite simple. To live is to run risks, and to a very great extent we are left on our own to protect ourselves as best we can. A contract obligation unperformed or a debt unpaid might be made criminal. But it is not. We are left to our own devices to exercise prudence in avoiding such risks in the first place, or to insure against them if we can, and we can resort to the civil remedies the law affords to redress the loss we suffer when prudence or negotiation have failed us.

Though there is no less certainty about the harm in this second class of crimes, the fact that these are not self-evident crimes indicates that the seriousness of the harmful conduct is less certain. For these crimes, people might have been left to their own devices in dealing with the wrongs that are done to them. Indeed, in most cases pursuit of civil remedies will still provide greater satisfaction to victims of these crimes when the resources of the perpetrator are sufficient to make such an exercise profitable. It is true that there are rights violated by these crimes, just as there are with those crimes that are self-evident, but these rights are deemed less important than the rights violated by the core crimes. In these crimes there is not an experience of suffering by the victim inherent in the criminal conduct, and in addition because universal restraint is less an issue, there are less compelling demands upon civic conscience, both of which again lower the tone of moral outrage for these crimes. The moral claim is less urgent, and plays an even smaller part in determining how wrong the crime is. In fact these crimes are largely the product of the draftsmen's skill in creating conditions and qualifications to transform into crimes those wrongful acts that were not criminal before the intervention of lawyers. Embezzlers, fraudsters, forgers, blackmailers, perjurers, and many others have their status as criminals depend upon the detail of the finely crafted harms that the authors of the criminal law have deemed appropriate for criminalization. This leaves a great deal that is wrong from a moral point of view without criminal liability, and ensures that even though there are no significant differences in what is deemed morally wrong, because of different qualifying conditions in the law there will be important variations from one jurisdiction to another regarding when it is that a particular wrong is a crime.

Even more problematic is the class of crimes in which the conduct made criminal has been discovered to be harmful. These crimes are created to provide protection against what has been discovered, and the subject matter might be anything from the environment and health to civil rights and securities trading. The harm might come to light as a scientific discovery, or it might emerge as part of a new appreciation of certain political, economic, or social conditions. Because these crimes are creatures of the political process, the seriousness of the harm and so the wrongfulness of the crime are matters that will depend on the prevailing climate of public opinion regarding the discovery, as well as considerations of expediency in the political arena. It is true that the public and communal aspect of these laws is prominent, and for that reason these laws have an element of civic obligation that imparts a tinge of the morally wrong to their violation. It is also true that the victims, once they have been identified, are morally entitled to the law's compassionate regard and to suitable protection from harm no less than victims of more obvious crimes who do not need to be discovered by the law. But these moral considerations must be seen in the context of the political process that gives birth to them. Viewed in this way, there is little substance to the claim that a crime of this sort is in essence a moral wrong rather than a more prosaic transgression that offends some measure of expediency enacted to suppress some harmful activity.

The two remaining classes of crimes are very different in their moral posture, though in both of them the crime, the harm, and the victim are all made to order.

The first group comprises those crimes that are on the books to enforce morals. The distinctive feature of these crimes is the nature of the wrong they are meant to address. The wrong is in fact independent of any harm that may be proposed as justification for having the crime on the books. There are strong feelings of disapproval that attach to the prohibited conduct, and that alone is deemed sufficient for such conduct to be made criminal. We are in the realm of the forbidden, most prominently occupied by sexual inhibition, but with such other sources of the forbidden as religion, social convention, and patriotism contributing their fair share. The absence of harm is, however, an embarrassment once there is entry into the legal arena, and so harms are contrived to support the case for criminalization. What are pressed into service are ominous and impalpable harms that remain hovering on a distant horizon, like homosexuality's destruction of the moral fabric of society; or else some harm that is all too real, but whose connection to the displeasing activities is equally speculative, like rape induced by exposure to pornography. When attempts are made to suppress these activities or to keep them out of sight, by laws against trafficking in forbidden materials or by confining the offending activities to restricted areas, what might be thought of as second-order harms, to neighborhoods, or to parks, or to bookshops, are constituted by violation of such laws. These auxiliary harms are in fact policy-grounded harms that belong to crimes of the next class.

It is more than a linguistic paradox that the enforcement of morals by the law is the weakest instance of the law dealing with what is morally wrong. "Morals" violations, when put to the test, do not show up at all well as purported moral wrongs. There are no basic rights of others that are violated. These crimes do not inflict suffering on others. And though they may well be disruptive of social solidarity, the laws that make a crime of these activities create prima-facie cases of transgression of individual rights. In doing that, they run afoul of the principle that the undertaking to abide by the law, which is the basis of a claim of moral wrongdoing, is limited to those protective purposes that give that undertaking its claims on everyone's allegiance. There is of course the further point that since liability to punishment must be proved beyond a reasonable doubt in individual cases, the need to have on the books laws creating such liability must be proved beyond a reasonable doubt, and morals offenses fall woefully short of meeting that requirement.

There is finally the other class of crimes in which the crime, the harm, and the victim are all made-to-order, this time, however, without there being any independent wrong to be dealt with. This is numerically the largest class of crimes in any well-developed legal system of the modern world. It comprises those crimes that are invented by government to coerce compliance with some policy of government that does not have any independently existing harm as the focus of concern. In most instances such laws are directed to dealing with narrowly defined problems and are far too limited to confer a general benefit.

Again there is scant reason for suggesting that these crimes are morally wrong. The basic rights of others are not violated. Suffering is not inflicted. And the morally binding undertaking of the good citizen extends only to abiding by the law in the interest of everyone being protected from harm or being benefited in some other way, not in the interest of ensuring everyone's obedience to the presumed will of the majority, or to any other will, whatever it might be, so long as it has been duly enacted into law.*

A pernicious confusion arises when it is assumed that if legislation is morally unobjectionable there is a *moral* duty of compliance by each citizen, when in fact morally unobjectionable legislation simply means there is no moral objection to enforcing it. There is of course a *legal* duty of compliance, and if the legislation is morally unobjectionable it is unburdened by any moral impediment to its enforcement against those who have a legal duty of compliance.

It is worth stressing as a final point that except for those crimes in which the harm is self-evident, the seriousness of the harm associated with the crime is very largely a matter of free-wheeling legislative discretion. Lawmakers are, of course, first and foremost politicians, and it is their own political fortunes and the fortunes of their party that exert the greatest influence on the exercise of that discretion. Crimes rooted in policies or in morals are treated as more or less serious, and penalties are made more or less severe, as political considerations dictate. Public opinion and the intramural process of political consensus within the legislature are what dictate decisions. More enlightened determinations of how morally wrong a crime might be are generally left out in the cold. Bismarck's observation should not be forgotten: No man should wish to know how sausages or laws are made.

Before concluding this discussion, a word needs to be said about the worst sorts of crimes that we are forced to confront. Though the five classes of crimes I have distinguished are meant to comprehend all crimes, it seems important at the end of their moral assessment to consider a special group of crimes that do not settle comfortably in any of the five classes, and indeed seem not even to be adequately comprehended by the notion of a crime.

These are the uncommon instances of the worst crimes, marked by sheer inhumanity and representing the most evil acts that humans are capable of. They are the crimes that really have no name (to make use of Churchill's arresting phrase), though we of course must give them names to make them amenable to the workings of the legal process. Some are the instances of individual depravity over time that looked at objectively give meaning to the otherwise uncertain concept of evil, even though we know there are explanations that will put what was done and the person who did it into more familiar territory. More worrying still are the depravities of those who have great power over their victims as political leaders, or as members of the organizations that carry out their schemes. Because of their positions of power and prestige, the leading figures are thought of first as protectors and benefactors who have adopted reprehensible means to achieve their goals, rather than as some species of criminal. Hitler, Stalin, and Pol Pot are convenient names to begin a very long list of such leaders in recent times, and a much longer list of underlings who carried out their plans with an insatiable appetite for depravity can be constructed by consulting the bountiful archival records of atrocities that our times have produced.

The harm done by these activities seems at first to have a grounding that is encompassed completely in our moral life, and for that reason we find the reduction of atrocities to mere crimes something of an embarrassment. The grossest infliction of suffering, no matter what great cause it is said to serve, goes beyond any condemnation that the criminal law is capable of producing, and we are left with unsatisfied moral outrage that we are obliged as civilized people to contain as best we can by treating these atrocities as mere crimes. But regarding these acts simply as moral wrongs of the worst sort does not do them justice. Even though the suffering they cause and the rights they violate provide grounds for moral condemnation, such condemnation is woefully inadequate. These are acts beyond the bounds of our moral life, acts that take place in the region of inhumanity where the human fellowship that is the foundation of all moral life has ceased to exist. Not knowing what else to do in a civilized community with its own moral life to consider, we adopt the forms of our criminal jurisprudence to deal with these atrocities as best we can by treating them merely as crimes.

8

Criminal Conduct and its Culpability

Harm can occur when no one is to blame. This is the case when no one had anything to do with it, like the harm to life on earth from unknown cosmic radiation. When any activities that can be connected with the harm turn out to be free of fault, once again no one is to blame. Or when the activities were far from faultless, but were the activities of someone who lacked standing to be treated as a responsible person, again (strictly speaking) no one is to blame. But stark, blameless misfortune is a fact of life that we accept only with the greatest reluctance. We are naturally disposed to look for someone to blame when something bad happens, and only with great disappointment after a fruitless search will we grudgingly admit that we were unable to find a culprit.

Much more often we do find someone who at the very least should have done something that was left undone, or should have done differently what was done, or (if we are really lucky) someone who did something that should never have been done.

There are great satisfactions in blaming. The criticism that otherwise might land on one's own doorstep is deflected onto others. Blaming confers a sense of superiority that critics enjoy over the objects of their criticism, and especially the sense of superiority that those who are in the right enjoy over those who are in the wrong. There is, moreover, an important practical side to blaming since many claims against others for recompense can succeed only if blame can be pinned on them. When something seems especially wrong and calls for more than recompense, those whom we blame, we also wish to punish. The satisfactions of blaming, the acknowledgement of wrongdoing with an apology, and any compensation that might be available are sometimes just not enough to make up for the harm. Never is that clearer than when a crime has been committed.

Blaming someone for murder, rape, or even shoplifting seems a laughably limp response. What is important, however, is that the person accused should not be able to show prima facie that he is not to blame. He is said to be blameworthy for what he is said to have done (which would indeed be feeble if meant simply as criticism), and sufficiently blameworthy to meet the requirements the law has set for the crime charged. *Culpability* is the preferred term of art for blameworthiness, and when an accusation is made, the real importance of claiming that the conduct in question was culpable is the service such a claim performs in denying that the conduct was not blameworthy.*

But what is it that connects a person with harm in ways that make blaming him appropriate? The answer (squeezed very tightly in a nutshell) is this: *his ability to control the events that produce the harm; his duty to exercise that control to keep the harm from occurring; and his failure in doing his duty.* If any of these elements are not in the picture, we cannot criticize a person by saying that he did something he should not have done, or that what he did he should have done differently, or that he failed to do something he should have done. It is true that we might choose to disregard the fact that a person had no ability or duty to exercise control over the events, and so, even though he was not in any way to blame for the harm that occurred, he still is to be held liable for it. Doing that, however, abolishes all normal rights of innocence with a single stroke and creates "strict" or "absolute" liability, which in the criminal law must always be seen as a very grave step.

This link between the person and the harm is *conduct*, which when it exists is an event, sometimes as simple as pulling a trigger, sometimes as complex as implementing a policy of genocidal extermination. It is of course a personal event, though many persons together may be involved in a single item of conduct (which is what *an act* is), and the person whose conduct it is may, as for example companies or governments, be an entity other than a natural person. Conduct comprehends only matters that are purportedly under or within the control of the person whose conduct it is. Whatever is done *intentionally* is the domain of conduct, though in general it seems a good idea to rely as little as possible on the overworked and much abused concept of *intention*.

We live our lives in a way that makes it unusual for harm to be attributed to what we do. Yet we do things with an awareness that in everything we do there lurks some risk of harm to ourselves or to others. Some items of conduct are associated with certain harms in a particularly intimate way.

Driving a car is a wholly innocent activity that is fraught with dangers which we avoid by adhering to conventions of safe driving. Other activities are seen as inherently harmful, and for them alarm bells will ring even if the harm happens not to occur. Regardless of the occurrence of harm, such conduct by itself will often attract criminal liability just because it *threatens* the harm. Sometimes, as with reckless driving, the conduct all on its own is made criminal. Sometimes, as with attempted murder, the conduct attracts criminal liability only derivatively from a crime that requires harm to occur if there is to be liability.

★ ★ ★

Attempted crimes are a fascinating species of crime and a gold mine for the theorist. Three outstanding problems in the law of attempts reveal a great deal about culpability, about how we judge how wrong a crime is, and why indeed we should think it is wrong at all. One of these problems concerns the punishment of attempts in relation to punishment of the completed crime. A second problem concerns liability for an attempt when commission of the completed crime was impossible. And a third problem presents itself when we consider what was done and try to locate the threshold for attempt liability.

The first of these problems appears when we notice that attempts are punished less severely than completed crimes even though the attempt consisted of conduct that was no different than it would be for the completed crime. Imagine two assassins with crossbows aimed at two prospective victims. Following exactly the same routine, the two assassins shoot at their targets moments apart. The first arrow strikes its target with fatal consequences. Only a chance movement of his intended victim made the arrow of the second assassin miss its target, yet the fate of the would-be assassin is affected almost as dramatically as the fate of the would-be victim. This does not seem right since there is an assumption that how wrong a person's conduct is must be judged by what was within his control, as well as a further assumption that how wrong the conduct is determines how great the punishment for it should be. And so of course it does not seem right that two persons bent on assassination should be punished differently when the outcome was different but everything they did was exactly the same. It seems to follow that in such cases there should be the same punishment for the attempt as for the completed crime.

Considerable ingenuity has been exercised in trying to explain how the difference in punishability might make sense. Unfortunately, the greater the ingenuity, the less satisfactory the explanation. What needs to be explained are the intuitive feelings about punishment for attempts that are reflected in the law, not how the difference can be made to appear rational when crime and punishment are appropriated as materials for philosophical invention. One proposal, for example, invites us to view those who perform exactly the same criminal acts as participants in a lottery in which winners and losers start out on an equal footing. Those who fail in their criminal endeavors are regarded as winners, and those who succeed are regarded as losers, with punishments meted out accordingly. Another proposal asks us to imagine that licenses to commit crimes are being auctioned, and the price to be paid in punishment is greater for licenses that permit completed crimes to be committed, based on the idea that a greater advantage over people who do not break the law is enjoyed by the criminal who succeeds in his attempt, though those who are unsuccessful must pay for the opportunity in any case. But neither of these exercises provides a way out of the dilemma that prompts them. The question remains why those who have done exactly the same thing should be punished differently when there is a difference in outcome attributable entirely to chance.*

Others have taken a different route, avoiding the search for some solution in principle and seeking instead an explanation of why people feel the way they do. Plato thought that when the harm did not occur we owe a debt of gratitude to the gods and celebrate the occasion with a kind of partial amnesty in the form of lesser punishment.* Adam Smith pointed to the lesser resentment that is natural when harm has not occurred, saying:

> The resentment of the friends of one who had been attacked with a design to murder him and had made his escape is not near so great as if he had been actually murdered. In this case the grief for their friend blows up their resentment and makes them demand the greatest rigour of punishment. In the other case their joy on the escape of their friend soothes and lays asleep their indignation.*

Here we have a great truth about conduct and punishment. We are ineluctably tied to our feelings in deciding when and how much to punish a crime. How wrong the conduct is becomes a subordinate consideration, and when the measure of punishment is to be decided, we inevitably find ourselves affected more by what has happened than by what has been done. It has been suggested that this is a matter of moral luck, but that is not right. It is rather a matter of luck pre-empting any opportunity for moral assessment. Chance, not culpability, is what drives the engines of punishment, for we need only deal with those feelings of grievance that arise in response to what has happened. When there is only an attempt, we are more relaxed and can recognize that the further suffering through more severe punishment that a moral assessment of conduct might allow would be gratuitous, and that such punishment would therefore itself be morally reprehensible. Even though the conduct of the two assassins is indistinguishable, we punish the failure less because, fortunately, we do not need to punish it as much.★

The second problem concerning attempts is no less instructive.

Sometimes it turns out that the completed crime could never have been committed even though everything was done that would normally bring it about—intending to kill him, someone pulls the trigger with the gun inches from the victim's head, but fortunately the gun just happened to be unloaded; or the intended victim just happened to be in the kitchen when the shots were fired into his bed in the middle of the night; or he just happened to have died minutes before the bullets were fired into his body. In each case the perpetrator was of course unaware of the impossibility and had every reason to believe he would accomplish the killing. These are what might be called cases of *happenstance impossibility*.

It is important to note that in assessing the conduct all of its elements must be taken into account, including whatever the accused knew or believed or thought he was doing, for those mental elements are at the heart of the control center that confers upon behavior the status of conduct. If he knew his gun was not loaded, the *threat of harm* posed by pointing it at the victim's head and pulling the trigger is different than it would be if he believed (incorrectly) that the gun was loaded (though of course the victim would *feel* equally threatened in either case). The law reflects this difference in the threat of harm that characterizes the conduct by calling one attempted murder and the other something less serious, though still a completed crime in its own right.★

There are other cases in which the facts also make it plain that the completed crime could not be committed, but in these cases what was done could never have brought about the intended result no matter what the circumstances, though the person who did these acts thought it could. These are cases of what might be called *manifest impossibility*—with homicidal intent, pins pushed through the heart of a wax model of the victim, or some incantation recited over a harmless drink to be served to the intended victim, or any of the numberless scenarios that a consummate belief in magic or religion might produce. It is no more than wishful thinking, but the criminal purpose and the commitment to achieving it through what is done is no less real than in cases of happenstance impossibility.

There are many cases falling between *happenstance impossibility* and *manifest impossibility*. These are cases of what might be called *implicit impossibility*, where, for example, the means employed are of an appropriate sort but grossly inadequate for the job at hand, as anyone who was serious about it would be expected to know—using a weapon with nowhere near the necessary range, trying to open a bank vault with hopelessly primitive tools, attempting to pass transparently bogus money as the real thing.

But when should criminal liability be imposed, and why?

Cases of happenstance impossibility are cases in which there is a serious threat of harm in what was done, and the threat exists even though the harm could not occur. Conduct of a kind that might have produced harm is what interests the criminal law, and the conduct here is of that kind since it was only by chance that the harm did not occur.

Cases of manifest impossibility, on the other hand, are cases in which the conduct posed no threat of harm, cases in which it cannot be said that what was done might have produced harm. When the threat of harm is lacking, the conduct fails to arouse criminal concern, though it might possibly call for some other sort of intervention to address the untoward aspects of such behavior.

In between we have the very broad class of implicit impossibility, running from cases in which impossibility results from mere technical ignorance to cases in which anyone can see that the project could not possibly succeed. Somewhere within the class a line must be drawn, but the principle is the same. Cases that merely amuse are on one side, and cases that alarm are on the other. Some cases will ring alarm bells and at the same time make us laugh, at which point we recognize that threats of harm can have a funny side even if the law is in no position to treat them simply as a joke.★

But what does this tell us about criminal culpability? In all of these cases of attempt there was the same dedication to achieving the criminal purpose and the same diligence in pursuing it. Nevertheless these cases exhibit dramatic differences in criminal culpability. These differences have nothing to do with the will to do what was wrong or the commitment through action aimed at achieving what was wrong. Whatever mistakes there were in any of these cases fall outside the moral realm, and are simply failures of knowledge or appreciation regarding things of practical importance in bringing about the harm that was the object of the exercise. Yet the conduct is criminally culpable in some cases but not in others. Criminal culpability, then, is not a matter of moral wrong. Rather, it depends on the presence of conduct that not unreasonably frightens and angers us. It serves as a warrant for punishing in the name of necessary protection, not moral rectitude.

The third great challenge for the law of attempts is deciding when the threshold of liability is reached.★ Smith has been nurturing a grievance against Jones and decides to kill him. He tells this to his wife, who is shocked and tries to make him change his mind. Smith thinks more about what he will do and finally decides to shoot Jones when he comes home at night. Smith buys a gun to carry out his plan. A few days later he goes to Jones' house and waits in the bushes, but when Jones appears Smith is embarrassed to find that he has forgotten to take the gun with him. The next night he returns with the gun, but his wife has removed the cartridges, and he is furious when he discovers that the gun is not loaded. On the following night he again waits in the bushes, this time with a loaded gun, but Jones fails to appear. The next day Smith learns more about what Jones was supposed to have done previously, has a change of heart, and abandons his plan to kill Jones. If Smith's wife had informed the police and they had intervened, at what point or points, if any, could Smith be charged with attempted murder? Would it make a difference if he only found out his gun was not loaded by pointing it at Jones and pulling the trigger? Would the abandonment matter? If not enough was done to incur liability, what more, as a minimum, would be necessary?

Under the common law, what was done must come dangerously close to the completed crime if there is to be attempt liability. Complete preparation, no matter how unequivocal, would not be enough by itself, nor would it be enough just to be on the way to the job—in the car fully prepared and driving to rob the bank, for example.

Most modern penal codes in the United States have adopted the less demanding test that is found in the Model Penal Code. Only a substantial step toward committing the crime is required once there is a clear and unequivocal intention to commit the offense. In some jurisdictions there are tests that place weight on the likelihood of a person changing his mind, or on whether an observer of the conduct in question who had no independent knowledge of the person's intentions would be left in any doubt about what the person intended to do.

The point of importance here is that these tests are concerned with whether a sufficient threat of harm is presented by the conduct in question, and the different tests take a different view of what constitutes a sufficient threat. From a moral point of view, however, it makes no difference whether one is in the car on the way to the bank when apprehended, or whether the arrest is made in the midst of work on a safe with an acetylene torch in the bowels of the bank. Rules regarding abandonment are to the same effect. A change of mind leading to voluntary abandonment can avoid liability if it takes place early enough. Turning the car around and going home might well avoid liability even under the substantial step test, though abandoning work on the safe after suddenly deciding that crime does not pay will not have the same happy outcome under any test. The harm is still sufficiently remote in the first instance, but not in the second. From a moral point of view, however, it makes no difference when the criminal activities are voluntarily abandoned so long as no harm has been done. In addition, what prompted the abandonment may well have moral significance—a genuine change of heart, or only cold feet on this occasion. But the law is indifferent to such considerations. So long as abandonment is early enough, the inner workings that are of moral significance make no difference to the law.

The three great issues underlying attempt liability show that criminal culpability and moral culpability are only distantly related descendants of a common critical practice. It is not harmful intentions in acting, no matter how settled those intentions may be, that makes conduct culpable for purposes of criminal liability. It is the threat of harm that such conduct poses that matters, with the caveat that the threat comprehends only what would naturally be perceived at the time of the conduct, and that the conduct comprehends whatever is known to the person whose conduct it is and can be said to inform his intention in acting as he does. By contrast, in judging the moral culpability of conduct it is the intention with which one acts that is of crucial importance.

★ ★ ★

Criminal culpability, however, does not play its most important role in the law of attempts. It features most prominently in ranking the wrongfulness of conduct by assigning degrees of culpability to what is done. As we shall see, this role has been misunderstood by those who treat crime and punishment as the themes of a great morality play. But first, a word about the part that criminal culpability plays in assessing conduct.

To appreciate how a person might be connected to some harm, we need to consider what contribution he made to those events that we take to be the occurrence or threat of the harm. Sometimes when terrible things happen those who at first we think are in some way involved turn out to be innocent bystanders. At other times we conclude that they do indeed bear responsibility, though not in every case to the same degree. They might actually have meant the harm and did what was necessary to bring it about. Or they might not have had as their purpose the occurrence of the harm, but could hardly be unaware that what they were doing would very likely bring it about. Alternatively, they might have been doing something notoriously dangerous with utter indifference to the possibility of harm occurring. Or they might simply have been careless and inattentive in doing something that was not dangerous if done with due care and attention, but otherwise could result in harm.

These different degrees of culpability are needed to allow us to articulate the different kinds of conduct that we wish to make punishable, for even short of complete innocence we recognize that not every blameworthy act merits treatment as a crime, and not every act that does merit such treatment is equally serious. I come home drunk, turn on the water, and stand watching while the tub overflows, causing damage to the apartment below. Certainly this is blameworthy, though not conduct ominous enough to qualify as criminal mischief. If in a mood of neighborly vengeance I do the same thing purposely, criminal prosecution in addition to a lawsuit might well follow since the conduct is of a more threatening sort. If the harm itself is greater—a fire rather than water damage—the same indifference to consequences that fell short of criminal liability before might now be enough for the law to intervene with arrest and prosecution for the campfire I made on the living room floor. Recklessness with fire in these circumstances is a good deal more dangerous than recklessness with water, and so the greater harm in prospect makes the conduct criminal even though its degree of culpability is the same.

The degrees of culpability for the various elements of criminal conduct are expressed adverbially—*purposely*, *knowingly*, *recklessly*, and *negligently* are the eminently serviceable designations used in the Model Penal Code.*

They are meant to ensure that what is done intentionally—the conduct in question—is sufficiently ominous to warrant the imposition of criminal liability. How ominous the conduct itself is will not, of course, be affected by the occurrence or non-occurrence of the harm.

What we have, then, are judicious limitations of criminal liability based upon the relation between conduct of a certain sort and the harm that concerns the law, to ensure that criminal liability will be possible only when there is a sufficiently robust threat of harm constituted by the conduct.

There are those, however, who think that the criminal law is and ought to be a way of dealing with occasions of serious moral defection. For them criminal culpability is a species of *moral* wrong, and punishment the natural response. I know of no term that is used more and explained less than *moral*. Its use is obvious, but its meaning is obscure, and like most mysterious things, its attractions are enhanced by its mystery. Here, as elsewhere in the book, I make no effort to dispel the mystery, a task that must be postponed to another day, though I hope to make clear what jobs I am doing when I use the term.

In criminal law theory the mystery is exploited through the use of the terms *actus reus* and *mens rea*, which in combination are the elements of criminal conduct. When put to proper use these terms designate what must be done to constitute a particular crime, comprehending those aspects of conduct that are readily accessible as events in the physical world, and those aspects of conduct to which others do not have direct access and so, like all affairs of the mind, must be inferred from what is reported and what can be observed, or be taken on a faith that is ultimately blind and based entirely on what the accused has to say about himself. It is obvious that the conduct of someone who makes a mistake that kills is not the same as the conduct of someone who intends to kill. When death is caused by a mistake, the conduct will be viewed very differently, and it does not matter whether the mistake was a result of lack of skill, inattention, ignorance, or false belief. Making a mistake in this sense means that a bit of what was done was not as it should have been according to the conscious design controlling the activity. This provides an excuse, for far from being entirely under our control, the world in which we live, including our own fallible selves, is endowed with abundant opportunities for mishap. The death intended and the death by mistake will equally be caused by what was done. *But keeping in mind the difference between mere activity and conduct, we see that the conduct in the* second case does not include the bit that caused the death, and so we deem that conduct less culpable, which is to say we recognize an excuse that downgrades culpability and perhaps even exonerates. And so it is with each degree of culpability, where arguments of exculpation can be advanced based on the facts of the accused's conduct in a world in which happenstance is a constant challenge.

However, a moral coloring is commonly given to the term *mens rea*, and the degree of culpability becomes the degree of wickedness. The maxim "*Actus non facit reum, nisi mens sit rea*" was given a classic moral rendering by Blackstone as "An unwarrantable act without a vicious will is no crime at all". This language represents the shift away from a world of harm that can be investigated and managed for better or worse by a legal system and other parts of government that seek to make the world a safer place. The shift is toward a world in which those who administer public power through the law carry on their activities guided by intuitions about human nature. Guilt is no longer just a synonym for criminal liability, and culpability is taken to entail feelings of guilt that are available for exploitation by those who administer the law. Remorse, repentance, and forgiveness are seconded from sin to crime. Reprobation, condemnation, and punishment of wickedness are seen as the mission of the criminal process. In this morally intoxicated environment it is not surprising that deciding how wrong conduct is will be heavily influenced by notions that traditionally have flourished outside the criminal law, mainly in churches.

Our moral life does indeed have an important part to play in the business of crime and punishment. The concerns of political morality carry great weight in deciding what limits to place on the exercise of public power in prescribing what is punishable, in enforcing the law, and in administering the institution of punishment. Moreover, when crimes are committed that violate the victim's basic human rights there is a moral wrong that those who exercise public power are not free to ignore. Many of these crimes will naturally engage the panoply of moral sentiments that constitute our moral life, and moving from anger toward understanding and conciliation may well result in moral growth for both victim and perpetrator. Through an appreciation of the harm he has done the perpetrator may experience some moral uplift, though this will depend on what his crime was really all about and how he feels about it now. But once again the question here is whether the criminal law ought to be designed and operated to vindicate moral attitudes, or whether it should be concerned with harms that need to be protected against and victims who need to be assuaged. Allowing culpability to take a moral turn invites the state into moral preserves where even in a mature democracy it has proven itself to be a poorly qualified manager and, still worse, a cynical manipulator of popular sentiment to serve the ends of political power.

Besides the usual threshold designations of culpability, there are other terms whose job it is to act as intensifiers. Some of these do find occasional employment at the definitional threshold, as when *malice aforethought* or *premeditation* is used in the definition of murder. Terms such as these might seem to support the suggestion that it is after all a moral assessment that is called for in determining liability. Even more convincing are terms like *cold-blooded*, *vicious*, or *atrocious*, which the law tends to avoid in drafting its texts, but which may seem to have great moral force when used elsewhere to describe a crime. Culpability is certainly affected by what these terms suggest, but is it *moral* culpability?

Murder in cold blood is worse than murder in the heat of passion, and it will be judged more culpable throughout the system, from police investigation to parole hearing. But in fact cold-blooded murder is worse because of the greater dangers that it represents: a death decided upon without regard to normal inhibition, and in its most dangerous form a contract commodity available to anyone for a price. A calculated cold-blooded killing is, however, in itself no worse *morally* than a hot-tempered murder by someone who allows himself to be carried away by his emotions, since in both cases the *moral* wrong consists in violating the same natural human right, in inflicting the same suffering, and in violating the same social undertaking.

But these three reasons why crimes *in general* may be morally wrong are not the final word with regard to particular crimes. When a crime is committed any proper moral assessment will include questions about *why* the perpetrator did what he did, presented in terms that make sense from the perpetrator's point of view at the time. We must know what the motive was to make proper moral judgments, or when there is no motive to explain the crime, we must understand the motivation. But the law can happily disregard these questions in determining guilt or innocence since it is only *what* was done, and not what prompted it, that determines the question of criminal liability.

If the criminal law really was based on a moral assessment of conduct, consideration of motives and motivations would dominate the proceedings.

What prompted a person to act as he did must surely be at the heart of any moral judgment of that person for what he did. This is true for any crime, and it is especially true for crimes committed by that portion of the population that are born into conditions of hopeless deprivation and violence, where crime is often regarded as the only practical means of obtaining certain satisfactions that others who are not so unfortunate take for granted as their birthright. But with rare exceptions, motives are not part of the definitions of crimes, and motivations never are. It would be unthinkable to allow someone to get away with the harm he does because it was done with a worthy motive—killing a tyrannical stepfather to restore a happy family life, for example; just as it would be unacceptable to create criminal liability for otherwise innocent conduct because a malign motive lurked behind what was done—taking a frail and aged parent for a walk in the cold weather hoping that its effects might hasten the day of one's inheritance. It is true, of course, that motives and the further explanations that make them clearer do influence discretionary decisions throughout the criminal process—decisions about whether to bring charges and, if so, for what crimes, what sentence to impose, whether to grant parole. But even in exercising their discretion, police, prosecutors, judges, and parole boards are interested mainly in the light that a motive sheds on the criminal danger inherent in the criminal conduct. A benign motive reassuringly tells us that what was done did not have the harm as its object. A malign motive tells us the opposite story, confirming our apprehensiveness, while a motive that is not straightforwardly malign but simply displays an indifference to harm in the pursuit of some other object, though hardly reassuring, will not ring alarm bells quite as loudly. Morally worthy and morally depraved are, however, quite beside the point.

Where, then, are we left in what some suppose is the pursuit of moral judgment through the criminal law? In its operation the criminal law is concerned with harm and the threat of it—what is needed to prevent that, and what needs to be done when it occurs. Confounding the criminal law with moral issues and turning it into a regime with a moral mission subverts the criminal law in two ways. It exposes the soft underbelly of social injustice and personal misery to which the criminal law remains indifferent. It is the condition of those people who most plausibly might be expected to commit crimes that is given prominence by moral investigation, and for the criminal law any engagement on these issues in the moral arena must surely be a losing battle. The other consequence is no less disturbing. It invites those with the power to dispose of our lives to engage in activities for which they are ill-suited, putting them in a position to abuse their power under the banner of a facile moral rectitude. By contrast, moral rights restraining such abuse of power are comprehensible and manageable, and respecting those rights turns out to be a full-time occupation for those who administer criminal justice.

9
More about Culpability

Once someone's conduct is linked to a criminally untoward occurrence and comes under scrutiny as a possible crime its culpability is of paramount importance in deciding about guilt or innocence. And if someone is found guilty, culpability again looms large in deciding on an appropriate sentence. Strange, then, that exactly what culpability is should remain an enigma, though all the while confidently invoked as the very touchstone of liability to punishment and (along with harm) pre-eminent in determining what the measure of punishment should be.

Early in the last chapter I suggested a formula for criminal culpability that had three elements. In this chapter I want to consider this proposal in a more leisurely way with a view to making culpability in criminal law theory a more intelligible notion. In the next chapter I take up the prevailing idea that a wicked or otherwise untoward state of mind is the key to culpability, and try to show that this is quite wrong. This mentalist notion encourages a view that I wish to discredit—the view that concern about culpability in the criminal law is concern about what is morally wrong in criminal conduct.

There are two reasons why keeping criminal culpability free of moral entanglements is important. One is that it helps us keep moral argument in its place, where it is less likely to contaminate questions of criminal liability with notions of moral wrongdoing that ought not to influence decisions about liability. We must be careful not to put people in prison simply because what they did was in some way seriously wrong from a moral point of view. The other reason, which is no less important, has to do with understanding why we are interested in culpability at all. Those who identify criminal culpability as a kind of moral defection are mainly interested in the *inculpatory* force to be derived from determinations of culpability. I want to suggest that it is not *inculpation*, but rather *exculpation*, that makes culpability such an important matter. Once good grounds for accusation have replaced good grounds for suspicion there is a quest for moral support to back up the raw feelings of antipathy that the crime itself has produced. According to the prevailing view, it is in the mind of the person who is accused that true evidence of moral unworthiness is to be found, and a theory of psychoculpability, as I shall call it, is spun out to make this seem plausible. That theory, and the misconceived moral criticism that it promotes, are what I want to argue against.

But first, criminal culpability as I see it.

The formula I proposed ran like this. When a harm that concerns the criminal law occurs, or when there is some threat of it, it is prima-facie appropriate to blame a person for that occurrence if, but only if (1) he had the ability to control the events that produce the harm or the threat of it; and (2) he had a duty to exercise that control to prevent or avoid the untoward occurrence; and (3) he failed to exercise that control.*

The first condition in this formula is of paramount importance. It points sympathetically to the very limited control that we have over what happens in the world, and particularly over what happens to us and to others whose fate concerns us as a result of our activities. Not really being masters of our fate is an enduring part of the human condition, and though we struggle with some success to push back the frontiers of the uncontrollable, as a practical matter our exposure to unwelcome events can be dramatically reduced only by practicing a tedious and deadening routine of safety above all else throughout our lives. Unexpected things that are unwelcome happen even then, and when they do we may well find ourselves unable to prevent the harm that is likely, perhaps even certain, to occur. Still, we are not entirely at the mercy of the Fates. Though we may be unable to prevent the harm, in many cases we may still be able to contain it, and perhaps even undo it.

We are of course all endowed with the wisdom of hindsight, and after the event we often know exactly how we might use the resources that were at our disposal to prevent the harm if only we could turn back the clock. That wisdom and those resources do not, however, give us the ability to control the crucial events unless we also have the ability to turn back the clock, which is rather more problematic. At that point the unwisdom of hindsight often asserts itself and tempts us to pass judgment as though the benefits of hindsight really were available at the earlier time.

But even if the wisdom of hindsight were at our disposal at the earlier time, all too often there is nothing we could have done to prevent the terrible things that happen to us. Most serious illnesses and many of the most serious accidents and natural disasters make that clear. There are forces at work in the world that we know nothing of until they show themselves, by which time the damage is done. And because we lack the know-how, there are forces that we cannot frustrate even if we are aware of them before the damage is done.

But what does our sad plight as victims of fate have to do with crime?

Among the many sources of harm in the world a prominent place is occupied by the activities of those who engage in dangerous or harmful conduct. Sometimes such persons lack the ability to control whatever the occurrence or threat of harm depends on. It may be that certain bits of the world that impinge on their activity are fraught with perils that they cannot cope with. The issue then comes down to whether the risk created by this inability is itself something the actor is accountable for, or whether the risk is something that is not his business and is properly regarded as resting in the lap of the gods. Resolution of this issue turns on whether or not the harm is expectable, whether or not it is the sort of thing that should come as no great surprise to anyone engaged in such activities. When favorable answers are forthcoming and we are disposed to say it was sheer accident, or some freakish occurrence, there is then an exemption from liability that bypasses questions of culpability and declares simply that the actor is ineligible as a candidate for blame.

More problematic are those cases in which the lack of control is due to some personal abnormality that reduces a person's ability to cope with challenges presented to him by the world within, or by the world around him. Physical handicaps can produce such cases, though because the inability is usually more obvious these cases are disposed of more easily. Much more common are cases in which the abnormality is mental, and because less palpable its authenticity is not as easily certified. These abnormalities include cases of automatism in which one has a consciousness but not a normal awareness of what one is doing—sleep-walking and hypnotic states are the most common examples. There are also psychotic breaks in which a person in a state of delirium or utter delusion has lost touch with reality. Whatever the cause, these are all cases in which the person clearly lacks the ability to exercise control *as the formula requires*, that is, *control over the events that produce the harm or the threat of it*. When the inability to exercise control is less radical, the case for exemption from blame is less obvious, though the abnormality will still serve as an excuse whose exculpatory force will depend on how great the inability to control is taken to be. We are now talking about the unhappy facts that are the basis of the more usual insanity defense, when severe mental impairment subverts judgment or self-control, but still leaves a person in touch with reality; or where there is a defense of diminished responsibility because of an extreme emotional state or some severe chronically debilitating condition affecting intelligence. We must also include here the general exemption enjoyed by those who are underage, at least to the extent that this exemption derives from a presumed inability to appreciate properly the consequences of one's acts, and so leaves a child unable to exercise sound judgment.

It is a fact of the greatest importance that our internal life may be a source of harm in two different ways.

We may be unable to react in an appropriate way when we are challenged from the outside. Uncontrollable and violent temper in response to provocation may leave a person unable to avoid doing harm. And there may be some chronic difficulty that makes it impossible to pay attention to what is happening or to maintain a sufficiently clear awareness of what one is doing as a consequence.

But in addition to such failures of interior infrastructure in meeting external challenges, there are dangers lurking entirely within ourselves. Our rages, our desires, our obsessional beliefs, our feelings of hatred, of persecution or of love, and a thousand other nameless and barely describable states of mind and feeling—all of these are events that need to be kept safely within bounds where they remain harmless. If we follow our imagination and act on our feelings we may land ourselves in serious trouble. It is crucially important that we exercise control over ourselves as we negotiate our way through the many opportunities that life presents us with. It is here that our restraining infrastructure must act upon the flow of our internal life to keep us out of trouble.

Though our resources of control are immensely complex and little understood, it is clear that the most important part is played by a secondary tier of controls that allows reflective mechanisms to prevail over those primary forces that left to their own devices would have us acting in ways that are heedless of the interests of others. Because an understanding of these reflective mechanisms is such a difficult business, we are unable to draw precise boundaries between normal and abnormal conditions of self-control, between an inexcusable failure to behave as we should, and a failure that we genuinely could not help.

Whether internally or externally grounded, whether through madness or because of a sudden power failure that leaves us in the dark, the inability to exercise control resonates as a plea of helplessness that entitles one to be excused. Lurking in the background is the rejoinder that one is nevertheless responsible for the consequences of one's inability—that one should have foreseen the possibility of a psychotic episode or a blackout, and should have taken appropriate precautions. And if one destroys one's ability to exercise control—by drink or by drugs, for example, the excuse will be fatally undermined unless one can somehow make the case that through no fault of one's own one lacked the ability to exercise control over the destruction of one's ability to exercise control.

This brings us to the other two conditions for criminal culpability in the formula I suggested.

Not everyone who has the ability to prevent what is harmful or threatening has a duty to do so. Intervention as a kind of Good Samaritan is an example that comes immediately to mind, since duties to act as a volunteer are not much favored by the law, and when recognized at all they are narrowly circumscribed. Of greater importance are those situations where one could have acted to ensure that some remote harm would not occur, and when it does, a finger is pointed with the absolute confidence of hindsight. By never allowing my car to be driven by anyone else I can ensure to a high degree that when I am not driving my car no one will ever be killed in an accident involving my car. But if I do allow it to be driven and someone is killed, my simply allowing it to be driven, without more, cannot support a claim that I am to blame. "*I'm* not responsible for *that*" is the kind of exculpatory claim that denies there was any sort of duty to exercise control over the events that produced the harm. There is no general duty to do whatever might be done to nip in the bud any possible harm that one might imagine. We have reasonable expectations and unreasonable ones, about risks of harm as about everything else, and it is the reasonableness of such expectations, not things as they happen to turn out, that determines culpability.

This last denial of a duty to prevent the harm that occurred is an exculpatory move that is conventionally discussed in the law under the rubric of causation. Unlike an excuse, it does not appeal to personal matters, and unlike a justification, it does not point to special circumstances. It is simply a declaration of non-involvement, at least not in any way that would raise reasonable expectations that harm might occur. It relies on notions of *expectability*, that common sense of what to expect without which we either remain inert or else feel threatened by possible perils in everything we do. Giving my car keys to my friend, when there is no reason not to, leaves the crash that kills him an hour later in the realm of the unexpected and leaves me not only blameless but exempt from consideration as a candidate for blame, even though there is not the slightest reason to believe that he would have been killed had I not given him the keys.

Justifications are also claims asserting that no duty existed to prevent the occurrence, or the threat, of harm. There must, of course, be something that needs to be justified, and only when there would normally be a duty to avoid harming would an attempt at justification be appropriate. It is the exceptional case that rests on exceptional circumstances. Despite the general duty to avoid harming, I do sometimes have a right to do harmful acts to save my own skin and even my property, and also to save others from serious harm. I also might have no practical alternative to carrying out orders that cause serious harm, and this again might justify what normally is unjustifiable. Carrying out one's public duties might involve inflicting some harm as, for example, when engaged in law enforcement activities, and in such cases there may be exceptions to the general duty to avoid harming. Even something less than a public duty may justify harmful conduct when there is a situation in which responsibility for care, safety, or discipline is at stake—parents, teachers, plane crews, prison guards, medical personnel, are all justified in certain circumstances in doing what otherwise would constitute an assault or some other crime against a person or his property. There is even a general justification recognized in the Model Penal Code for a "choice of evils", when one acts to avoid a harm believed to be greater than the harm which the law that is being broken seeks to prevent.*

★ ★ ★

Duties to avoid harming are carefully circumscribed in the criminal law. There are various degrees of culpability, and only if conduct is sufficiently culpable to satisfy the requirements of the law will a particular crime have been committed. If a person's conduct is less culpable than the law requires it to be for criminal liability, no duty to avoid doing or threatening harm will have been breached since no such duty existed. If I go into a shop where I am given five pounds of apples instead of the three I paid for, and I never happen to notice the mistake, I commit no crime when I take the apples home and never pay the difference. That is because the law of theft does not include a duty of care to be observed by purchasers in the interest of preventing such losses to sellers.

Many crimes admit of different degrees of seriousness. The harm in all of them may be the same. But the culpability is different.

Acting purposely is more culpable than acting knowingly, which in turn is more culpable than acting recklessly, which in its turn is more culpable than acting negligently. So, according to the Model Penal Code, for a homicide to be murder, the death must be caused purposely or knowingly, or even recklessly if the circumstances manifest an extreme indifference to the value of human life. Manslaughter, however, is constituted by reckless conduct causing death, or when death is caused under extreme mental or emotional disturbance "for which there is reasonable explanation or excuse", with reasonableness to be judged by putting oneself in the actor's shoes. Finally, negligent homicide is constituted by death caused negligently, that is, it is caused by a failure to take account of a risk so substantial that the failure constitutes a gross deviation from the standard of care that a reasonable person would observe.*

Each of these different grades of homicide incorporates different duties to avoid killing. We have a duty to restrain ourselves from homicidal acts in the face of homicidal wishes, desires, temptations, inclinations, or whatever else might describe what it is that leads us to have a conscious design to kill someone. We also have a duty to avoid engaging in activities that make it practically certain that death will occur, whether we want it to or not. Either sort of conduct will do for murder. Furthermore, we have a duty to pay attention to the substantial risks of death that are created by things that we might do, and to refrain from acting in ways that create such substantial risks on pain of being liable for manslaughter if death occurs as a result. Finally, we have a duty to carry on acceptable activities in a manner that takes account of its risks in a reasonable way. A breach of that duty resulting in death means liability for negligent homicide. Just which of these duties has been breached determines how culpable the offending conduct was and so just what sort of crime, if any, may be charged.

It is a self-evident truth that killing someone on purpose is more culpable than killing simply through indifference to the risks in what one is doing, or through carelessness. Our dispositions to apportion blame in this way are fixed and unshakeable. But why are we committed to this scheme of apportioning blame? As it happens, deaths caused by negligent or reckless conduct are (in that order) much more common than deaths caused deliberately. The reason is simple. There are innumerable instances of law-abiding activities that can and do prove fatal when carried on in an unsafe way—in our cars, in our hospitals, in our factories, in our homes—in fact almost anywhere. There are in addition a great many instances of risk-heightening activities that we think of as reckless; unacceptable conduct that risks lives—other people's and one's own—though still not the straight-forward taking of lives that normally brings the strongest inhibitions into play. Because negligent and reckless conduct cause far more deaths, such conduct represents a greater danger from a social point of view, and it would therefore not be entirely unreasonable to view carelessness that resulted in death as meriting the greatest blame, with conduct indifferent to risks not far behind when such conduct proves fatal. After all, with the huge numbers of traffic fatalities each year a notorious fact, why couldn't he have been more careful, and why did she take such chances?

But the likelihood of death occurring, as a notorious social statistic, is not the key to culpability. Something related to *conduct*, not chance, is at the heart of culpability, and so what was under the actor's control is what matters. Death caused by negligence, or even recklessness, is death caused by what happened, what went wrong, rather than being an outcome that was the object of the activity, or as we say "intended". For that reason, culpability is not as great.

Still, we need to know why the degrees of culpability we recognize belong in the order that we take to be self-evident. I suggest there are two reasons for this.

The first relates again to duty. The greater the degree of culpability, the less onerous the duty that must be discharged to avoid harm. Consider homicides. Acting with the aim of killing someone, or being aware that it is practically certain that what one is doing will kill someone, or carrying on what is manifestly a life-threatening activity without giving a damn about the possible fatal consequences—the dangers of any of these homicidal activities are much more within the control of the actor and so more easily avoided than are those lapses that constitute negligent homicide, or that constitute the recklessness of manslaughter when one has disregarded certain risks and, in so doing, gambled with other people's lives. Because it is so much easier to avoid killing when there is greater control over the crucial events, failing in one's duty to avoid killing in those circumstances is more culpable.

When there is murder we are inclined to say that there was no excuse for what happened, no fortuitous element that made the difference. When there is only manslaughter based on recklessness, the duty to avoid killing was somewhat harder to observe since there was only the intention to carry on an activity that was not itself homicidal, though admittedly it did have clear homicidal risks toward which the actor displayed indifference. When there is negligent homicide, the risks were not as easily avoidable since it was not some notoriously dangerous activity with unacceptable risks that was being carried on, but rather an activity with acceptable risks carried on in an unacceptable way with regard to those risks. One sees the same idea borne out in finer assessments of culpability. Murder in the first degree—with premeditation, malice aforethought, or whatever other intensifier of culpability the law might prescribe—is more culpable than second degree murder which lacks these special features. The reason is that opportunity for aborting any inclination to kill is even greater when the conduct is more considered. When there is *wanton* recklessness, which increases culpability, the dangers are more manifest, easier to appreciate, and so easier to avoid. The same holds true for the greater culpability in *willful* negligence, which leaves the perpetrator less surprised and in a better position to have prevented what happened than when there is some more ordinary variety of carelessness with tragic consequences. On the same principle, strict criminal liability seems unfair because liability is imposed even though it is impossible as a practical matter to prevent the harm from occurring—a case of zero culpability, in which discharging whatever duty there might be is impossibly difficult.

The other reason we grade the culpability of criminal conduct as we do relates to the feelings it produces. Harm through the carelessness of others, or through their willful disregard of risks, is indeed far more common than harm deliberately inflicted. But when doing harm is a purposeful activity, the offending conduct is a more dangerous and more frightening proposition. There is a will and an intelligence dedicated to achieving the harmful object, which means there is a pursuit of harm that strives to overcome whatever obstacles may be in harm's way, including whatever measures of self-protection might be adopted by a prospective victim. As for harm done knowingly, though not purposely, it is only a bit less culpable because by definition harm is still a virtual certainty as a result of the conduct in question, even though the focus of will and intelligence has been shifted from ends to means. By contrast, cases of recklessness lack a will and an intelligence devoted to causing harm, though at the same time there is a deliberate lack of will and intelligence devoted to preventing harm in the hazardous situation that has been created by the actor. Recklessness therefore stands intermediate between conduct devoted to harming and the negligent conduct that merely fails to include certain prominent risks of harm among the concerns that govern perfectly acceptable conduct. And so we have a scale of conduct posing threats of harm, with its culpability measured by the extent of personal involvement in bringing about the harm. Feelings of fear and anger, and the animosity that is produced by such personal involvement, are of a corresponding intensity, with the strongest feelings reserved for those whose dedication makes their threat the most daunting.

I have suggested that the greater the degree of culpability, the easier it is to avoid committing the offense, for the simple reason that as one ascends the scale of culpability there is increasingly greater control over the events that produce the harm. This is less remarkable than might at first appear, since the same principle is at work with regard to exculpation by way of excuse. All of those excuses that claim an inability to do otherwise—"I couldn't help it" in its various forms—are claims of lack of control over the crucial events, perhaps because of personal deficiency or impairment, perhaps because of external forces that made compliance with the law impossible, or perhaps because of a lack of opportunity that had the same effect. The excuse is most telling when control over events is unreasonably difficult, if not truly impossible, in which case claims of culpability tend to vanish from the scene.

Claims of ignorance or mistake are the bases of a different class of excuses that oppose ascriptions of culpability more directly.

If the purpose, or knowledge, or belief, or recklessness, or negligence, required for an offense is lacking because of a person's ignorance or mistake, he has a good defense. Again, it is a matter of control over events. When, because of what he does not know or what he incorrectly believes, a person is not in a position to exercise control over events as the law requires, he has a good excuse for what he does when acting in accordance with his faulty belief about the way things are. The principle needs a good deal of qualification to make it serviceable as a source of legal rules, but the broad principle is all that need concern us here. It is true, of course, that being able to show that a person acted under some misapprehension and did not do on purpose what the law prohibits may still leave him open to a lesser charge based on lesser culpability. The housekeeper may have thought the poison was only sugar and didn't mean to kill the old lady, but in fact it was ludicrously irresponsible for her to have used a sugar bowl to store the poison and then to have absent-mindedly put it on the tea tray. Furthermore, when someone acts in ignorance of a law that has not had sufficient promulgation, or acts on a suitably authoritative, but mistaken, statement of the law, there is once again the makings of an excuse that the law recognizes. But whether it is fact or law about which there is mistake or ignorance, the exculpatory claim that is available points to an inability to discharge one's duty under the law. Once again a paramount principle of fairness asserts itself in these circumstances to excuse for failing to do what one could not do.

It may seem strange to explain culpability in terms of failing in one's duty to exercise control over ominous events. Murder, for example, seems not to be any sort of *failure* to exercise control over events. If anything, it seems a matter of exercising one's control to produce the awful outcome one has in mind, or at least the awful outcome that one is bound to know is imminent in what one is doing. But the whole business of culpability becomes much less mysterious if we think of murder as a failure to exercise the restraint that one is duty-bound to exercise in the face of errant impulses, obsessions, feelings of grievance, desires for vengeance, the lure of money, feelings of righteous indignation, or even religious or patriotic aspiration—whatever it is that makes the difference between not doing the terrible act and doing it.

In viewing crimes as a failure to do one's duty, the emphasis is shifted from those supposedly wicked or otherwise untoward states of mind that conventionally loom large in explaining why this crime was committed by that person, and instead the emphasis is placed on the failure to exercise self-restraint by employing those mechanisms that people normally use to keep themselves law-abiding when crime beckons—allowing habits of obedience to have their influence, or containing vindictive fantasies within the imagination where they may run with free rein to exhaustion, or perhaps submitting to the influence of awesome moral precepts, or pangs of conscience, or self-respect, or even just responding to one's fear of the consequences.

★ ★ ★

I have been discussing criminal culpability. But most occasions of blame do not involve even the slightest suggestion that a crime has been committed. Sometimes there is a definite moral tone to such blame, when it seems appropriate to say that what was done was morally wrong—unfair, unjust, unethical, dishonest, disloyal, untrustworthy, exploitive, humiliating, cruel—often in personal relations, but in many institutional settings as well. More often, however, blame carries with it no suggestion of moral opprobrium, but rests on some alleged *fault* in failing to do what one ought to do or doing what one ought not to do, with *ought* appealing to non-moral standards. Consider, for example, the bridge builder whose bridge, though perfectly safe, sways when those who paid for it think it shouldn't. Or the goalkeeper whose momentary inattention lets the ball in. Or the chef who cuts corners and produces an inferior dish. Or the lawyer who doesn't ask the right questions in cross-examination. Or my clumsy inattention in spilling the wine. In these examples there is no occasion for moral criticism, nor is there any suggestion of conduct that might concern the criminal law. Since there are no prospects of the sort of harm that the criminal law could be interested in, any thoughts of criminal culpability would be quite inappropriate.

Moral culpability is different from both the criminal variety and the ordinary variety that abounds in everyday life. Fear and anger on the victim's side, with a special tinge of animosity, and often some shame on the perpetrator's part, are the hallmark feelings characteristically associated with criminal culpability, while embarrassment is deemed appropriate when the faults of ordinary culpability are pointed out to those who are at fault. Moral culpability, however, makes use of *guilt* as its main emblem. It is true of course that guilt has been adopted as the law's term for criminal liability, but the legal and the moral uses of the term parted company some time ago, so that legal guilt and moral innocence are eminently compatible, as are legal innocence and moral guilt. Billy Budd and Jesus Christ are notable examples of the first, while the second is well represented by the many imposing figures who with considerable respectability and legal immunity torture or butcher their way through the pages of political, military, and religious history. Guilt in the moral sense enjoys the primacy that conscience and moral sentiment enjoy over rules, even rules of the highest political authority, and if I claim that you are morally culpable, regardless of what legal liability there might be, I am, among other things, claiming that you ought to feel guilty. For your part, though you may dispute your moral culpability, once you acknowledge it you cannot deny that you *ought to* feel guilty. In the moral procession there is then an array of standard measures that allow a release from guilt, or at least a substantial abatement of its effects, through such things as apology, confession, remorse, repentance, suffering, reparation, and forgiveness.

But the distinction between criminal and moral culpability cannot be drawn so simply. More is needed to avoid confusion.

The first thing to note is that feelings of guilt may be irrational, in which case their presence is not a sign of culpability. It is quite understandable that a person should feel guilty if he harms someone. But he may be justified in causing the harm, or may have a perfectly good excuse, and though this will normally moderate feelings of guilt, the brute fact of causing harm will often sustain some feelings of guilt that linger on. Arguments are presented to attack or defend a judgment of moral culpability, and a critical dialogue develops according to rational procedures. If moral culpability is then established, we ought to *feel* guilty, and not just think that we are. But if claims of exculpation prevail and we are exonerated, we ought not to feel guilty. If we do, the feelings, even if quite understandable, are irrational, and they tell us nothing about culpability.

But what about criminal conduct and the feelings of guilt that we have, or that we should have?

When commission of a crime consists of conduct that we have good reason to think should make us feel guilty regardless of what the law has to say, there is moral culpability. This includes instances of those self-evident crimes that need no legal recognition to make them crimes, as well as certain wrong conduct that might or might not be deemed a wrong worthy of criminalization. Though we can be assured that something morally wrong has been done, in neither case do the feelings of guilt enlighten us about criminal culpability.

The situation is further complicated by another important element: the *authority* of the law. People feel guilty, and upon careful reflection think it right that they should, just because they have broken the law. Even though there is a clear distinction between how people feel about their conduct and how they feel about the fact that they have broken the law, they are disposed to feel guilty about their conduct when it violates the law just because it is a violation of the law. This seems unremarkable when one remembers that feelings of guilt have their *locus classicus* in what is experienced as a defiance of authority. Indeed the law depends very heavily on exploiting such feelings to maintain its status as constituted authority in a community whose laws cannot always withstand independent moral scrutiny, even (perhaps especially) when they reflect overwhelming popular sentiment.

But feelings of guilt that derive from transgressions of authority are fundamentally different, from a moral point of view, from feelings of guilt that derive from the conduct that happens to transgress. It is what has made it possible for people in Tokyo with normal law-abiding attitudes to go about their business of trading shares based on insider information openly and with a clear conscience, while traders with the same law-abiding attitudes in New York avoid disclosing the fact that they are acting on information obtained through insider channels. If they are caught and their criminal acts are exposed, they will feel guilty about what they have done because it violates the law, but it would be most unlikely that what they have done would make them feel guilty if the law in New York had been changed to leave insider trading a lawful activity, as it has been in Tokyo. It is also a matter of whose law has been broken. Our spies do not feel guilty when brought to justice in the other country, and their spies likewise have an easy conscience when convicted for the same activities under our espionage laws—provided, of course, the spy in each case is not a citizen spying on his own country. Espionage against a foreign power is more like a hero's work than a criminal's, and the authority of the law carries moral weight only for those who feel they owe it an allegiance. This last point will of course have much wider implications within any political society with regard to its disaffected members.

Criminal culpability, then, does not call for feelings of guilt, though it is clear that those feelings will be appropriate on many occasions of criminally culpable conduct because the crime also constitutes a moral wrong. Criminal culpability has to do with *control* over those aspects of *conduct* that might loosely be called *endangerment*, a notion that puts the stress on the *harm* the criminal law is purporting to deal with, be it real or imaginary, self-evident or speculative, threatened or experienced.

10

Psychoculpability

Criminal culpability is normally thought to be a species of moral culpability. But feelings of guilt and the conduct that makes such feelings appropriate are not the reason. Rather, there is a belief that the true source of moral wrong is located in the realm of the mind, and the terms that we use in assessing criminal culpability—"purposely", "knowingly", "recklessly", "negligently"—are thought really to be making a cryptic reference to what had been going on at the time in the mind of the person whose conduct we are judging. Whether intended or not, the way these terms are explained provides encouragement for this idea.

Take, for example, the definitions that appear in the Model Penal Code. A person acts *purposely* when it is his *conscious object* to engage in such conduct or cause such a result, or when he is *aware of* the attendant circumstances, or *believes or hopes* that they exist. He acts *knowingly* if he is *aware* that his conduct is of such a nature or that such attendant circumstances exist. A person acts *recklessly* when he *consciously disregards* a substantial and unjustifiable risk; and he acts *negligently* when he should be *aware* of such a risk and he fails to *perceive* it. The states or processes of mind suggested by these terms in their characteristic employment in the criminal law are taken to be signs of something morally wrong in the realm of the mind.

Such episodes in the mental life of the accused are of course not enough by themselves to create criminal liability. For a crime to be committed we must wait for these hidden affairs of the mind to erupt into criminal acts in the observable world. Typically we have a picture of the criminal mind thinking its criminal thoughts or at least lapsing into what the law considers a sufficiently incautious state of inattention. For crimes that are serious business, the mind then moves ahead into a condition of commitment known as intention, which is an especially arcane region of the mental realm, and from

there into that even more mysterious region where mind and body inter-
act—the will. The whole person then makes manifest the criminal
collaboration between mind and body, and the crime is committed.

But why sit idly by? If the criminal mind can be identified before the
criminal act takes place, and it is the criminal mind that is the source of
the culpability on which liability is based, why not recognize liability at
this earlier stage? Surely there must be certain cases where the criminal
mind has declared itself with unmistakable clarity. Intervention at that
point would keep prospective victims from harm, and would even help
the mental perpetrator by keeping him from committing the full-
blooded crime that would take place if he is allowed to act on his criminal intentions. The venerable maxim of the law is *Actus non facit reum nisi
mens sit rea*—an act does not create guilt unless there is a guilty mind—
but there is here no suggestion that a mind cannot create guilt without a
guilty act.

But those who are attracted by the notion of a guilty mind usually stop
short of advocating criminal liability without something more in the frame.
There are several good reasons for this. One is a certain lack of confidence
in the only possible source of evidence—disclosure by the would-be perpetrator. Actions speak louder than words, and without actions we cannot
be sure that words alone express a sufficiently serious intention. Then there
is the possibility that however serious the intention may be, when it comes
right down to doing it (and perhaps even at an earlier time), a person may
change his mind. There are, after all, many good reasons for changing one's
mind about committing a crime. And finally, the prospect of law enforcement for crimes of the mind is a frightening one. Do we want what amounts
to thought police, and a system of law enforcement that can proceed just on
evidence of what someone heard someone else say? There is a long and terrible history of such regimes, and of the inquisitorial methods that are
cheerfully employed to invade those private regions that in any decent
society are inviolable.

But though the law cannot act just on what is going on in the mind, on
the orthodox view it is still goings-on in the mind that provide true enlightenment about what makes criminal conduct morally wrong. The various
exculpatory claims of a personal nature that the law recognizes as defenses
are given an interpretation that fits this view. On this view, when there is a
good excuse of some sort, it turns out that in fact affairs of the mind were
not really what at first they seemed to be.

It might be that we misunderstood the intention of the accused when he put the counterfeit money on the counter—he only meant it as a joke—or perhaps he didn't even realize the bills were counterfeit. Perhaps someone accidentally substituted the deadly poison for the perfectly harmless substance that it resembled, and so again there were only innocent intentions where we had suspected foul play. Or perhaps a person's mind was disordered in some way that makes it ineligible to serve as the author of a crime—perhaps it could not form a proper intention, or perhaps it could not even understand what was really going on. Exculpation takes place, on this account, when we find the relevant mental elements to be quite different from what we had supposed. We find the mind to be innocent, and normally the person whose mind it is will be as appalled as we are by the misadventure that we at first thought was a crime.

There are several obvious points to be made against this model of psychoculpability.

Whatever might happen to occupy our mind in its solitary operations is normally spontaneous in its origin, and it continues to live a life of its own. To some degree we can control our thoughts, but that is not what we are expected to do. How then can we be held responsible for these goings-on in the mind? Because of its spontaneous nature our mental life is not meant to be judged in the same way as our conduct, and so it enjoys a blanket exemption from criticism.

A second point is this. People are not normally aware of their state of mind when they do things. Their state of mind is something they can talk about retrospectively, but at the time they are normally occupied with what they are doing and what is happening. One can hardly be expected to do anything about what one is unaware of. What sense can it make, then, to treat a person's state of mind as the essential inculpatory ingredient of his untoward conduct?

In addition to lack of control and ignorance, there is a third point that undermines psychoculpability. If a mental state is to serve as the foundation of wrongdoing and the issue of criminal liability turns on the existence of such a mental state, surely there must be reliable evidence of the existence of that mental state. But in fact mental states are notoriously inaccessible and notoriously evanescent as well. Though others may draw inferences, it is only the person whose state of mind is at issue who can provide direct evidence, and his lack of awareness at the time only compounds the difficulties of proof that are anyway inevitable because of his monopoly of information at the source and because of his interest in protecting himself.

Is it really possible, then, that it is untoward states of mind that must be proved to establish culpability? Is it not possible that so-called states of mind are in fact nothing more than a further description of *what was done*, to reassure us that it was in fact just the conduct that we claim it to be, and to tell us that exculpation is therefore not possible? In fact the kind of evidence introduced to support such a claim makes it clear that the issue here is what, exactly, were the events over which a person was exercising control, ie what precisely was his conduct, not what were his states or processes of mind.

★ ★ ★

One sort of "mental state" does, however, seem exempt from these points against psychoculpability. Surely one does know one's *intentions* when one acts, or at least there is a sufficient awareness to satisfy the concerns of the criminal law, even though as one acts one's mind is normally occupied with things other than one's intentions. One's intentions seem almost by definition a matter of genuine choice, in any event no less than one's conduct. And what one's intention was can be talked about after the event with a kind of confidence that is lacking when trying to recall one's thoughts, beliefs, hopes, desires, expectations, and all the rest of what is put about as the mental states with which one acted. It is true that in exceptional cases people are genuinely bewildered by what they did and can give no explanation that makes sense of it. There are also cases in which people can explain themselves up to a point, after which they are more or less in the dark, as when I am perfectly clear that I intended to take the umbrella that I knew was not mine, but can't really say one way or the other whether I intended to return it. Though intentions may sometimes be elusive in this way, on the whole they are available and fit to play their part in those determinations of culpability, or responsibility, or liability that must take place later.

Intention presents itself in different guises according to the role it is to play, and to keep confusion at bay some crucial distinctions are required.

Having an intention is a good place to start. We do commit ourselves to doing things, sometimes publicly with a declared intention, and sometimes privately with a resolution that only we know about. Intentions of either sort may be more or less settled depending on the depth of our commitment to what we intend to do, depending, in other words, on how easy it would be for us to change our minds. Good intentions, presumably unful-filled, are said to pave the road to hell, though for bad intentions unfulfilled it seems there is nothing to fear. And while it is true that we may sometimes be held accountable for our stated intentions on which others rely, even then it is only what we have done and not simply our intentions that pro-vides grounds for any kind of serious criticism, inside or outside the crim-inal law.

What one has when one has an intention to do something is no more than a plan of action to which there is some significant degree of commit-ment. Believing that John *intends* to do something may be a surmise based on what we think we know in spite of John's silence, or it may be based on a public declaration that leaves no room for doubt. That being said, it must be added that behind the public declaration there may be a private mental reservation that makes the true state of affairs different from what it appears to be.

Turning now to a different locution, one is tempted to suppose that when something is done *intentionally* there is an internal plan of action that has been implemented in the outside world. Doing something *unintention-ally* is then taken to mean that what was done had no such plan behind it, with a strong suggestion that it will therefore have come as an embarrassing surprise to the person who did it. But such an interpretation is seriously misleading. All we can say with confidence about something that was done *intentionally* is that it was not done *unintentionally*. That, however, is saying a great deal. It is saying we can take what was done at face value and assume an appropriately critical stance, and that the person who did it can expect no help from the excuses that are lurking in the undergrowth, ready to spring into action once it is conceded that what was done was the outcome of those uncontrolled forces in the world that surprise us and remind us of our limitations. How we explain what is done unintentionally calls for a study of the whole person, often with particular attention to how he func-tions in a social context in which mistakes are a common occurrence and avoiding them an exercise in social skills. The mind has a huge part to play in all of this, but not as an unseen *éminence grise* whose influence behind the scenes becomes apparent in what we do intentionally.

Different still is one's *intention-in-acting*. Did he mean to turn off the life-support system, or was he just trying to disconnect the television? Did he mean to kill the man crossing the road, or was he simply trying to avoid hitting a plastic bag that he thought was a dog? Sometimes one's *intention-in-acting* is the fulfillment of an intention that one has, and some-times it has no such antecedent. In either case, deciding what the *intention-in-acting* was is reaching a decision about how to describe what was done. Conduct, unlike mere behavior, is always purposeful, and it is important to understand in each instance of apparent untoward conduct just what pur-poses were being pursued. Mistakes that are the basis of an excuse can only be identified by referring first to whatever is the *intention-in-acting* that properly describes the conduct in question. And a false accusation based on a misunderstanding of what really was done is likewise corrected by refer-ence to the true *intention-in-acting*.

Finally, there is the particularly mischievous notion of *intent*, or as it appears in criminal law theory, *specific intent*. Beyond the *intention-in-acting* that describes the conduct that has taken place, it is sometimes important to determine what further purpose was being served by what was done. The uncertainties surrounding conduct may relate to prospective harm, and an extended description of the conduct may be required to resolve the ambiguities in what has taken place with reference to what may yet occur. Unfortunately, a mentalist interpretation often creeps in at this point, and it is widely assumed that the phrase *with intent to* in the definition of a crime signals the law's interest in what is going on in the mind of a person who engages in certain conduct. It is a common misconception, and by no means peculiar to criminal law theory. Consider the following example.

New York Times columnist Tom Wicker wrote about the Chicago trial of those charged in connection with public disturbances at the time of the 1968 Democratic Convention. One provision of the law under which an indictment was obtained made it a crime to cross a state line *with intent to cause acts of violence*, and Wicker commented:

The defendants here are the first to be tried under a provision of the 1968 Civil Rights Act that made it a Federal crime to cross a state line with the intent to cause a riot or a disturbance. The constitutionality of this statute has yet to be determined, but the Chicago trial clearly suggests—as, indeed, does the language of the act—that what it seeks to prohibit or penalize is a state of mind, not an overt act.
Ironically, it is also pretty clear from this proceeding how difficult it is to prove a state of mind, long afterwards. It is probably more difficult for the prosecution, on whom rests the burden of proof, than for the defendants, which is why Mr. Schulz sounded so preposterous in his efforts to show that Rennie Davies was saying one thing to Roger Wilkins while "thinking other thoughts".

Nevertheless, if the issue of a trial actually comes down to "other thoughts", rather than to actual words and deeds, the deeper question may be whether even "the burden of proof" any longer means anything.*

It was of course not the object of the law to find what was in the accused's mind at the time he crossed a state line, much less to make his criminal liability depend on what was in his mind at that time. Specific intent is simply part of the description of the conduct that is required for the offense to be committed, namely its purpose, and it makes clear the prospective harm that is of interest to the law. In doing what he does, the actor has a purpose that makes the act an act of that kind rather than of another kind—crossing a state line to incite a riot rather than to sell ice cream. That purpose is the specific intent of the act. But having a purpose as one acts does not mean that one then has a purpose in mind. One *may* have a purpose in mind, but that is rather an unusual case. It is normal to have a purpose in mind when, as one acts, one must give close attention to what one is doing or to how one is doing it in order not to have things go awry. If one travels unfamiliar roads, and crossing the state line at certain points rather than others will affect one's ability to cause a riot as planned, then, naturally enough, one might well have one's purpose in mind as one seeks out the right crossing point and then crosses.

Even more extraordinary than having one's purpose in mind is a case in which one is thinking about one's purposes as one acts. This is normal when, for some reason, one's purpose is not entirely settled, as, for example, if one were still undecided about whether to run the risks of causing a disturbance in Chicago or whether simply to visit one's mother in the suburbs. But neither having the purpose in mind nor thinking about it is necessary for the purpose to be the specific intent of the act. Having boarded a bus in Pittsburgh, one may immediately fall into a deep and dreamless slumber which lasts all the way to Chicago, and one may still have crossed state lines with intent to cause acts of violence.

Evidence one way or another for the existence of a specific intent is publicly available, as is evidence of any other feature of the act. Why one traveled to Chicago may call for inference and surmise from things said and done, as well as from circumstances that would normally prompt a trip of one sort or another. The evidence is no different from that available to determine the purpose being pursued in any other act; and certainly determinations of purpose are commonly and confidently made in many kinds of legal proceedings, as well as everywhere else. States of mind, which are private, largely inaccessible, and a subject only of speculation much of the time, are not what we must know about to know about specific intent. Far from creating opportunities for abuse of prosecutorial power through intrusion and speculative conclusion, the requirement of specific intent provides protection against wrongful prosecution by describing in greater detail the act for which there is said to be liability so that it cannot be confounded with some other act which in other ways it resembles, though not in purpose.

This conception of specific intent helps make sense of what is known in criminal law theory as "the doctrine of transferred intent". That doctrine supports liability in a case where, for example, the accused, intending to kill a certain person, shoots at him and, because of poor aim, causes instead the death of another person whom he had no intention of killing. In its most appealing version, conventional theory holds that there is liability for murder, since both the state of mind and the act of the accused satisfy the requirements for murder; and because, in addition, the act of the accused was the cause of the death. To those who object that since a different victim was intended his state of mind was not the required one, conventional theory replies that the difference is immaterial, since what is required for the offense is simply an intention to kill some person.

The trouble with this is that in the case at hand the accused did not intend simply to kill someone—anyone at all. If he had, there would be no difficulty in holding him liable, since the law does not require that a particular person be intended as a victim. Wanton, indiscriminate killing that is indifferent to whom the victims may be is readily accepted as full-fledged murder. In the case of the unintended victim, however, the accused did not intend to kill the person he did kill, nor did he intend to kill just anyone (which would include the victim), and so he did not have a "state of mind" that in relevant respects is the same as the one he would have if the victim were intended.

The difficulty here stems from the mentalist account of transferred intent upon which the analysis relies, and is remedied by a recasting that makes use of specific intent as we now understand it. The act of the accused in this case can be correctly described as shooting with intent to cause death, and that act satisfies the act requirement for murder. The offense of homicide (and not merely attempted homicide) requires in addition that the act cause the death, and this requirement is also satisfied in this case. Thus, the difficulty to be found in conventional theory vanishes once the accused is seen to be acting with an intent to kill; and once it is understood that the intent is part of the act and not some state of mind that may have accompanied it.

★ ★ ★

Other issues of importance are plagued by mentalism. The law of attempts has proved particularly hospitable since in many cases it appears that it is only *a belief*, albeit a mistaken one, that stands between freedom and years in prison. Some cases of this sort were discussed in the last chapter, but to make clear what the proper role of a belief really is I revisit one of the classic inventions in the literature of attempts.*

We are told that on her return to England from the continent, Lady Eldon was discovered to have secreted in her coach some lace purchased abroad which she believed to be French lace and thus dutiable, but which was in fact non-dutiable English lace. On the orthodox view she faced liability for an attempt to smuggle, even though the crime of smuggling was impossible, since her mistake was a mistake of fact. That case is contrasted with a variation in which the lace is indeed French. Believing correctly this time that it is French, Lady Eldon again has hidden it. But French lace has in fact just been removed from the duty list, though Lady Eldon does not know this. On orthodox principles there presumably would be no liability for attempt here, since this time her mistake was about the law, and simply believing that what one is doing is against the law cannot create criminal liability for it when in fact it is not against the law. Even commentators who reject the orthodox distinction of fact and law among impossibilities have acquiesced in finding liability in the first case but not in the second, though they do not deny that this seems paradoxical.

There is indeed cause for dissatisfaction with such a result, for in fact either the harm has been threatened in both cases or else in both cases Lady Eldon's conduct does not pose a threat of harm. On either alternative both cases should have the same result. Which result is the correct one depends on a more ample understanding of the penal law under which Lady Eldon is to be charged. It is not possible here to argue for one or another interpretation of that smuggling provision, since no text of the law is provided by the inventors of the cases, nor is there any indication of exactly what policy the law was meant to serve. The possible alternative interpretations can be made clear, however—and for our purpose that is enough. These cases, then, can be analyzed in the following way.

If Lady Eldon's mistaken beliefs had significance at all, her beliefs had the same significance in both cases. In the first case, believing wrongly that the lace was French, she hid it. In the second case she wrongly believed the lace to be on the duty list, and, once again, because of her belief, she hid it. It is true that in both cases she believed that she was hiding a dutiable item, but her belief about what she was doing does not in itself have any inculpatory significance from a legal point of view. It is also true that in both cases Lady Eldon's belief that the lace was dutiable prompted her to hide it. This act of secreting the lace was done intentionally, but only if this act posed a threat of the harm that concerned the law was it culpable in the eyes of the law. The question of whether harm was indeed threatened by the act depends on exactly what harm it was that the law had concerned itself with.

It might be decided that undeclared introduction of a dutiable item is the harm, and that dutiability of the article is necessary only for commission of the completed crime. A threat of the harm (and so a criminal attempt) is then constituted by merely secreting in order to introduce free of customs something *believed* to be dutiable, whether it is or not. This seems a plausible view of the harm intended to be dealt with in an ordinary smuggling provision, and it would be supported by argument that the government policy to be served by this law is discouragement of evasive practices. On this assumption about the law, both Lady Eldon cases would sort with the picking of an empty pocket as an instance of an attempted theft since her conduct, like the pickpocket's, is dangerous with respect to the harm that the law seeks to prevent, even though under the circumstances the harm could not occur.

A second possibility is that, under the law, dutiability of the article is necessary for the attempt as well as for the completed crime. Under this view, the completed crime would be undisclosed introduction of an article in fact dutiable, and the attempt would be conduct tending but failing to accomplish that. This conception of the harm being dealt with in an anti-smuggling law is plausible in a country where customs control is efficient and schemes of evasion are rare. In such a country there might still be concern that if no law prohibiting evasion were on the books, evasive practices to avoid payment of duty would grow, and for that reason there is a law punishing the undisclosed introduction of dutiable items. Because evasive practices are rare, however, there is no need to punish mere secreting of items that are not dutiable but only *believed* to be, and a construction reflecting this fact can fairly be placed on the law as enacted. The harm, in other words, is non-payment of duties, and that harm is not threatened unless the item is dutiable. If the law were to be viewed in this way, there would not be attempt liability in either Lady Eldon case.

Beliefs, though themselves without inculpatory force, may still affect culpability, and it is important to avoid confusion on this point. Lady Eldon's belief might be quite different in a way that would be most helpful to her in avoiding criminal liability. Suppose, for example, that she had hidden some very expensive lace bought in France, even though she believed it to be exempt from duty, for it had always been exempt, and only very recently (unknown to her) had it been made dutiable. She had hidden the lace to keep knowledge of its purchase from her husband, since he often criticized her extravagance and she feared that he might make a scene if it came to his notice in the course of a Customs inspection. If charged, Lady Eldon might well protest that although she failed to disclose the item as the law required, she honestly believed that the lace was not dutiable and that she was therefore not required to disclose it. Under either of the two versions of the law just suggested, this might well avoid liability. But under a third version, which made undisclosed introduction of dutiable items an offense, and hence acts of concealment at Customs for whatever reason an attempt, her claim would not avoid liability. Whether it is accepted or rejected, however, Lady Eldon's claim is a plausible one that bears good credentials as a recognized mode of exculpation.

At this point an error having grave consequences for criminal law theory is commonly made. It is assumed that when Lady Eldon's belief counts in her favor, it is because the belief shows that her mind was innocent; and that a belief counting against her similarly has the significance it does because it shows her to have had a state of mind that was not innocent. But the belief itself is not a reason for blaming or exempting from blame in the criminal law.

If Lady Eldon has an honest and reasonable belief that the lace is not dutiable, as a practical matter she is unable to conform her conduct to the law, since she has no reason to believe she may be violating it. In addition, what she does intentionally—her conduct—is then in some measure less dangerous, for her activity is not guided by any evasive design. It is for these reasons alone that her belief furnishes grounds of exculpation. Lingering doubts on this point might be dispelled by imagining that a law reform commission is considering a change in the law so that no longer would it matter that someone in Lady Eldon's position believed that the dutiable item she hid was not dutiable. Considerations of fairness to persons not engaged in acts of smuggling will likely be weighed against the government's interest in more efficient and economical Customs control. The less ample freedom from regulation that will result from casting a broader net will be considered in the light of the benefits to accrue from a law more easily enforced. But it is virtually inconceivable that one item on the commission's agenda would be the assessment of the wrongness or dangerousness of certain beliefs and of the importance of punishing persons who entertained such beliefs when they acted in accordance with them. Unfortunately, however, it would be an item of the highest priority for any law reform commission that took seriously the mentalist explanations of attempt liability to be found in many standard texts.

★ ★ ★

The antics of another English lady have been the occasion of similarly strange conjectures, this time about a variety of things going on in the lady's mind, and whether they were enough to make her a murderer.

Mrs Hyam set fire to Mrs Booth's house after pouring petrol through the front door letter-box. She did this to frighten Mrs Booth into leaving town and terminating her engagement to a man with whom Mrs Hyam had previously had an affair. Unfortunately, two of Mrs Booth's daughters died in the fire, and Mrs Hyam was convicted of murder. Her conviction was ultimately upheld by the House of Lords by a three to two majority, with considerable diversity in the views expressed by the judges.*

At the heart of this case, as judges and many commentators have seen it, is the moral significance of what Mrs Hyam knew and what Mrs Hyam's intention was. It was accepted that she only meant to frighten Mrs Booth and did not intend any more serious harm. And it was conceded that Mrs Hyam was aware that what she did put the lives of the occupants of the house in extreme danger, with fatal consequences quite predictable. What moral weight then should be attached to what Mrs Hyam knew and what she intended, and would that moral weight be great enough to satisfy the standard for murder set by the law? Her intention was also to set fire to a house that she quite rightly believed to be occupied, and that item in her mental history must count quite heavily against her morally. This raises questions about how many different intentions Mrs Hyam had, and in any case how can we tell whether there are two intentions or only the one that we already know about being described in two ways. And if there are two different intentions, which is the one that was being fulfilled by what was done. Can Mrs Hyam's "foresight" of the harm (as legal parlance puts it) be somehow transmuted into an intention, or must the two mental states remain two separate and distinct features of the mind? The pursuit of such questions was implicit in the decision of the case.

Moral psychology has a long and distinguished history in religion and philosophy. Its speculations are, however, an unaffordable luxury, or worse, in the criminal law. The criminal law is not helped by being told what difference there is morally between an intention to kill and an intention only to do what is likely to kill. It is not the moral truth about the conduct that matters. What matters *is* a moral concern, but it is a concern belonging to political, not personal, morality. What is at stake in the criminal law is a person's life, liberty, dignity, and reputation. Political morality dictates that these things may be compromised by the state through criminal liability only when necessary to protect people as they live their lives together in that curious mixture of conflict, cooperation, and interdependence that is life in society. It is what Mrs Hyam did intentionally—her conduct—that needs to be judged under a body of law that meets this requirement of political morality. It is not a question of whether Mrs Hyam's less harmful intention leaves us with a moral deficit that makes the homicide something less than murder. The question to be answered is whether conduct posing such a threat to life should be treated as murder when it causes death (as it would be under the Model Penal Code) because culpable in the highest degree, or whether it should be viewed as posing the lesser threat that reckless conduct poses, to be dealt with then as a less culpable homicide. The dangerousness of what was done intentionally, not its wickedness, is what must be assessed, with proper credit given for any exculpatory elements that may be in the picture.

★ ★ ★

There is an unmistakable air of absurdity about what I have called psychoculpability, and one wonders what accounts for its long and vigorous life in criminal law theory. My suggestion is that it flourishes because of a paranoia that is rooted in fear of crime. The mentalist version of a criminal mind confers respectability on nagging suspicions of criminal dangers that one cannot see but which one feels certain are lurking in the shadows waiting to strike. We are disappointed when we seek confirmation—we need only shine a light and we see no one is there. But belief in an evil that is harbored beyond our reach in the dark recesses of another's mind will always provide reassurance that our fears are not misplaced.

11

Persons and Choices

When judging culpability, is it possible that it is the person, rather than his conduct, that deserves the most attention? Conduct must of course be paid attention to first, for conduct constitutes the crime. But the person who committed the crime matters even more. After all, it is the prospect of punishing that person for the crime that is of paramount concern at every stage of criminal justice.

Knowing the sort of person we are dealing with is reassuring in a number of ways.

Crimes are only relatively brief episodes in the midst of lives that are otherwise law-abiding. This is true even when the episodes are repeated, and even when the offender lives a life of crime either as a professional or as an habitual offender without professional standing. Numberless opportunities for crimes of all sorts are ignored by people who commit crimes, just as they are by people who don't. Moreover, crimes only rarely encapsulate a person or his life and tell the whole story in some essential way. Looked at simply as the act it is, the criminal episode itself seems too meager to justify the comprehensive long-term horrors that serious criminal liability entails for the actor. But there is a measure of reassurance if we go behind the act and search out those traits of character that make the crime seem quite natural for the sort of person who committed it. We then can feel we have a substantial case against the person that justifies what we do to him, with the criminal act left to serve a more modest role as clear, tangible evidence that it is indeed a suitably bad person that we now wish to punish.

Looking more carefully at the person has the further virtue of helping good people in time of need. We are all creatures of clay who might in moments of stress or weakness do some foolish thing that puts us on the wrong side of the law. If that should happen, we would like to be able to introduce our good character in evidence to help make clear that what we did was an aberration and quite out of character. We are then entitled to be treated differently, so we say, for the criminal episode is not rooted in the person we truly are. This also comforts us by making it clear that we are not one of *them*, preserving our position on the right side of what is the most frightening and the most enduring divide within any society.★

It has also been suggested that character provides a broad foundation for exculpation in general. If a person acts in response to serious provocation or is forced to do what he does, if he must act to avoid serious harm, if he is overcome by emotion or is simply out of his mind, in all these cases he is in no position to act in accordance with his natural inclinations. What he does is out of character and does not represent him as the person he truly is. Those considerations that militate against making the acts of the moment a basis for life-destroying punishment again come into play as we moderate or suspend blame. After all, do we really want to treat as criminals those people whose criminal acts are out of character? It is true, of course, that just because a person is a genuinely decent sort he cannot expect exoneration when he foolishly allows himself to succumb to temptation or fails to exercise self-control. There is more to judging the culpability of criminal conduct than judging its origins. But when one simply cannot be expected to be one's characteristic self—terrible threats, imminent danger, intolerable humiliation, mental collapse—surely acting out of character is then a claim that matters and that might even carry the day. In these cases crimes were not committed because of failings of character, but rather in spite of a good character that unfortunately could not govern on this occasion for reasons that remind us that we are only human.

Even if the culpability of an act is not in general to be determined by reference to character, what about the possibility of a person's badness nevertheless influencing judgments of culpability negatively? Can the person he is have an inculpatory effect that makes what he does more culpable? And can the person he is undermine those exculpatory claims that otherwise might help him or even let him off the hook entirely?★

It has been suggested that racial or religious hatred, or homophobic loathing, might intensify the wrongfulness of crimes of violence that are motivated by such hatred or detestation. The suggestion is that emotions are not forces that are morally neutral or morally blind, and that those beliefs and attitudes that make us feel and act as we do cannot escape moral scrutiny any more than our conduct can. When the vile act partakes of the actor's vileness, his vileness counts against him additionally when he is judged for his act.

Then there is the exculpatory effect of provocation. The law makes an allowance for reactions to provocation when the reaction appears objectively to be a risk inherent in the provocation. In that case, a suitable measure of exculpation might be in order. So, provocation may reduce murder to manslaughter, as, for example, when a husband kills a man that he finds in bed with his wife. But if a man finds his girlfriend in bed with another man, killing the other man will not be seen in the same light by the law even though the emotions that prompt the act are every bit as strong. In a similar vein, the law will not confer exculpatory significance on the very strong emotion of a hot-tempered person responding with a violent assault to some petty insult, though the same emotional state may well reduce the charge if the violent response was provoked by some intolerable humiliation. In these cases it is said that the person is being held to a standard that reflects the norms or values that everyone is expected to assimilate as part of the process of becoming a morally sound person.

There are other examples of how judgment of the person can influence judgment of his conduct. Murder may be equally premeditated when it is the compassionate act of a son who is concerned to relieve the dreadful and seemingly interminable suffering of his father, or when the son kills the same suffering father because he wants to get his hands on his father's money sooner rather than later. It is the moral quality of the person that governs the outcome when in its discretion the law treats these two cases differently, so it is said.

Self-defense provides another instance of community norms supposedly showing a person the way to moral enlightenment, though this time community norms are themselves less uniform and less certain. How much force a person may use to defend himself, and under what conditions it may be used, has always been controversial. There has been renewed interest in the question of whether a person who is threatened by an assailant must retreat if that can be done safely, or whether he may stand his ground and use whatever force seems necessary to defend himself. Standing one's ground as the alternative to a safe though humiliating retreat has widespread support in the law, though, controversially, not where a wife who is confronted by yet another beating from her husband uses deadly force to stop him instead of simply leaving the house. Whatever the legal rule may be, the theorist's suggestion is that acting so as to enjoy the legal benefits of self-defense is a matter of personal morality which the law may vindicate or may treat as contrary to the prevailing moral norms of the community. Shall personal honor, when affronted by an aggressive intruder in one's own home, be forced to take a back seat to concern for the intruder's life and limb, or shall it be allowed to prevail over concern for the value of that life? Shall the self-respect of the abused wife prevail, or shall regard for her husband's life? The legal conclusions reached in different legal communities may be different, but no matter what the legal rule may be, on this view it is a judgment about moral values a person ought to have incorporated and be influenced by in deciding what to do in such a situation, and hence it is a judgment about the person.

Duress is another possible defense that is said to turn on matters of personal character. A bank teller alone after hours may be scared out of his wits by an elderly lady who suddenly appears brandishing her umbrella and threatening to strike him with it. He follows her instructions, empties the cash drawers into her bags and opens the vault so she can help herself to more. If accused of complicity, he might well have a hard time establishing a defense of duress even though he provides compelling evidence that he was far more frightened than a colleague in another branch, who received only sympathy when he complied after a loaded gun was put to his head by another bank robber the week before. Community standards of *"reasonable firmness"* are what are said to be at stake, and people are expected as part of their moral development to have formed characters that exhibit such firmness when confronting threats of harm.

★ ★ ★

Judging persons, rather than conduct, is beset with major difficulties, and what might be called character theories of criminal culpability do not travel an easy path.

First, there is the matter of responsibility for the sort of person we are. Several questions lurk beneath the surface. Just what sort of person are we, anyway? To what extent are we ourselves responsible for being that way? Given that we are what we are, is it really fair to expect us to act out of character and somehow do what a person with a better character would do, in effect holding us responsible for not being different than we are?

What sort of person we are and how we became that way are fascinating questions, but they do not lend themselves to answers that enjoy anything like the certainty required in criminal proceedings. Biographies bear ample witness to the complexity and subtlety of these questions. Contradictions of different elements of character abound, and even the most careful examination of a person and the life he lived often leaves us wondering just what sort of person he really was. This is true to a considerable extent within the covers of a single biography, and is even more evident when several different biographies of the same person are considered together. In fact, an abundance of conjecture about these matters is at the heart of any serious biography. For the purposes of the criminal law questions about acting in or out of character must be avoided since we are too uncertain about the contours of anyone's character, and equally uncertain about when and how, if at all, a person might act in contravention of his natural dispositions.

It is perfectly true that coming to some sort of conclusion about a person's character is an easy exercise. Reporting such conclusions with supporting evidence is an activity carried on in many organizations, including those agencies that are responsible for preparing pre-sentencing reports in a criminal justice system. But such assessments are not based on investigations that tell the story of a person's character in anything like the depth and detail that would be required to determine whether a person should be found guilty of a crime when his fate hinges on an issue of culpability. Was someone's criminal record, his history of unemployment, and his dissolute behavior, a true indication of his character, or only a superficial history of reactions to psychological problems he had or pressures on him in the life he was forced to live? His biographer and his psychoanalyst might be able to illuminate that question, but nothing reliable enough for determining the outcome of criminal proceedings is ever available to tell us just how the crime he is charged with relates to the person he is. What he has done previously can often tell us something of practical importance about how he behaves in general, and this can help clear away ambiguities and uncertainties in what he has done now. This is not because we know more about the person he truly is, but because we know more about what that person is disposed to do, which may give us a somewhat more secure foundation for calling him to account for what has happened now. But that is all.

There remains a further question whose attractions are perhaps more philosophical than practical. Can a person be held responsible for the person he is, or for any particular personal traits that are said to bear on issues of culpability? Do we really have sufficient control over those influences that make us the person we are, and can we modify or counteract their effects? If not, it would seem that forces beyond our control can make us and keep us seriously handicapped in our efforts to abide by the law, even though we may still choose to do so. Because of this irremediable handicap it would seem that we then should be entitled to some dispensation when we break the law. The claim would be one of diminished responsibility based on being a certain sort of person that one could not help being, a person strongly disposed to doing certain things that the law punishes.

Clearly most people most of the time can do something to change themselves in ways that represent self-improvement. And once they are developed enough to appreciate and resist bad influences, people can keep themselves from becoming worse than they might be, though it is certainly more difficult for some people than for others, depending mainly on personal circumstances and the inner resources they possess once they have reached a point of moral emancipation in their development. This leaves us uncertain and unable to give an unequivocal answer to the question of whether we can rightly be held responsible for the sort of person we are. Fortunately, for purposes of determining issues of criminal liability we do not need to know the answer. All we need to know is whether we are responsible for those *acts* of ours that make us answerable to others. We do of course recognize that people are sometimes not responsible for what they do, or that even if they are, it would not be fair to hold them responsible because of the circumstances in which they did it. But the capacities and the opportunities that are lacking when we come to those conclusions make no reference to character-traits. The sort of person he is may *explain* why he behaves violently or dishonestly, but it has no part to play in helping us decide whether he is entitled to an exemption for what he did.

It is important that we have ways of summing up those things about people that seem important and that provide us with ways of understanding their behavior. But it is important to remember that what we are summing up is only what we happen to know about how a person acts or reacts, including both what is said and what is done. The evidence that can be introduced to establish a character-trait, while perfectly manageable for the ordinary purposes of life, is far too unfocused and selective for the purposes of any criminal proceedings in which disposing of a person's life depends on how an issue of culpability is decided. If there is a history of dishonesty or violence, that may be very important as a context in which to assess claims relating to the culpability of what was done in the instant case. But it will be important then only as it affects the *credibility* of these claims, and not as some added ingredient of wrongfulness belonging to the person rather than his conduct.

Attention to the person has, however, a sinister side that makes it something more than a snare and a delusion. Demonizing those who commit crimes is an activity pursued relentlessly by newspapers and politicians as well as by the public at large. Among certain professionals the study of "criminal types" has a long and ignoble history, as does, more popularly, the belief that members of particular groups have a disposition to crime. Furthermore, there is always an eagerness to indulge in the reassuring fiction that in general dispositions to commit crimes emanate from a flawed moral constitution, and that explanation relying on the facts of social or psychological pathology diminishes our moral vigor and our resolve to punish crime. Not surprisingly, these views breed, and are nurtured by, superstition and prejudice about people who commit crimes. Perhaps worst of all, they result in discriminatory practices in law enforcement that regularly put innocent people at risk.

In one of its most insidious forms, attention to "bad sorts of persons" takes place when the police are confronted with a case in which evidence is in short supply and a plausible suspect is needed. Disreputable elements in the community are canvassed for likely candidates, and one or more are selected, with those having an arrest or a criminal record enjoying preferential status. Individuals whose life-styles are particularly unsavory or whose appearance and demeanor is perceived as menacing are at a particular disadvantage. Such people are brought in for questioning, bits of evidence mysteriously appear, and in due course one of them is charged after standard techniques of interrogation produce further bits of useful information. It is, after all, easy enough for people experienced in criminal scenarios to use any information from whatever source to create a plausible story that tells how and why the crime was committed by the undesirable character who has finally been selected for the part, quite often after a positive identification in a notoriously unreliable identification parade. At the heart of this approach to law enforcement is the relative ease with which character traits that fit the crime can be imputed to the sort of people that are selected as perpetrators. In addition, being undesirables, these people become victims of two pervasive assumptions that tend to allay any misgivings. Even if a person like this did not commit *this* crime, surely he committed others. And in any case, the community is a safer and pleasanter place with such people out of circulation. These attitudes in law enforcement enjoy the warmest support among the public at large, where lack of contact with injustice makes ignoring it a good deal easier. As far as the agencies of law enforcement are concerned, it is closure of cases that is of paramount importance, and in the absence of sufficient hard evidence a warm welcome is given to speculation and surmise about a person out of which a plausible tale can be woven leading to conviction. The tale need not be, and usually is not, told to a jury, and most often it is not subject to any critical examination in court. It serves, rather, as a potent weapon in plea bargaining to extract a guilty plea from innocent people who are frightened when they consider how plausible the fabrication will seem in court if they decide to dispute it and are portrayed there as the disreputable people they are in the eyes of the world.

No less insidious is the abuse of prosecutorial power to find some crime, or even to contrive to have some crime committed, so that someone who is considered a bad person by the prosecutor can be made to face criminal charges. It is hard to imagine a more notorious or a more spectacular example than the investigation of the President of the United States by the office of the Independent Counsel, which culminated in the impeachment of President Clinton.* After fruitless years of searching for materials out of which a crime might be fashioned for purposes of bringing an indictment, an attempt was made to force the President to lie under oath in order to avoid hugely embarrassing disclosures. This grotesque episode in the nation's history rested on certain notions about faults in the President's character that had considerable currency and that were given a big boost by stories of his numerous sexual exploits. Although the very high profile of the victim in this case is unequalled, the abuse of prosecutorial power is commonplace. It shows itself whenever the person becomes the primary object of interest and the crime becomes a weapon to be used against him.

In a US Supreme Court case decided in 1988, Justice Antonin Scalia wrote a lone dissenting opinion attacking the constitutionality of the Ethics in Government Act of 1978, which established the office of the Independent Counsel. With amazing prescience he addressed the sort of abuse of investigative and prosecutorial power by the Independent Counsel that later took place during the Clinton administration, and quoted a speech delivered in 1940 to a conference of United States Attorneys by Robert Jackson when he was still Attorney General. Jackson spoke about the temptations to *any* prosecutor of "picking the man" and then "putting investigators to work, to pin some offense on him". Any prosecutor, Jackson said, "stands a fair chance of finding at least a technical violation of some act on the part of almost anyone", and so, he continued, "the real crime becomes that of being unpopular with the predominant or governing group, being attached to the wrong political views, or being personally obnoxious".*

Temptations to abuse the awesome discretionary powers with which police and prosecutors are endowed are a good reason to treat the crime as all important. But beyond that, it is not at all clear why the criminal law should ever need to concern itself with an assessment of the person's character when really it is only an assessment of conduct that concerns the criminal law. That assessment can be made in an entirely satisfactory way just by considering the facts that bear on conduct—what sort of threat of what sort of harm was there in what was done intentionally. The person behind the criminal conduct is an endless source of fascination, but such preoccupation quite wrongly suggests that the criminal law can be understood as a mechanism for moral eugenics whose aim is to rid the community of persons of bad character.

For those who are understandably concerned that crimes are only brief episodes in otherwise law-abiding lives, there is little consolation in a search for the bad person lurking beneath the crime. Only in quite exceptional cases will the perpetrator turn out to be the substrate of evil that is required to silence our conscience as we contemplate the massive punishment that we are visiting on him. The more ambitious the investigation, the more complex and equivocal the results. True comfort lies in moderating our institutional response to crime in ways that enable us to recognize the criminal episode for no more than what it truly is in the full context of the person's life.

★ ★ ★

What of those inculpatory and exculpatory claims that are supposed to make reference to personal traits and values in order to heighten or diminish the culpability of the criminal act? First, the inculpatory claims.

Should the bigotry and hatred that fuels a violent attack on a member of some despised group insert itself into a judgment of how wrong the crime is so that what is morally reprehensible about the perpetrator makes his crime worse? It is easy to accept that a racist or homophobic attack is more serious than the same angry violence prompted by something more mundane. But is it something about the crime—the kind of threat that is constituted by such conduct, and the grievous assault on sensibilities that is part of such a crime—or is it something deplorable about the perpetrator that is revealed by his crime? Attacking people because of what they are does have a special added horror. There are several reasons why. First, in such cases there is nothing a victim can do to avoid being a prospective target of such attacks. Second, such an attack is an assault upon part of a person's identity, and for that reason is especially hurtful. Third, the attack is all the more intimidating when, as a member of a group that is a minority in the community, a person is attacked because he is different from the majority in ways that matter to the majority. But nothing about the character of the person who makes such an infamous attack need be referred to in order to explain why the attack is especially infamous.*

A person's character is equally irrelevant to an understanding of exculpatory claims. A closer look at the examples discussed previously makes this clear.

It was suggested that a person who reacts with inappropriate violence to a petty provocation has not assimilated the community's norms, and that it is this defect in character that leaves him bereft of the exculpatory help that the provocation might otherwise provide. But surely it is a judgment about conduct, not character, that determines what reactions to provocations will be allowed, or will at least be regarded as a less serious violation of the law. How menacing a reaction is can be judged only in the light of what provoked it. If it is quite understandable that someone might react in that way, we feel much easier about that item of conduct, and see it as not the serious threat it would be if considered out of context. But if the triggering event seems trivial, we view it as a pretext rather than a provocation, and the violence that follows is viewed as a menace that must be dealt with by the law. What matters is our view of what happened and how threatened such conduct makes us feel, not what this reveals about the person provoked with respect to deviation from community norms.

Then there is the son who is tormented by his father's suffering and risks a charge of murder when he acts to bring the suffering to an end. He displays tragic nobility of character, while the son who takes his father's life in the same circumstances to get his hands on the old man's money shows himself to be a despicable person. But that is not what matters when discretion is exercised to treat these two cases of premeditated murder differently. It again is the conduct of each that matters. In the first case there is certainly not a callous disregard for the life that is taken, almost nothing at all that is menacing in what was done, and so there is conduct that we can live with quite comfortably even if we feel we cannot afford to let the unauthorized taking of a life pass unnoticed as a crime; while in the second case we have conduct that is very menacing indeed, conduct that can fairly be described as seizing an opportunity to kill for money where the chances of being exposed seem remote.

It was suggested that killing in self-defense is governed by legal rules that make implicit reference to the moral values of the defendant, and that only if they accord with the moral values enshrined in the law will this exculpatory defense be given effect. With due regard to the moral significance of the threat he presents, the life of the aggressor is weighed in the moral balance against the honor, dignity, self-respect, proprietary rights, or whatever else of moral value to the defendant he would sacrifice by retreat, and if on balance the defendant is found morally wanting, his defense will fail.

But again, it is not an assessment of the person that decides the issue, but an assessment of his conduct in the circumstances. Self-defense raises issues of competing interests to be accommodated where once again there is a situation of harms in opposition, this time harm that is threatened opposed by harm that is inflicted to put an end to the threat. Whether the harm inflicted is justified is determined by assessing the seriousness of the threat, adding to this the collateral elements that would be suffered by retreating to escape the threat, and weighing that against the harm inflicted. This is not to deny that moral values have a part to play in reaching a decision—life, honor, dignity, and proprietary rights are all charged with moral concern. The point is only that conduct, not persons, raises the moral issues.

Next there is duress, and the matter of reasonable firmness in resisting pressures to commit a crime. Is it really a matter of having a sufficiently strong character when the chips are down, and standing firm in the face of all but the most terrible threats when knuckling under means committing a crime? Is this then a feature of the good citizen's character, part of what it means to be law-abiding, avoiding crime not only in good times when it involves no risk, but in bad times as well when avoiding crime might have certain unpleasant consequences?

But again, a test of character is not the issue. It is harms in opposition that is the crux. Does the conduct constituting duress pose a sufficiently serious threat of harm to allow the person threatened to engage in the harmful conduct constituting the crime? Obviously the seriousness of the crime has an important part to play, as does the seriousness of the threat, with regard both to the kind of harm threatened and to how much of a sense of its immediacy and unavoidability was created. Striking a suitable balance between the harm threatened and the harm done to escape that threat is the aim of the law, and it makes no difference whether the person who pleads duress happens to be an appalling coward or a person of unusual firmness in the face of danger.

Mental disorder as a defense has also been explained in terms of character. In an illuminating article one writer has put the matter this way:

What is the difference between a sane person who kills for monetary gain, and someone in the grip of a paranoid delusion who kills the person he believes is persecuting him, such that the latter, but not the former, should be acquitted of murder? The former's action, we suppose, flowed from an intelligible motive for whose sake he was prepared to flout a basic legal and moral value which he could nonetheless understand: the latter's action, by contrast, displayed neither his excessive concern for an intelligible end, nor a disregard for values he could understand; it rather reflected the radical distortion of his thoughts and emotions from which he was suffering. But this is surely to say that what makes the former person culpable is that his action flowed from an intelligible set of attitudes and concerns (from, that is, certain character-traits) which renders the action both intelligible and culpable.*

But of course a person who is legally insane when he commits his crime may through his crime manifest his reprehensible character traits no less clearly than a person who suffers no such disability when he commits the same crime. The insane person might be suffering from delusions and thinks the person he kills has a hoard of gold coins under the mattress. He kills "for monetary gain". Insane persons may have perfectly intelligible motives from which they act in committing the crime, and these motives may be as much a reflection of character as they are in the case of sane counterparts. The difference between the two lies in some radical incapacity that, for example, leaves the insane person unable to put the brakes on once the idea has taken hold, or unable to have a realistic appreciation of just what it is that he is doing. The same rapacity that was in evidence previously when the person was sane was also at work driving him on during the episode of insanity, and it prompted the crime just as it might have if he were sane. But that rapacious trait of character is without relevance one way or the other in determining the question of culpability. The incapacity is all that matters.

Where, then, does all this leave us? Quite simply with conduct, properly understood, as all that is necessary to determine matters of criminal culpability. And with concern about the character of the person whose conduct it is, otiose at best, and quite likely an encouragement to abuse of power and miscarriages of justice, as free-wheeling conjecture about people's underlying dispositions takes the place of those familiar and reliable procedures that assess their conduct in the light of concrete evidence relating to the crime.

★ ★ ★

The shadowland between a person and his conduct is occupied by his choices. Or so it seems. I do something. There is no question about who did it, or about what was done. But did I choose to do it? Or was it more a matter of something seemingly thrust upon me completely unawares, like a sudden collision with something that appeared out of nowhere; or perhaps something that burst forth from me, quite as much a surprise to me as to anyone else; or just something that seems to have happened unexpectedly in the course of what I was doing, or as a result of it, but in any case not at all what I had in mind? It is customary to dispatch these incidents to some hinterland of accountability occupied by things done that one did not choose to do. These are acts that have a good claim to be treated as excusable, acts superficially associated with the actor, but at the same time subject to a radical dissociation. They stand in contrast to proper acts that are fully-fledged because a matter of *choice* and therefore without any element of surprise for the person whose act it is.

But the separation is not quite that neat. We sometimes choose to do things against our will, not at all what we want to do, but what we feel compelled to do in the situation in which we find ourselves. And so we discern a conflict between what we would choose to do and what we have chosen to do. In such a case we say that what we did was not a matter of *free* choice, suggesting that choices can still be choices even though what is chosen is, in no uncertain terms, dictated to the person whose choice it is. These are cases that range from the relatively easy choice of doing what is ordered at gunpoint to the painfully difficult decisions that are made when we realize some terrible sacrifice is the only way to avert something that is even more terrible.

In these cases we are not at all surprised by what we did, and we are not able through an excuse to distance ourselves from what has happened. Instead, we invoke the exceptional circumstance and say that we were justified in what we did because exceptional circumstances call for exceptional measures. Perhaps we have no license to kill some innocent person even to save ourselves from certain death; or, more generally, to do whatever might be necessary to escape harm, no matter what the cost to others. But neither are we to be judged under standards that prevail when things are normal since we are in a situation that is far from normal. Judgments must respect the fact that choices are sometimes forced upon us; otherwise the notion of acts freely chosen will lose its significance.

But what of choosing itself? When we choose, quite freely, to do something, is there something in the choosing that enhances the right or wrong of what we do? If we *choose* to do good, and not simply do good, is the act somehow given moral elevation? Or, even, as Kant apparently thought, is it only the good act chosen as such that can in any case be esteemed as morally worthy? Perhaps my perfunctory hand-out in response to a plea for some money from some poor person in the street—hardly more than a mindless reaction to a mildly annoying intrusion—will not receive full marks, or any marks at all, on the moral scorecard. Similarly, is there something about *choosing* to do something bad that makes it worse than simply doing it? When I break the law with full knowledge of what I am doing, is there something about my *choosing to break the law* that makes it worse than simply doing what happens to break the law? Good things that are prompted by a sense of what makes them good do seem more creditable morally, and bad things done with a relish for their badness seem especially discreditable. But does that in any way bear on the concerns of the criminal law? Since it is the threats and the harmfulness of conduct, not sentiment or attitude, that is the concern of the law, these matters of moral concern seem irrelevant. Two people commit exactly the same crime, both of them fully engaged in committing the crime, and both without a shred of excuse or justification. One of them hates the police and enjoys breaking the law, which he has quite deliberately chosen to do as an act of defiance. The other is not interested in breaking the law and is only interested in what his crime will accomplish, and so in that sense has not chosen to break the law.

Whatever the moral distinctions that may be made, within the ambit of criminal jurisprudence there is no reason to regard these two lawbreakers differently. The notion of choice that matters for criminal liability is a different sort of notion altogether. *Choosing* is not the expression of some sentiment or attitude, nor is it the expression of a wish or a preference by word or deed; nothing at all like ordering in a restaurant or making a move in a game of chess. What matters for criminal liability is that the perpetrator did not lack the capacity *to choose* to conform his conduct to the law, or did not lack a fair opportunity *to choose* to do so. The significance of *choosing* in this context can be appreciated by considering what its elimination would mean.*

Lacking the capacity to act in conformity with the law, or lacking a fair opportunity to do so, is *more than enough* for an excuse. If someone commits a crime instigated by others while he is in an altered state of consciousness for which he is not responsible, or when he is physically overpowered and used bodily as an instrument to commit a crime, there is surely an excuse. But requiring such a massive loss of self-determination is setting the standard too high. Not having the capacity or fair opportunity *to choose* not to engage in criminal conduct sets a lower standard that lets people off the hook when there is merely an impairment or interference that makes it *unreasonable* to require a law-abiding course of conduct, though admittedly such a course of conduct was perfectly possible. People who are legally insane can and usually do avoid engaging in criminal conduct, but when they do not we take into account the unreliability of their resources for engagement with reality and for self-control, and conclude that though hoping for a law-abiding course of conduct is not unreasonable, requiring it is.

Here, then, is what we may conclude about choice in the context of criminal culpability. Unlike the case with moral judgments, the choice in choosing to do wrong has no inculpatory role to play. *Choice* does, however, help us to articulate in a more sensitive way the conditions that make exculpation appropriate and allows more moderate conditions of inability to be recognized as grounds for exoneration.

12

Consoling Fictions

When it comes to crime and punishment, everyone has a theory. Like Molière's M. Jourdain, who did not know that he spoke prose, many people do not know they have a theory, at least not until their views are examined and they are confronted with the evidence. Others have reasons for their views readily at hand and are more than happy to explain why they hold the views they do, but have little interest in subjecting the reasons they give to critical examination. At the summit are the professional theorists who examine each other's theories with a sharply critical eye, exploring crime and punishment as a subject for scholastic disputation, and with a quiet faith that through some mysterious process their work will benefit those who labor in the nether regions where the sordid machinery of criminal justice must grind on as best it can.

And so, at the bottom of the heap, we have the low-brow theories implicit in the stories of crime and punishment the mass media produce to feed an insatiable public appetite. In more elevated regions we find the middle-brow theories of those whose work appears in journals of opinion and who write books for an audience with more discriminating tastes, as well as those theories that can be discerned in the arguments of lawyers and the opinions of judges. While in the upper reaches, where theory itself is the business at hand, high-brow theories of considerable sophistication are produced and criticized in the hermetic atmosphere of the academy. But neither the plain man nor the professor enjoys immunity from those strictures of conscience that surround crime and punishment. Crimes must be punished, yet punishment is itself a crime cloaked in respectability. The pain of this moral dilemma is relieved by emollient fictions and evasions that are quietly insinuated into theory almost as secret ingredients. Here are four examples.

Idealization of Punishment

Punishment is not an invention of the law. And if punishment, like torture before it, fell into disrepute and were rejected as an institutional practice in the legal system, punishment outside the law would still flourish, not only as part of family life, but wherever discipline or wrongdoing is a matter of importance and there exists some authority to deal with it. Why then is such a great fuss made about justifying punishment according to law? Surely if there is anything for which punishment is appropriate it is crime. And surely the determination of guilt and the meting out of punishment is nowhere prescribed and practiced more scrupulously than in a legal system.

The agonized concern that prompts endless attempts to justify legal punishment has two sources. One is an awareness of what takes place in prison and elsewhere as a result of imprisonment. The other source of concern is the fact that it is the law that is responsible for this orgy of indecency and destructiveness, the law upon which we all depend for protection of our interests, the law whose word must be regarded as the final word in settling disputes, the law whose final word must be obeyed. Punishment according to law is the most terrible punishment that can befall us, and it is punishment at the behest of an authority in whom we must place our trust for protection against the injustice of others, as well as the vindication of our own just claims. No wonder we try to make criminal punishment seem a more familiar and more amiable part of life, like all punishment to be avoided for oneself, but like all punishment really quite an acceptable practice when administered to others who deserve it.

The awfulness of criminal punishment is disguised in three different ways.

We have, first of all, *the concept of punishment* to cheer us. It elevates our minds from the sordid detail of what goes on in the name of punishment, and in a realm of abstraction allows us to think in a more dispassionate way about exactly what we mean when we talk about punishment, and what confusions we must be careful to avoid. Being clear about the essentials, we can talk in a more precise way, deciding, for instance, whether what is called punishment is really punishment if the person being "punished" is known to be innocent; what the difference is between punishment and other things bearing some resemblance to it, like punitive damages or preventive detention or involuntary civil commitment; and when a penalty or deprivation that the law imposes for some wrongdoing is properly regarded as punishment.

In this realm of abstraction, we can replace "punishment" with a term like "sanction" to remove emotive distractions and lower the temperature of discourse to a point where being made to work on a chain gang and being made to suffer a trade embargo are seen to be in essential respects the same. It is rationality working in the service of an escape and pre-empting the place of a more troubling rationality. Instead of ideas employed to deal with experience in an orderly way, without loss of contact or distortion, but in a way that allows us to think through the whole of the experience, there is a more comforting rationality that allows us to feel better about what we are doing by allowing us to ignore those elements that tend to upset us.

Closely connected to denaturing by abstraction is muddling by association. Since punishment abounds everywhere, why not view the homey varieties that we are all familiar with side-by-side with the terrifying variety that we want to come to terms with. And so everyone's experience of a fine for illegal parking is reassuring when used as a paradigm for punishment at large. In the academic literature, we find as analogues of what we do when we send people to prison such things as parental punishment of a child by making her sit quietly on the stairs after she made noise and teased a sibling; tutorial punishment of students in an Oxford college for not attending chapel; and even punishment for misbehavior on the ice by being required to sit in disgrace in a penalty box before thousands of spectators at a hockey match. Being sent to bed without supper and serving a five-year prison sentence are equally instructive examples of punishment, and this helps reconcile us to the dreadful things we do in imposing punishment for crime. After all, it is only the far greater wrongfulness of crime and the thoroughly wholesome principle of punishment proportional to wrongdoing that accounts for these two examples of punishment appearing to be so different. In contrast to techniques of abstraction, which suppress the awful truths, association makes criminal punishment seem a friendlier business just by stressing the supposed similarities between it and what we ourselves are familiar with in the routine of ordinary life where certainly there is no element of torment or lasting damage to those who are punished.

Finally, there is diminution. Punishment is a prominent feature of human life everywhere and in every age. It abounds in myths and religious tracts in every culture. As a theme in literature it even takes precedence over crime since no crime need occur for fate, or wanton acts of human vengefulness, to inflict punishment upon hapless victims. Put in this very grand context, punishment within a legal system seems restrained and admirably civilized, particularly with regard to considerations of justice, but even with regard to the relatively humane treatment that most legal systems provide when compared to the utter barbarity that the human imagination can produce when freed of legal constraints.

But of course there is no abiding solace to be found in contemplating what is even worse. We have our own standards to guide us, and even if God Almighty does not respect them in what he prescribes and in what he is said to have done in biblical texts, they remain the standards we live by. It is the numbing effect that such texts may have that is troubling. Most people do not have any experience as prisoners themselves, nor do they have any other experience of what goes on in prison, and so they are deprived of the only enduring antidote.

Sentencing to Perfection

What a noble pursuit is the quest for the truly right sentence. It has engaged the efforts of many theorists who are dedicated to making sure that justice is done—not overdone or underdone, but done exactly as it must be done if it is justice in more than name. Justice must consist, above all else, in making the punishment fit the crime, or so one would suppose.

Even if everyone agreed about what criteria are to be applied in the search for such fitness it would be no easy task to get it right. In fact there is vast disagreement about what the right criteria are. No one disputes that some crimes are worse than others (though exactly how much worse is a bewildering question), and no one disputes that sentences should reflect that fact. But even these unexceptionable principles become a nullity in practice when the likes of the fashionable three-strikes-you're-out sentence is mandated by law. Indeed, they are undermined whenever any consideration extraneous to the crime that has been committed comes into play in arriving at a sentencing decision.*

Three-strikes-you're-out is now the law's most dramatic detour from efforts to make the punishment fit the crime. But it has always been accepted that a person's criminal record (indeed even his police record) may influence his sentence even though these are reports of facts that have nothing to do with the crime for which he is now being sentenced. Three different thoughts encourage this. One is simply that people who have committed crimes before are more likely to commit them again, and so should be kept out of circulation for a longer time as a contribution, admittedly modest, to a safer social environment. A second thought is that persons with a criminal history are worse persons and therefore ought to be punished more severely than those whose lapse from innocence is without any precedent—though it is not clear whether the rewards of previous innocence are being denied the recidivist or whether he is being given an extra measure of punishment because, by this additional crime, he has shown himself to be a worse person than the crime alone would indicate. (At this point there emerges once again a deep controversy between punishment of the person *for* his conduct and punishment of the person *because of* his conduct and what that tells us about him. It raises again the fundamental question of whether it is conduct or persons that dominate in decisions about the extent of criminal liability.) There is a third thought in departing from punishment just to fit the crime, and it has to do with the need for those benefits which are supposed to be provided through punishment itself or are supposed to be made available as a concomitant of serving a sentence. It is assumed that someone who continues to commit crimes requires more extensive rehabilitation to make him law-abiding like the rest of us, and a longer sentence is needed to allow such extended rehabilitation to take place. Silly as all of this may be, and especially in the real world of prison life, these thoughts do guide the architects and the craftsmen of sentencing as they go about the business of conceiving and imposing sentences.

But there is much more to interfere with making the punishment fit the crime. It is widely supposed that making an example of someone who commits a crime will put a brake on the commission of such crimes by others. When some crime seems particularly prevalent, both the penalties on the books and the sentences imposed may be increased in an attempt to somehow diminish the overall attractiveness of such crimes. As with most simplistic products of the mind, there is no real interest in finding out what happens when these notions are put into practice and whether stiffer sentences really do make a difference. Nevertheless, the idea continues to flourish because of the release from anxiety and rage that it provides for a community plagued with crime when it is believed that the perpetrators are being locked up and the key is being thrown away.

Matters are further complicated by the widespread practices of plea bargaining and of rewarding cooperation with the authorities by reductions in sentence. Plea bargaining need not mean a complete abandonment of the matching of crime and punishment so long as there is a genuinely sustainable charge of a lesser crime and a sentence that reflects its seriousness. Much

more often, however, it is a game of threats and incentives to induce a guilty
plea that allows the case to be disposed of in a way not unacceptably embarrassing to the authorities and not unacceptably distressing to the defendant.
Cooperation with the authorities—typically as an informant or as a witness
for the prosecution—can result in immunity from prosecution or in a
reduced sentence following a guilty plea, and when the reduced sentence is
not matched by a reduced charge, once again there is a sentencing practice
that is heedless of the principle that punishment must fit the crime.

It is universally accepted that a repentant sinner is to be treated more
charitably than an unrepentant one, and this has its counterpart in sentencing. If the defendant accepted responsibility for what he did, if he seems
genuinely remorseful, if he does whatever he can to repair the damage,
restore what has been taken, and do whatever else might be possible by way
of reparation to the victim, he is entitled to have that considered in his favor.
Conversely, he will have it held against him that he refuses to acknowledge
that what he did was wrong and he may even be penalized because he continues to protest his innocence.

Yet another complication is introduced when alternatives to time in
prison are among the sentencing options. Sentences can be suspended, and
besides probation, there are many varieties of conditional discharge, including those that provide for reparations to victims. There are fines, and there
are a variety of community sentences as alternatives to imprisonment or
any other sort of custodial sentence, as well as quasi-custodial sentences
outside of prison within the community. A good deal of ingenuity has been
shown in devising dispositions that will do less damage to the offender, will
help relieve the public purse of the huge burden that imprisonment
imposes, but will not let the public feel that justice or public safety has been
compromised. But when a crime is neither shocking nor an occasion for
sympathy rather than condemnation, it can be a daunting task to decide
what kind of disposition is most appropriate, a task that further complicates
the quest for just the right sentence.

As if all of this were not enough, an array of further challenges must
be met.

Each convicted person presents his own idiosyncratic problems to be
taken into account at the time of sentencing. Ought not health or age or
effects on a family to be considered when there are plainly inhumane consequences in prospect? And should not the background of the person being
sentenced be considered when it is clear he should have known better, or

when he really couldn't be expected to behave like someone who had a normal upbringing? Is the right punishment for the crime really so great a moral imperative that it trumps the moral imperatives that constitute the core of decency in everyday life?

Closely connected to this is a problem that confronts those theorists who wish to explain how a proper match can be made between the crime and the punishment. To make a match it is obviously necessary to measure in some way the severity of the punishment. But no matter what elements of suffering or deprivation are taken to be appropriate when measuring punishment in the abstract, there are bound to be very great variations in the effect of any measure of punishment as it is experienced by different individuals. In so far as the particular effect in each case can be anticipated, is it not incumbent upon the one who passes sentence to use the individuated assessment rather than the more general one based on notions that do not depend upon how any particular individual will experience his punishment? After all, we are interested in the seriousness of the particular crime that has been committed, with all of the mitigating or aggravating factors that belong uniquely to that particular criminal event being given the weight that is due them. Why should the punishment not be subject to a similarly unique assessment of severity that takes into account whatever we can reasonably estimate to be the suffering and deprivation that the perpetrator of this particular crime will experience?

I have just referred to the aggravating and mitigating factors that are taken into account in determining the seriousness of the crime. But just what these factors are, and which of them ought to be included, is a matter of considerable controversy. How great a weight ought to be given to the harm that happens to occur as a result of the criminal act, regardless of what was intended or what might reasonably have been expected? How great a weight ought to be attached to what the perpetrator had in mind, regardless of what he actually accomplished? When does the reason he did what he did matter, either to make what he did better or to make it worse? And in general, is what matters more the seriousness of the kind of harm that a kind of crime involves, or what we think of as "the state of mind" of someone who by his conduct brings about the harm. It is a question whose answer will tell us, for example, whether the kind of difference that distinguishes robbery from burglary is more important than the kind of difference that distinguishes murder from manslaughter. In short, there is no consensus among theorists regarding the way that seriousness of criminal conduct is to be determined, and so the seriousness of one crime compared to another often remains controversial.

The sentencer's headaches are still not at an end. It is axiomatic that there must not be disparity among sentences. Nothing, not even proportionality, is more important as a principle of justice than treating like cases alike and different cases differently according to their difference. But how can there be any hope of avoiding disparity when there are such great difficulties in determining just how serious a crime is in any case, in determining how severe as punishment a sentence is in any case, and just how sentences ought to be influenced by an assortment of relevant considerations that bear on neither of these questions?

In view of all this, what can we say of the ideal of the right sentence, of punishment that truly fits the crime while at the same time reflecting the many other considerations that compete with straightforward notions of seriousness and severity to determine a sentence?

The right sentence as an exuberant moral ideal is an illusion. The disagreements that endure at the heart of the issue of seriousness and the miscellany of disparate constraints that bear on the sentencing decision make the idea of imposing the right sentence a matter of *faute de mieux* rather than the achievement of some moral excellence. As earlier discussions make clear, there are many pitfalls to be avoided, some concerned with injustice and some with inhumanity, and passing a sentence that avoids them is meeting an important demand of political morality. When sentences are seen simply as a matter of grim necessity, a cog in the great anti-impunity machine that was suggested earlier in the book, the sense of noble purpose that animates so much of sentencing theory is dispelled. What is called for are the negative virtues of balanced judgment and restraint. Getting it right can mean nothing more than not getting it wrong, which seems a truly heroic achievement when one considers the very strong feelings which depend for their abatement on the punishment a sentence represents and the ill-assorted uses to which a sentence is put. It is the supreme challenge for judicial discretion, and only by meeting the challenge can the demands of political morality be satisfied.

Belief in the virtues of objectivity can hardly be misplaced when one considers the great diversity of views among judges about everything that is important in deciding on a sentence. Judicial discretion is nowhere more untrammelled than when deciding on the appropriate sentence under laws that do no more than prescribe a range within which the sentence must fall. Everything, therefore, depends upon the particular preconceptions and predispositions of the judge who happens to be dealing with the case, and surely the sentence a convicted person receives ought not to depend on that. But is it possible to devise a scheme that both excludes judicial idiosyncrasy and allows the many considerations that ought to be included in sentencing deliberations to have their proper influence?

Sentencing guidelines to achieve this have been widely adopted in the United States,* but have been held by the Supreme Court to be advisory only and not mandatory as they were intended to be, since they have the effect of redefining the crime at the sentencing stage, with the new elements the guideline introduces not subject to proof that would satisfy a jury beyond a reasonable doubt, even though they may increase a sentence beyond the maximum allowed by statute. But there is an even more fundamental objection. To achieve uniformity among sentences the guidelines must ignore the *individual's story* that illuminates the significance of each of the features of the crime and of the defendant's history which the guideline uses in calculating a sentence in each particular case. Taking that individual's story into account, with all of its special circumstances, is something only the judge can do when he exercises his discretion. And without considering that story, the opportunities for injustice abound, since only through the explanation it provides can the plausible first impressions that the guidelines embody be shown to be incorrect. In the most general terms, what seems to be needed instead is, first, a thorough ventilation of all of the issues over which sentencing discretion may properly roam, with a view to arriving at an enlightened consensus in the form of a detailed policy statement. Then it would seem sensible to require detailed sentencing opinions to support sentencing decisions in each case, which in turn must be subject to appellate review to ensure that this enlightened consensus was being respected. Only then could a sentence that avoided the pitfalls of injustice and inhumanity hope to become the general rule and not the exception.

What I have suggested here forecloses any hope of achieving *the* right sentence, a sentence that in itself is something of positive moral worth. I am suggesting that a more modest effort to minimize in a piecemeal way injustice and inhumanity is the best we can hope for. But that is no small thing.

Judgment from Nowhere

Not all crimes are the work of criminals. Even the most serious crimes are sometimes committed by people who not only think of themselves as law-abiding but who display a robust commitment to keeping on the right side of the law. Murders among friends and family, for instance, are commonly the acts of law-abiding citizens whose crimes are a sharp (though not always unexpected) departure from lifelong habits of obedience, conformity, compliance, and allegiance that characterize the good citizen's relationship to the authority of the law in its various forms. These crimes are straightforward crimes that tell us a great deal about personal fragilities and nothing about personal commitments, save how little those commitments can mean as a bulwark against criminal conduct.

But it is not these straightforward crimes of the law-abiding that I want to talk about now. What interests me here are those normally law-abiding people who are threatened with serious criminal liability because what they did seems wrong now even though at the time it seemed right. In saying it seemed right at the time I am not suggesting that they made some terrible mistake (for which they may or may not have been responsible) which we now can see and which leads us to judge what they did quite differently. On the contrary, when I say it seemed right at the time, I mean that it would be reasonable enough for anyone in their shoes to act as they did even though once we view what they did (or indeed once they are able to view it themselves) not *from* the circumstances in which they found themselves but only *in* those circumstances, what they did seems wrong. It is, in other words, a matter of seeing them just as they were, but not adopting their viewpoint at the time. There can be a great difference in the way things are seen at the time by people who are part of what is happening, and the way things are seen by an observer or (more likely) someone reviewing the evidence of what happened after the event. For the theorist the different viewpoints and the conflicting views that emerge from them are bound to be disturbing. After all, in the most difficult situations in which people find themselves, they often have only what seems right to them at the time to guide them, and what seems right at the time may well turn out to be wrong even though it is the view that anyone in that situation might be expected to have.

When I say it seemed right at the time I have in mind more than one kind of case.

There are first of all those people who would say that no matter how profoundly upsetting it might be, it just seemed the right thing to do at the time, suggesting that what was done was dictated by a moral reading of the events. It seemed the right thing, for instance, to take one life rather than many as one hurtled down a steep road with no brakes but with a choice of whom to avoid hitting; or in a hospital fire deliberately neglecting the old people in a geriatric ward in order to save the children in a pediatric ward; or not ignoring the anguished pleas of a soldier wounded in combat who wished to be killed quickly to put an end to his horrible and apparently hopeless suffering.

But claiming that it seemed the right thing to do will sometimes be a bit rich. Sometimes the best we can say is that it seemed all right to do what was done, that all things considered it seemed safe enough, though of course there are always risks of one sort or another and one must be sensible in assessing them. Appearances can be deceiving, and the question then is whether those appearances should really have been relied on. It may be easy enough to see through misleading appearances when looking at the facts with detachment later on, but is it right to expect such perspicacity from the person who is involved at the time?

Rape accusations are a gold mine here, as well as a minefield. At one extreme there is the notorious case of several men who after an evening's drinking together proceeded to the house of one of them and had forcible intercourse with his wife against her will, claiming afterward that they believed the husband when he had told them earlier that his wife would resist as part of a kind of kinky play-acting that made the sex more exciting for her.★ At the other extreme are cases in which the woman expresses a genuine unwillingness to have sex, but in the sort of intimate setting in which women who might be persuaded often express an initial reluctance; and in the face of the woman's increasing passivity, which the man inter- prets as acquiescence, he presses on, though in fact the woman never really does change her mind. It seems plain enough that a genuine belief main- tained in the face of evidence to the contrary will not suffice. There were certainly some grounds for believing that the wife's resistance might be a sham as her husband had suggested—such things are not unknown—but hardly grounds enough for proceeding without some further evidence from the wife in view of the momentous consequences should the wife's resistance and not the husband's story turn out to be genuine. But when a man and woman are in an intimate situation of their own making, there is a measure of plausibility in the man's claim that it seemed all right to have sex without an express retraction of the woman's previous refusal, even though, in view of her unretracted refusal, he can hardly mount a case that will confidently withstand a prosecutor's critical examination concerning the crucial issue of consent. Once again it is what anyone in his shoes might do, yet in spite of that, as we see it now he seems to have done something wrong.

Finally, there are cases where even from the actor's viewpoint at the time there were important considerations weighing heavily against what was done, but in spite of that there is a plausible claim that he had a right to do what he did. Imagine, for example, killing in self-defense with a preemptive strike when in a situation that was genuinely alarming for the person feeling threatened, though in retrospect it appears that the danger that seemed so great, so frightening, and so immediate may have been more imagined than real.* Not only self-defense, but acts of self-preservation can produce such cases—killing someone to survive on his flesh and blood, or to put a stop to his consumption of precious oxygen until rescuers can reach the air pocket, when otherwise death by starvation or by asphyxiation seems certain.* Of course what one does is wrong, and notoriously wrong, but still in the circumstances, wasn't there a right to do it? "I have a right to act to save my life before it's too late" seems a plausible enough claim when the appearance of imminent mortal danger is perfectly authentic, and insisting that there be sufficient evidence to confirm that death is imminent seems unreasonable. "I have a right to do whatever is necessary to survive, even taking his life, when it's a matter of my life or his" seems a perfectly plausible claim when heard as the voice of the person struggling to survive. But notice the change in moral mood when the tense changes to the past and the claim begins "I *had* a right...", suggesting a kind of ambivalence between the view he had when he was involved, and his view now when he is detached. An even more striking mood change takes place when the claim is in the third person, signaling unequivocal detachment. It is this utterly detached claim that is judged in court, a claim inviting a certain serene deliberation that the person whose conduct is being judged could not have hoped to enjoy in the midst of his predicament.

All of these cases turning on a purported right have a common theme. The participant's view at the time is highly charged with immediate concerns that preclude the balanced deliberation required for sound judgment, whether moral or prudential. It is not simply that his view of the matter is different. The matter itself is different, and inevitably so, because involvement then and there calls for action, not judgment; and the kind of action called for is governed by stresses and urges, and especially by those instincts that keep us from being victimized by our deliberations when deliberation becomes a frustrating or hazardous occupation. Our view at the time is customized to suit the needs of the occasion.

Even though these crimes are not nearly as common as those less problematic crimes of the law-abiding that result only from human frailty, there is a particular fascination and even a certain sense of urgency in finding the right answer for these prima-facie crimes that consist of conduct that seemed right at the time. The main reason, I think, is that they are what might be called crimes of predicament, and even though we do not expect to find ourselves hurtling down a hill in a car without brakes, or desperate to survive in a mine shaft or a lifeboat, or even being faced with criminal liability resulting from a sexual encounter, there are enough predicaments and enough experiences of danger in our lives to make us feel that we too might one day find ourselves in trouble with the law just for doing what we had a right to do.

The theorist seeks escape by a flight into detachment. It is (to adopt Thomas Nagel's striking phrase) the view from nowhere that allows us to transcend the idiosyncratic features of any particular viewpoint and the predicament from which it stems, yet leaves us able to take account of all of its detail. The idea is to strike a pose of moral objectivity that is sympathetic to the plight of the person who is now accused of a serious crime, but does not let that person's perfectly understandable view at the time determine the judgment of what he did. Some theorists allow very liberally for the legitimate self-interest of the participant to determine his actions, and in situations of difficulty grant him the privilege of causing or risking great harm to others when there truly seems no other way to prevent great harm to himself or to other prospective victims. Other theorists are less sensitive to the participant's predicament and display a greater concern for those who are harmed, or are threatened with harm, relying instead on principles that purport to promote the general welfare by imposing criminal liability. But even wholly sympathetic theorists resort to moral premises to decide the issue, and employ an argument about the moral status of what was done to determine the question of criminal liability. So, for example, Hobbes affirms an inextinguishable privilege of self-defense because of a self-defense proviso that must be included in any social contract that makes abandonment of a state of nature plausible. Put another way, any promise to perform the impossible would be void. To be "tyed to impossibilities is contrary to the very nature of compacts" says Hobbes.★ But in the lifeboat, in bed, in the car out of control, we have man once again temporarily in a state of nature because he must rely on what comes naturally rather than on the guidance that comes with deliberation. The possibility of exculpation rests not (as Hobbes seems to suggest) on a proviso that must be included or read into any social compact, with the good moral grounds that such an escape clause provides. Exculpation is rooted in the very facts of life that make such a proviso necessary.

In a discussion of these matters, Jeremy Waldron considers a hypothetical case in which an extremely dangerous terrorist uses a hostage as a human shield in an attempt to escape from a building surrounded by police operating in a shoot-to-kill mode. The terrorist convinces the hostage that either they escape together or they die together, and arms him with a pistol for added firepower in their attempt to escape. Suddenly they are confronted on the stairway by an armed police officer, and all three start shooting to kill. Waldron suggests that the hostage may be in some difficulty with a claim of self-defense, first, because the force he is defending against is not unlawful; and second, because it is worse from a social point of view that the terrorist should survive rather than be killed by the policeman. Discussing Hobbes' theory, Waldron asks why we find it difficult to accept Hobbes' view that "the law of nature" provides the ultimate justification. The answer, he says, is that for Hobbes "there is no *moral point of view* in the state of nature" (the emphasis is Waldron's).★

I have taken this excursion to suggest the great difficulty that all theorists have in abandoning a position of detached moral deliberation when the issue is criminal liability for those who at the time they acted are convinced they had a right to do what they did, and in whose shoes any of us might well have done the same thing with the same sense of right. Even Hobbes, whose argument rests ultimately on what are taken to be indisputable facts of human nature, speaks in terms of rights of nature that must be respected by the law when acts of self-defense or (arguably) other acts of self-preservation are being judged. There is a law of nature to which any law of a lesser order must defer. But when a person who was in a dire predicament, or perhaps only confronted with a difficult choice, tells us that he felt he had a right to act as he did, he is asking us to come to a conclusion through sympathetic identification with his plight. If we might act the same way if in his position, or at least would not consider that we were acting wrongly if we did act that way, why should we condemn him for what he did? What kind of morality is it, anyway, that exploits unfortunate circumstances to send people to prison?

The answer, I think, is that such a morality would be a very bad morality indeed. But fortunately it is not one that does in fact provide the reasons why suggestions of criminal liability are plausible in these anguished situations. The life that has been taken or the personal security that has been violated cannot be ignored as a source of grievance in its own right. Simply engaging in a sympathetic identification with the person responsible for the harm in his predicament at the time may well result in moral vindication. But there are then the further claims of the innocent victims (and prospective victims) to be considered. It is an issue of political, rather than personal, morality, so that even if the case for what was done is stronger than the case against it, that fact alone cannot be allowed to carry the day. Consideration must be given as well to the turmoil that a system of criminal justice is meant to keep at bay and that will erupt if the victim's interests are not given proper consideration. This is not good news for the theorist seeking consolation through some moral judgment of the conduct of the accused. Quite often that conduct enjoys moral innocence even though properly judged by the law to be guilty, with the detached judgment in court only an artifice designed to serve the needs of the system by ensuring against impunity for what now seems a crime. Discretionary dispensations from punishment (and even from prosecution when the system and the public can stand it) will reflect the moral truth. Furthermore, when the victim's grievance has been undermined by complicity or some other adverse feature of the story, the moral truth is likely to carry the day in court without reservation. But that is another story.

The Consolation of Evil

Sympathetic identification has severe limits even when it is only moral exculpation that is sought. If a predicament is so dire that the drastic measures taken might well be adopted by anyone who found himself in it, or the dangers sufficiently ambiguous to allow what was done, it is a case in which sympathetic identification tells a story that carries the day morally, even though, alas, the law may not be in a position to follow suit. When, however, there is simply desperation, but not the immediacy that is necessary to license harmful action, it is not an exculpatory wind that fills the sails of sympathy, even though the desperate plight that explains the crime deserves the greatest sympathy. People may be desperately poor, desperately unhappy in a dreadful marriage from which escape seems an impossibility, or tied to work that is both intolerable and an unalterable part of their life. If theft or murder is committed in a desperate attempt to escape, there is ample room for sympathy. But the kind of sympathetic identification that will make the crime seem *right* will be lacking so long as there still are those opportunities and abilities that make compliance with the law a realistic possibility.

Yet leaving it at that seems too abrupt a departure. Even when there are no obvious grounds for sympathy, nothing lamentably compelling in the circumstances of the crime, there is still the nagging truth of *tout comprendre, c'est tout pardonner* to haunt us as we look more deeply into those circumstances and increasingly come to understand the person whose crime it is. How much greater still is the poignancy when our sympathies are instantly engaged by the misery that produced the crime. Though in neither case will sympathetic identification lead to moral exculpation, there is nevertheless a subversive influence at work that threatens to undermine the moral foundations of criminal justice. In a more extreme form our extended understanding becomes deeply subversive. How can we, after all, condemn and punish acts that we can see ourselves doing if, *per impossibile*, we not only were in those circumstances but were that other person, influenced not only by the circumstances but subject to all of the influences that make him the person he is and that explain why he did it. It is no longer a *sympathetic* identification that governs our moral appreciation, but rather an *empathetic* identification. We are not simply putting ourselves in his shoes, which allows us to appreciate the natural effects of his situation on anyone who might find himself in it. We are putting ourselves in his skin, which allows us to appreciate the particular effect on him as the person he is. It is not simply seeing ourselves in that situation and working out with a suitably disciplined imagination what *we* would be likely to do. It is understanding what *he* did by taking on board not only his circumstances as he saw them, but also all those idiosyncratic features of the person he was that played a part in his doing what he did. In sympathetic identification we make common cause with whoever might be in such a predicament. In empathetic identification we make common cause only with the person who actually was in that predicament.

But if we are to live together we cannot afford the luxury of judging each person's acts with an understanding that best suits his personality and his personal history. Harm, and threats of it, have a life of their own that must be paid attention to. Concern about harming one another also rests on a compassionate regard for the person. The sympathy for victims that is inherent in judging harming and the threat of it as morally wrong must trump the sympathy evoked through empathetic identification with the person who does or who threatens the harm.

Clearly the very idea of either a sympathetic or an empathetic engagement with someone who has committed a crime is alarming since it threatens to weaken the hostile response that is the foundation of criminal justice. To put a stop to such subversive activities the notions of evil and wickedness are invoked. Placing certain conduct beyond the pale forecloses the possibility of respectable identification with it, and so exculpatory inclinations are nipped in the bud. But beyond this know-nothing position, there is a moral insight that must be taken seriously. Certain acts *are* in fact beyond the pale, and although understanding will inevitably moderate our attitudes, we do still wish to keep these crimes beyond the pale. The unspeakable crimes of the holocaust, the hideous crimes of terrorism, the barbarities of slaughter and suffering deliberately inflicted in our time in every part of the world, are all amenable to understanding and to the softening of attitudes that inevitably follows. But we have good reasons for resisting this more mellow view, lest our moral sensibilities become corrupted. These monster crimes, however, are a very long way from the crimes that fill our prisons with people whose problems have landed them there. Having recognized this, we find ourselves uncomfortable with the thought that we must override our understanding and our compassion in order to serve the emotional needs of an angry and fearful community who view these crimes in a victim's perspective; or because we must be careful to keep the law from becoming an empty threat. And so, to make ourselves feel better, we are happy to smuggle in the notion of evil from beyond the pale to reassure ourselves that to some extent all serious crimes partake of the same intolerable essence. But there is a high price to be paid for this comforting self-deception. It leaves our moral vision severely impaired, even to the point of moral blindness. This makes no difference for those crimes that are truly evil and so morally opaque. But most crimes deserve to be treated as morally transparent, in which case a loss of moral vision becomes a serious handicap.

13

Guilt and Convictability

My aim has been to dislodge the moral evaluation of criminal conduct from the dominant position it occupies in philosophical discussion of crime and punishment, and also to suggest that punishing crime is not an activity that rests on some indestructible moral bedrock. But these efforts are not to be construed as a general disparagement of moral concerns in the criminal law and its administration. Far from it. Because crime is such a serious matter and because criminal punishment is so terrible a fate, the moral issues that are involved require urgent attention. These issues, however, lie mainly in the domain of political morality, where improving things *morally* is a matter of improving the conduct of those who have power over others.

There are two important issues of political morality that I want to discuss in this chapter and the next, one having to do with how law enforcement and criminal justice is carried on when a crime is committed, the other concerned with criminal punishment when viewed as a morally disturbing institution at the heart of political society. In dealing with both of these issues I hope to encourage a conception of political morality that makes judgments of morally right and morally wrong less important than judgments of morally better or morally worse with respect to practices that exist to serve practical needs, always mindful that these practical needs stand as obstacles in the path of moral improvement. For that reason Clemenceau's trenchant observation about military justice is equally incisive when applied to criminal justice: criminal justice is to justice as military music is to music.

★ ★ ★

Everyone agrees that when a crime is committed it is the job of the authorities to bring the guilty party to justice. It is generally believed that this is what the police are determined to do, and such a belief is well supported by what the police understand their job to be. But though their understanding of their job is unwavering, the police are less steady in their determination that the party brought to justice must indeed be the guilty party. Their understanding of their job and their performance of it are often at odds. Quite simply, when confronted with a crime, the forces of law and order have an overriding interest in identifying someone who can be convicted for it, and then building a case that will result in a conviction. That is what will satisfy the community's deepest need when who committed a crime is uncertain, and it takes precedence over all other considerations.

Obviously the person who committed the crime is the preferred candidate for conviction. But unless that person confesses straight away, has been caught in the act, or is otherwise known to be the perpetrator, it is a matter of considering the circumstances and deciding who is a likely candidate, or when the circumstances are unilluminating, a matter of using whatever clues there might be to find a likely candidate. Once a likely candidate is identified, a combination of interrogation and further investigation is pursued to construct a case against him. There may be genuine doubts remaining, but unless the doubts make the case seem too shaky to be taken further, they are left to be resolved by lawyers, judges, and jurors at a later stage. Convictions are of paramount importance. The public want someone to be found guilty and punished; and police and prosecutors want to have as many crimes as possible disposed of as quickly as possible in a way that leaves no room for public dissatisfaction.

Convicting those who actually are guilty is preferred by the police and everyone else for several reasons. The guilty should be punished for what they have done. Leaving them at large leaves them free to commit further crimes. And if someone who is innocent is not the sort who belongs in prison anyway, putting him there seems a terrible thing to do. These considerations are heartily endorsed by police and prosecutors, and they stand resolutely in the way of any temptation to try to convict those who are believed to be innocent even when there is a good chance of gaining a conviction. But believing someone is not guilty, and having some lingering doubts about his guilt, are two very different things.

The police are a professional organization performing a public service. There are goals whose attainment measures professional success, and these goals are determined by the needs of the community for which the police perform their services. When responding to incidents of crime the police seek to apprehend the perpetrator and obtain evidence that will lead to his conviction. Many cases require investigation to determine who commit-ted the crime, and the investigation will normally be concluded at a point at which there is a story that is deemed sufficiently plausible in view of background information as well as the more immediate evidence relating to the crime. There may well be other stories that are equally plausible, or more plausible, for which evidence that is no less persuasive could be obtained if the investigation were taken further. The police, however, are not scientific investigators and are not interested in extending their inves-tigations to explore these alternative possibilities in the interest of being as certain as possible that they have the right person. Resources are limited, speedy closure of open cases ("results") is deemed of the greatest impor-tance, and one sufficiently plausible determination is all that the system (and the public) requires. Though it is not uncommon for investigators to blow hot and cold and change their minds as they follow up leads, they are quite resolute in sticking to their guns once they feel they have made a good enough case against someone, even though miscarriage of justice is a live possibility if other known avenues are left unexplored.

The task of gaining a conviction is easiest if the person to be charged seems the sort who might well belong in prison, or at the very least is some-one whose absence from the community would be considered a gain rather than a loss. People believed to be engaged in criminal activities are good candidates. There are also many varieties of undesirables who can easily be thought of as dangerous because of their eccentric appearance and behav-ior, or even if only because their desperate circumstances suggest that they may do harm out of desperation. These people are good candidates, and particularly if they have some sort of psychological vulnerability that will make it easier to get them to say what the police would like to hear. If there is a criminal record, so much the better. Indeed, having a criminal record makes one a star attraction. Those in the business of fighting crime can salve their conscience with the comforting thought that even if the person they have fingered did not commit this crime, he almost certainly has commit-ted some others. A belief that social sanitation is the overriding goal of law enforcement lends support to this approach. Crimes become a pretext for bringing criminal types into a custodial regime so that the community will be a safer place for the rest of us.

In their efforts to make a case, the police interrogate suspects in order to produce damaging admissions, or even better, a confession. Interroga-tion by the police is a harrowing experience at any time if there is any suggestion that one might be in some trouble. When it is made clear that one is a suspect in connection with a serious crime, it is one of life's truly frightening experiences. Techniques of interrogation are designed to intimidate and to trick. Both are often combined in some version of the familiar good-cop bad-cop routine in which one interrogator appears to befriend the increasingly threatened suspect, intimating he wants to help him in order to gain his confidence and get him to talk. The process of interrogation is in fact an ordeal intended to produce a confession, or at least to produce enough information to allow the police to charge the suspect then and there, or if they are not even that lucky, to provide them with leads for further evidence.

Looked at from a moral point of view, the interrogation of suspects is itself suspect in the extreme.

For one thing, it is not clear why procedures designed to elicit information at an early stage in the criminal process should be very different from procedures available for the same purpose early in civil proceedings, where both parties have a right to find out what the basis of the other party's case is. Both civil and criminal procedures have as their purpose the eliciting of information bearing on prospective liability. Claims of criminal liability, whether tentative or well supported, must have some foundation, and it seems only fair that a suspect have the opportunity to challenge the basis of such claims at the earliest possible time, and certainly once things have moved beyond the stage of preliminary enquiries to a point at which the person being interrogated is not free to get up and leave. Instead, the system normally postpones disclosure of the full evidence that ultimately constitutes the prosecution's case until the time of preparation for trial, which means that persons accused of a crime are unable to know in sufficient detail exactly what the case is that can be mounted against them at the time they are forced to make the momentous decision whether to plead guilty or not guilty, a decision that disposes of the great majority of cases without the need for a trial, mainly through plea bargaining and other mechanisms designed to induce guilty pleas.*

It might be suggested that although those who are being interrogated by the police have no right to compel disclosure of information that the police already have, the apparent unfairness is redressed by the privilege to remain silent enjoyed by those who are interrogated as part of the general protection against unwilling self-incrimination that is fundamental in the law. If relevant questions need not be answered by the person against whom there are claims of possible criminal liability, why should those who are asserting these claims have to answer questions asked of them? But such a suggestion misses the point of crucial importance. The authorities who point a finger in the context of possible criminal liability are making a threat of terrifying proportions—being branded a criminal for all those not yet so branded, and for everyone a massive deprivation of liberty and the basic dignities of life that a prison sentence entails. Early disclosure of the information the authorities are relying on may well allow those who are threatened in this way to explain why that information does not warrant the conclusions that have been drawn from it, putting an end to the threat. But the authorities are in a very different position. They are not confronted with any dreadful prospect, and the suspect's right to withhold information does not frustrate the possibility of remedying a frightening situation. The charge of unfairness in not requiring police disclosure is not a charge of procedural unfairness, a charge that there is not a level playing field. The charge is one of substantive unfairness, of people being threatened and kept in the dark so that they cannot find out what they need to know in order to extricate themselves from their predicament.

The grand prize of police interrogation is a confession. But everything about interrogation in custody by the police conspires against the reliability of any confession that may be obtained from someone who has not confessed already.* The intimidating setting of a police station and the very fact that it is the police who are asking the questions, the fact of the interrogation being conducted while in custody, and the hallmarks of intensive interrogation by the police—threatening, humiliating, sinister, devious, and above all, a relentless testing of endurance—all of these features make any confession manifestly unreliable. The ordeal of interrogation is, however, the easy option and is especially attractive given its great virtue as an instant disposition of the case if a confession is obtained. Macaulay memorably captured the thought well over a century-and-a-half ago in his comments on the proposed Indian Penal Code of 1837 when he observed that it was easier to sit in the shade and rub pepper in the eye of a suspect than to search in the heat of the countryside for evidence.

Since confessions obtained under these conditions must *always* be tainted by suspicion of unreliability, it is difficult to understand why any such confession cannot later be retracted in open court out of the hearing of a jury, and be voided without further ado, with the confession itself and the fact that it had been made both inadmissible in evidence. There is fundamental legal protection against being required to incriminate oneself, and if subsequently, in the protective setting of open court, one retracts a confession made in circumstances that are inherently coercive and bewildering, it seems plain enough that only the retraction should be given effect. Instead, however, courts and legislatures contrive to preserve what can be relied on as a knockout piece of evidence in the face of what is acknowledged to be its manifest unreliability and its subversion of the protection against self-incrimination that is a cornerstone of criminal jurisprudence, fearful of destroying such a splendid instrument for obtaining convictions.★

The culture of convictability pervades the criminal process in many ways and at every stage. Eyewitness identification is one of its most valuable resources, and a notorious source of miscarriages of justice.★

Identification parades are commonly used by the police to help witnesses identify perpetrators. Having decided that some person might well be charged as the perpetrator, the police ask the victim or others who claim they saw the perpetrator to pick him out in a line-up of (say) half a dozen, or even a dozen, people who are put on display for this purpose. People who claim they saw what happened are of course disposed to pick out a person resembling the person they have previously described to the police, and with a target already in their sights, the police are not disposed to take great pains to ensure that each person in the parade conforms in every outward detail to the description previously given, so that only a recognition of *the person*, and not of those details, will be the basis of any identification. That, of course, is what any responsible scientific investigation would require in order to minimize the chances of mistaken identification.

There are other serious faults to be found in identification parades. When there are a number of witnesses who claim they can identify the perpetrator, it is not unusual for their descriptions to vary in some details. To have a reliable procedure it would therefore be necessary for the police to have each person in a parade resemble in outward details of appearance (such as clothing) the person described previously by the particular witness who is being asked to make an identification. This might well require a group different in outward details of appearance to comprise the parade for each witness, which again is not something the police are disposed to bother about. To allow the reliability of identification evidence to be tested it would seem sensible to require as a condition of admissibility that an audio-visual record be made of the entire procedure, including the questions and comments that are put to the witnesses, and then have this recorded version shown to the jury in court, with the police witness introducing it subject to cross-examination with regard to matters bearing on its reliability.

Since wrongful convictions based on mistaken identifications are notorious, a number of suggestions to remedy this have been made by experts, based on the results of solid empirical research. The police, however, are more interested in obtaining positive identifications than they are in avoiding false positives. It is not surprising, therefore, that proposals aimed at reducing the number of false positives have received a generally unenthusiastic response in law enforcement circles, and procedural reforms that offer greater protection to the innocent are generally not given serious attention.

Sequential viewing of line-up members one at a time has been found to be much more reliable than viewing them all *en bloc* since the sequential viewing requires the witness to compare the person he sees now with the person he remembers, with the aim of recognizing that person, rather than comparing the various members of the line-up to see who *most closely resembles* the person he has in mind and then trying to decide if he recognizes him. It has also been suggested that the identification parade be a double-blind procedure, with both the witness and the police officer who is conducting the enquiry unaware of who the suspect is, so that subtle indications from police to witness, perhaps unintended, will not be possible. Since witnesses are normally keen to "get it right", such hints from the police tend to exert a strong influence. Typically, however, the police respond with indignation to the double-blind suggestion, claiming that it is an affront to their professional integrity.

A further suggestion that has been given short shrift by law enforcement authorities is that procedures for obtaining identification evidence be left to experts who understand the pitfalls and can be relied on to minimize the opportunities for error, much as other forensic experts do, and that they then present the evidence in court as expert witnesses. Other suggestions to protect the innocent have been similarly ignored. It has been suggested that witnesses be allowed to choose more than one member of the line-up as possibly the person who was seen, since this will give a truer picture to the jury of the witness's confidence in the identification that has been made. And since identifications become much more reliable when they are made from a much larger selection—larger than could be put together in the flesh—it has been suggested, as it turns out once again by voices in the wilderness, that video clips be used to allow witnesses to view a "live" parade of (say) several dozen participants in order to make it more likely that genuine recognition is the basis of any identification.

It is important to note, moreover, that the police are not required to produce a full record of witnesses who claimed to be able to identify the perpetrator, so that those other identifications that did not suit the case that is being brought would be available to a defendant to challenge the credibility of the identifications that are relied on by the prosecution. This suggests a more general problem of great importance. Unlike the corresponding situation regarding disclosure in civil proceedings, the police cannot be required to open their files and disclose to an accused person all of the information they have that might be used to undermine the case against him. But a person who stands accused should be in a position to test the evidence against him by resort to other evidence that the police have and that has not been made part of their case because it would tend to undermine it. Other witnesses may have told stories that are inconsistent with the story told by those witnesses who are being used to make the case against the accused. There may have been tests relating to forensic evidence whose results have been inconclusive or clearly negative, but only a positive result has been put in evidence. And although in a minority of jurisdictions there may be an obligation on the prosecution to disclose all that it knows which will exculpate or mitigate, or more modestly (as in England) whatever it believes may undermine its case, it is the police who will have the essential raw materials upon which proof and refutation depend, with what is given by the police to the prosecuting agency most often selected with care to make as strong a case as possible. In short, the police are left free to build a highly selective case against the person who in their view offers the best opportunity to obtain a conviction, and they need not weaken their case by disclosing countervailing evidence or evidence of other possibilities that they have chosen not to pursue.

Making a case means producing credible evidence. But the credibility of an item of evidence cannot be determined in isolation. Not only does it require a context that allows it to be seen as evidence of some particular proposition, but it must be seen in the context of all of the available evidence bearing on that proposition, including evidence that tends to undermine it. When it comes to making their case against someone whom they have targeted, the police devote themselves to making the best case they can by deploying evidence that is helpful, but without investigating matters that might produce countervailing evidence that would undermine its credibility. That is something the system leaves to the defense at a later stage, though of course, even when there are particularly favorable financial circumstances, it is well beyond the ability of any but the wealthiest criminal defendants to begin to match the resources for investigation that are available to the police. And of course by the time a defendant embarks on any investigation of his own, the evidence will be largely dissipated and no longer available as it was when the police came on the scene at the time of the crime.

All of these points relate to police activities that are well within the law. But there is a police practice outside the law that is too well-established to be treated simply as a regrettable departure and not a part of the system. When the police are convinced that the person they have targeted is engaged in some criminal activity on a regular basis, they will often spare themselves the inconvenience of having to search out the evidence, not to say the embarrassment of not being able to find it. In such cases the police come armed with the evidence themselves and then find it where they have planted it. Of course such evidence is worthless if the defense can establish the true facts in court. But such police practices are not normally carried on in front of witnesses other than fellow officers and a hapless defendant whom everyone would expect to say that the incriminating item was planted on him or placed in his possession. To the police (and to a friendly court), the challenged evidence is merely a token formality to help convict a person who has been marked as convictable based on independent considerations.

Returning to the game when played according to the rules, one finds a worrying practice with regard to prosecution witnesses. It is considered perfectly proper to obtain the testimony of an otherwise reluctant witness—typically an alleged accomplice or co-conspirator—by promising leniency or immunity from prosecution; or in the case of someone already serving a sentence, a significant reduction in the time still to be spent in prison. It is, of course, a condition of this deal that the testimony will be favorable to the prosecution's case along lines that are indicated in advance.*

But imagine if a corresponding practice were allowed for the defense. Imagine if defense witnesses could be threatened with a terrible fate or offered release from terrible things they were already being made to suffer, and told they would escape these things only on condition that they gave testimony favorable to the defense. How could we possibly consider such testimony to be reliable? Indeed the practice is so deeply corrupt that the very suggestion of admitting evidence obtained under such conditions is shocking. Yet this is exactly the kind of evidence that is regularly relied on by the prosecution in seeking convictions for many serious crimes. It is notable that such interference with witnesses is a criminal offense. In England, for example, it plainly constitutes the offense of attempting to pervert the course of justice, and in almost any legal system such conduct is likely to attract serious criminal liability under laws protecting the administration of justice. There is no reason in principle for police and prosecutors to enjoy an exemption from liability since their interference with the administration of justice is equally pernicious, yet their interference is thought to be in the public interest, and so deserving of immunity. This, however, misconceives the public interest, which is not in seeing that convictions are obtained, but that justice is done.

As it happens, the testimony of witnesses is something of a luxury, and in fact the most important part of the criminal process in both the United States and Britain requires no witnesses to give any testimony. Criminal trials are a *pièce de résistance* of the entertainment media, but only a very small portion of our prison population can include in their curriculum vitae a conviction after trial. Most people in prison in the United States and Britain are there because they consented to the terms of a plea bargain offered by the prosecution. In both the United States and Britain, a lesser charge and/or a lesser sentence is offered in exchange for a guilty plea, and in both countries a cornerstone of the criminal justice process is the practice of imposing harsher sentences on those found guilty after trial and measuring leniency according to how quickly and cheaply a case can be disposed of through an early guilty plea. It follows inevitably that the weaker the prosecution's case, the greater the sentencing discount on offer and so the greater the chance of convicting someone who is innocent. In accepting the offer the defendant avoids the risk of having to spend a significantly larger part of his life in prison. The risk is heightened by the generally inadequate legal resources that he has at his disposal to defend himself at trial, a fact not lost on the lawyer who advises him and who is likely to recommend that he enter into the plea bargain once terms that do not seem unreasonable have been negotiated. Defendants naturally rely on the advice of lawyers, who are seen as figures of experience and authority in what is largely a mysterious and terrifying process, but who in fact, like the prosecution and the court, find it in their own best interest to dispose of a case as economically as possible.

The bargaining process not infrequently begins with the initial charge inflated beyond what the evidence will support if a fully competent defense were mounted against it. But there are even more serious faults in the process. The defendant normally does not yet know in sufficient detail what the case is that can be presented for him, partly because he does not yet know in sufficient detail what the case against him is, and partly because at this stage there has not yet been an exploration of his case in anything like the depth required to mount a proper defense in court. What legal issues may be raised, what expert witnesses and what witnesses of fact he may call, what their testimony might be, and what physical evidence might be available, is most often still largely undetermined, and so he is still in the dark about what his prospects really are. Very often he is someone who has a guilty conscience about some other wrongdoing, or feels frightened by what he supposes the rigors of a trial to be, or has a criminal record that he fears will somehow work against his chances of acquittal, or is just someone who thinks (quite rightly) that he, or the information about him, will not make a very good impression on a jury. All of these factors regularly influence people to plead guilty as part of a plea bargain even though they have not committed the crime with which they are charged, or may have a good defense that avoids liability for what they have done.

But what conception of justice can accommodate such a state of affairs? If a guilty plea willingly entered is enough to satisfy the requirements of justice, then the requirements of justice have been satisfied. But if justice requires that a guilty plea be entered only when it is made by someone who is in fact guilty, then justice has not been done.

I have sketched a picture of enforcers of the law in hot pursuit of convictions. The tactics they employ with the blessings of the law are designed to produce convictions that will appear to be sound, both within the organs of the legal system and outside in the community at large. But these tactics are seriously flawed from a moral point of view.

People are accused but not fully informed about the basis of the accusation. Information that might help them clear their name is kept from them. Possible perpetrators other than the person targeted are left uninvestigated once the police have settled on a person that suits their purposes even though the evidence that has been assembled does not foreclose the possibility of someone else being the guilty party. Evidence is treated selectively to create as strong a case as possible against the person who has been targeted, with countervailing evidence suppressed and not given the weight it would have if elementary standards of scientific objectivity were observed. Identification procedures are arranged to maximize the chances of obtaining the positive identification sought by the police, and the very real hazards of misidentification are generally ignored. Reluctant witnesses who are themselves liable to prosecution are coerced by the threat of it into testifying for the prosecution, or are bribed by the promise of an early release from prison if they are already serving time. Conditions of interrogation that make a confession manifestly unreliable are standard, yet if the confession is later retracted it may still be admissible and weighed by a jury along with the retraction. And to top it all off, large numbers of people are made to accept the dreadful fate that is offered them by the authorities in order to protect themselves from the possibility of an even worse fate, even though they have not had a proper opportunity to show that, appearances to the contrary notwithstanding, any such fate for them would be a terrible injustice.

As one might expect, these tactics result in a large number of people who are not guilty spending time in prison.* Popular perceptions, however, are quite different, and it is generally assumed that miscarriages of justice are a rarity—something inevitable in any system subject to human fallibility no matter how great the precautions that are taken to prevent an innocent person being sent to prison. Miscarriages of justice have their own special *frisson*, which the media are happy to exploit, though not beyond a point at which the system itself becomes too transparent and the abiding faith in law enforcement that the public cling to is threatened. Fear of crime and the will to punish it make it easy for a decent society to turn a blind eye to the unfairness and injustice of the methods employed to achieve public satisfaction. The blind eye that sees no evil leaves the authorities to get on with the job as they think it should be done with as little hindrance as possible, lest the job not be done properly, or even worse, not be done at all.

It would be naive to suppose that legal constraints upon law enforcement procedures could ignore the special problems that are presented by certain sorts of criminals. There would, for example, be a danger of prospective witnesses being intimidated, or even eliminated, by certain sorts of prospective criminal defendants if the information the police have were freely available to them. Ruthless interference with the administration of justice is to be expected especially from certain sorts of professional criminals engaged in organized crime. Yet it would be a mistake to assume that most of those people who commit crimes with some regularity would abuse a right to a disclosure of evidence by interfering with the administration of justice in ways that parties in civil proceedings would not, and an even greater mistake to assume that in general people accused of a serious offense are disposed to do that. In the small number of cases where there is reason to believe that the danger does exist, exceptional rights of non-disclosure could be invoked by the authorities through an application made to a court, with a hearing to deal with the application no more demanding than when there is an application for bail.

We do well to remind ourselves that the American Bill of Rights is the principal ground-plan of the country's political morality, and that placing restraints on the powers of law enforcement is the most prominent concern exhibited in that collection of basic protections. The immense growth of constitutional law expanding these protections against abuse of law enforcement powers testifies both to the steady elevation of a collective moral consciousness and to an increasing recognition of the truth about criminal justice in practice. It has always been understood that the powers vested in those who enforce the law were easily abused. Because crimes in prospect are so greatly feared and the general sense of impotence and vulnerability in the community is so profound, constituted authority is looked to as a refuge and a protector. Crimes that are committed raise the temperature to boiling point and excite a punitive frenzy. Those who enforce the law need little encouragement. They are not pressed unwilling into service as law enforcers, but choose such a profession because it suits them. Their careers are advanced not by scrupulous moderation in observing the restraints on their power, but by success in those law enforcement activities that contribute to community satisfaction. Community sentiment is itself subject to constant manipulation. It is exploited by the media, who can always be confident of the cash value of crime. It is also constantly exploited by politicians, who can be confident that fear of crime and promises to do what is supposed to put a stop to it are a rich source of political capital. No wonder abuse of law enforcement power has been such a prominent constitutional concern.

★ ★ ★

Pressures against the protective bulwarks are immense and unrelenting. Fairness and justice in seeking to convict only those who are guilty is overwhelmed by the urgent need to convict someone who can be marked as guilty with sufficient credibility. To make this easier, measures that are morally regressive are proposed. In England, for example, the venerable right to remain silent when questioned has since 1995 been compromised by allowing later statements in defending oneself to be impugned by the earlier silence, although clearly it is in the interest of justice to allow any-one being questioned in such forbidding circumstances to have the opportunity not only to consider his position carefully with the benefit of legal advice, but to continue to remain silent until he is in a position to understand how the answer he gives may be used against him by those who are interested in pinning the crime on him.★

Even more disturbing are certain measures enacted in England in 2003.★ Protection against being made to answer again for the same crime after being previously acquitted was modified to allow further prosecution for serious crimes when there is "compelling" new evidence.★ Double jeop-ardy is a horror that has not been allowed since the beginning of the com-mon law in England, was prohibited by Roman law, and, according to Demosthenes, was an impermissible practice among the Athenians. Protec-tion against it is, of course, also enshrined in the American Bill of Rights. But such a restriction is a handicap to the authorities in their pursuit of convictions. Having only one bite of the cherry, they feel they must make it as good as possible, with a case they are convinced has a good chance of standing up in court. But with double jeopardy no longer a bar, weaker cases can be used to help extract guilty pleas, the message being that if we don't get a conviction this time we can try again, and in the meantime a sword of Damocles will be suspended indefinitely over you and your lib-erty. It would also add immense weight to the chances of gaining a convic-tion the second time around and make a mockery of the presumption of innocence when it is made clear to the jury that this new prosecution is based on new evidence that the Court of Appeal (as the legislation requires) has already determined to be "compelling", a term which the government White Paper in 2002 helpfully amplified by telling us it is evidence "that strongly suggests that a previously acquitted defendant was in fact guilty".

Jury trials were curtailed in the 2003 Act.★ Any complex fraud case or any such case requiring a lengthy trial might be tried by a judge alone, as may any case where there is a serious risk that the jury will be subject to bribery or intimidation. But this is the thin end of the wedge. Jury trials are regarded by government as a nuisance. They add expense to the system, but beyond that they interfere with the process of obtaining convictions by requiring everyone on the jury, or a large majority, to be convinced beyond a reasonable doubt of the defendant's guilt. A judge, on the other hand, will make up his mind, and that is the end of the matter. No different insights and perspectives to be reconciled around a table in a jury room among people whose collective experience of the world is broader than any judge's could possibly be. The judge will of course be able to decide much more quickly, and will certainly wish to do so in the interest of expediting the business of the court. If a defendant who is acquitted subsequently commits a newsworthy crime, the judge who acquitted him may well find himself in an uncomfortable position, though members of a jury that acquitted would not, and concern about this in the back of the judge's mind will help the chances of conviction when there is trial by judge, rather than jury. But most important of all, judges in criminal courts are permanent participants in the criminal justice system, which is a complex professional organization that must rely on cooperation among its members to discharge the various responsibilities of the organization. Judges must therefore maintain sympathetic engagement on a continuing basis with police and prosecutors. The criminal justice system is quite naturally perceived by the judge as a mechanism for dealing with criminals. True enough, his job, among other things, requires him to make sure that innocent people are not found guilty. But contrary to the objective presumption of innocence that the law insists on, the judge as a member of the organization is likely to operate with a subjective presumption of guilt—if really we are to presume the defendant is innocent, why on earth has he been charged and indicted by those other perfectly responsible organs of the system? Jurors, however, are one-off participants who have no organizational affiliation with criminal justice and do not think of themselves as functionaries who must keep faith with the agencies of law enforcement. In short, they are less disposed to give police and prosecutor the benefit of the doubt, and so represent a more formidable obstacle to gaining convictions.

Jurors are, however, more easily swayed by common prejudices, and it is the most deep-seated of prejudices that the 2003 Act seeks to exploit in order to make convictions easier when there are jury trials.* Subject to the judge's discretion in allowing it in, a defendant's criminal record could be put in evidence to show *a propensity* to commit offenses of the kind with which he is charged, and evidence is similarly allowed in to show a defendant's general *propensity* to be untruthful in order to discredit the defendant's denial of the truth of the prosecution's evidence against him.* There is no single item of background information that is more likely to persuade a juror of guilt than the fact that the defendant has done it before. He is seen as a criminal, and, as such, he is not given the same consideration as someone who has no record. Having previously crossed the great divide, he is assumed to have an inclination to commit such a crime, or at least to be lacking the inhibition that keeps the rest of us from committing it. But the biggest boost to convictability does not take place in the courtroom. The *threat* of being able to introduce the defendant's criminal record, or evidence of a propensity to be untruthful, is the most formidable feature of the change in the law. As a lever in obtaining a plea of guilty, the threat has unsurpassed power. These enhanced prospects for disposing of cases will, of course, further encourage the police to target people with helpful criminal records, or indeed people who have told lies in the past and who can be persuaded that when this is made known, no jury will believe them now.

I have described these measures as morally regressive because they sacrifice fairness and justice to promote convictability. They are often said to be in aid of "victim's rights" by politicians pandering to populist sentiment, and this was indeed the line taken by the British government in enacting these radical changes in the law. An imaginary balance is suggested between the rights of those accused of crime ("criminals' rights" is a term in vogue among politicians) and the rights of victims, or more broadly, the rights of the rest of us ("the community"), who are enlisted as prospective victims. But of course what we all have a right to is simply an effective system that enforces the law fairly and justly, and not a right to have the emotional satisfactions of someone being convicted and punished. As to actual victims of crimes having rights beyond that, there is a very good case to be made for public compensation for the harm suffered, not unlike compensation from the government available to other sorts of victims of misfortune in an enlightened society. Whatever the satisfactions of conviction and punishment may be, unlike compensation, they provide no actual benefit to victims to make up for the harm that has been suffered.

14

The Decline of Punishment

Consider what the criminal law might be without punishment: a declaration of the community's most important rules of conduct, confident of the allegiance of those for whom habits of compliance are natural, but useless as a measure of social control for the community at large. Even those who treat the law with respect would more easily succumb to temptation when the right opportunity presented itself. And in such a denuded condition the law could offer no protection against harm. Predators would treat the law with utter indifference and would feel completely free to follow their inclinations. Their victims would be enraged by what they suffered, and without the law to requite their suffering would feel free to wreak vengeance themselves as best they could according to their own undisciplined notions of what had happened and how best to even the score. People would, moreover, pursue their own selfish interests heedless of those laws that are meant to implement the many policies of government that are needed to secure and to promote the general welfare. With society and its members left in such a hopelessly unprotected state, no government could hope to have its authority and its laws taken seriously. Government, as we know it, would be impossible.

This is not a happy message. Criminal punishment appears to be indispensable, but it is not a social practice that can fill us with pride. It destroys lives, inflicts terrible suffering, and degrades those who become its victims—the innocent family as well as the perpetrator—not only while it is being administered, but for as long as the person to whom it has been administered is known by others to have suffered it. Its standard form is imprisonment, and in that form it combines the essential features of some other notorious social institutions that also pose questions of political morality. I have in mind four such institutions that also violate basic human rights and are widely regarded as morally deplorable, though, like criminal punishment, in spite of being deeply objectionable, they have all enjoyed considerable respectability. Viewing criminal punishment in their company helps make it seem less a moral fixture and more a feature of social expediency.

Slavery and criminal punishment both involve a massive deprivation of personal freedom through limitation of movement and the exercise of custodial powers that are intended to pre-empt control of every aspect of the victim's life. Criminal punishment puts emphasis on confinement, while slavery stresses the performance of work, but the two tend to coalesce when punishment takes the form of forced labor and slavery is carried on in ways that are designed to prevent escape. Their kinship is recognized in the Thirteenth Amendment of the American Constitution, where "slavery" or "involuntary servitude" is prohibited, but penal servitude is mentioned as the single exception to what is being made unlawful.

Next there is torture. The intentional infliction of suffering is its essential feature, and though it is not now fashionable to make suffering seem an important part of criminal punishment—"hard treatment" is the bleak euphemism that now appears with great frequency—without its suffering criminal punishment would not be worthy of its name. In torture the suffering is administered in a concentrated form, typically to overcome resistance to disclosure of information, or to induce some declaration, or to extract a confession. Torture aims to make the consequences of refusal intolerable. In the case of criminal punishment, the suffering is more diffuse and takes place over a much longer time. Its purpose is to ensure that enforcement of the law is a matter to be taken seriously, so that the fact of enforceability will tend to have an aversive effect on those who experience crime's temptations. Its purpose, however, is not only prospective, and it is not only directed to those who might think of committing a crime. The suffering that is inflicted on those who commit crimes provides general satisfaction in the community by assuring everyone that people who are convicted do not get away with their crimes when they are punished, as indeed they would if what followed conviction was only some anodyne program to help improve the convicted person, and so was punishment in name only.

War is another institution with features that remind us of criminal punishment. Both require that lives and perhaps life itself be sacrificed to protect certain interests from the harm that is threatened by people who are marked as the enemy—in one case it is the enemy within, and in the other, the enemy without. Both institutions cultivate intensely negative attitudes toward the enemy through stigmatization and demonization, which helps to maintain public support for the brutality that is inherent in the institution's practices.

Finally, there is capital punishment. Like slavery and torture it can be viewed as an institution in its own right since plainly it is not needed as punishment for crime and exists to provide social satisfactions that are entirely gratuitous. Capital punishment concentrates feelings of hostility and vengeance and seeks their gratification. It insists that nothing less than death will satisfy the demands of justice. This means that nothing less than death will even the score. And with reference to the crime for which it is usually imposed, the death penalty is virtually unique in being able to even the score by reciprocating in kind. In seeking to gratify the feelings of victims and their public, punishment by imprisonment also may be said to even the score, but without the gratuitous satisfactions that payment in kind provides. In its finality, capital punishment forecloses redemption. Though this seems to distinguish it from punishment by incarceration, even here there is an underlying similarity that becomes clear when one considers how redemptive features in a prison regime must always take a back seat to the punitive elements. Imagine how different an inmate's life would be if all that mattered was what was good for him in dealing with whatever causes him to commit crimes, with all punitive elements eliminated from the custodial regime while such a program of *genuine* rehabilitation was being carried on. Ignoring the need to even the score and leaving the feelings of victims unassuaged, toleration of such a regime could hardly be expected no matter how well it worked.

Slavery, torture, war, and capital punishment—like criminal punishment—are institutions whose practical importance explains why they have existed or continue to exist in spite of being widely perceived as morally repugnant. To allow their practical benefits to continue without strictures of conscience, justifications have always been needed to make these institutions more palatable.

Labor produced by a person one owns is cheaper than labor that must be paid for as it is produced. There may be costs of acquisition initially, but the economies of the slave system make the costs of maintaining slaves much less than the costs that workers who are not slaves would incur to maintain themselves, costs that as a minimum must be paid as wages to workers who are free. In addition, there is a big bonus for slave-owners. Any comprehensive slave system will include the benefits of slave reproduction, adding more people to the workforce on an ongoing basis without additional acquisition costs, and representing a cash crop in the form of an excess beyond requirements to be sold at auction to other slave-owners.

But when slavery in the modern world fell into disrepute, as it did in the United States, it was not defended primarily on economic grounds. The welfare of slaves became the principal theme when the institution felt it must justify itself. It was said that slaves were being transformed from heathen savages into decent Christians, though admittedly not with the trappings of literacy that might encourage them to entertain dangerous aspirations. When it was suggested that it was wicked to appropriate their labor without paying them for it—perhaps all the more wicked as they became more Christian—the defenders of slavery pointed to the miserable lives of industrial workers in the North, where exploitation of wage earners in an unprotected labor market meant that living conditions and work conditions were worse than they were on those plantations in the South where slaves were cared for properly. It was, in other words, the welfare that slavery afforded to slaves—body and soul—that made slavery acceptable. Should their welfare be deemed less important than their freedom, slavery could no longer be justified in this way, and if the arguments based on welfare turned out to be spurious, this purported justification would likewise turn to dust. With a new moral consciousness that perceived slaves as fellow human beings, the blessings of freedom took precedence over concerns for welfare, while at the same time the humbug and hypocrisy of paternalistic justifications became apparent as the realities of slave life became more widely known. At that point political morality asserted itself against the institution of slavery, first by attacking those laws that conferred rights of ownership over human beings, and then by enacting laws that recognized and protected the equality before the law of all members of the political society, which included those who had been slaves as well as those who had been masters.

Torture appears in different institutional forms in different societies, and attempts to justify it take different forms.

Judicial torture was part of the legal system of many European countries for four or five hundred years, from the thirteenth to the eighteenth centuries, and enjoyed a respectability comparable to that of serious criminal punishment at the present time. It was employed in the most serious criminal cases to provide greater certainty when an accusation rested on the testimony of just one witness, or was based only on circumstantial evidence. Whatever evidence there was in such a case still had to be weighty enough to create a presumption of guilt before torture could be administered. To seal the fate of the accused the confession under torture would have to include details that only a guilty person would know, thereby ensuring the confession's credibility. As a legal procedure, torture represented an advance in rationality, supplanting the ordeals of fire and water that were designed to call forth the judgment of God to settle the matter of guilt or innocence through His determination of the ordeal's outcome. Torture also had a place within the legal system as punishment when extreme suffering was thought to be the appropriate response in dealing with misdeeds of a particularly vexing sort, and especially in executions expertly designed to intensify the victim's agonies and have them continue as long as possible.

Apart from its more respectable life as an institutional practice within the legal system, torture has had a long and notorious history as an adjunct of the law, and an even longer and more notorious history as an instrument of political power outside the law. As an adjunct of the law it has been employed by the authorities to obtain confessions as well as information that would implicate others when a crime is committed. More sophisticated methods of causing distress have replaced the crudities of the traditional third degree, and at the same time courts have become more scrupulous in examining claims of forced confession. Outside the legal arena, purely political concerns enlist torture for purely political purposes in the guise of dealing with crimes against the state, and in police states, torture is routinely used as an instrument of self-preservation by the government, to intimidate and to punish any opposition, as well as to elicit information about real or imagined enemies of the regime. One must also include here the use of torture to gain information that is said to be needed to prevent a catastrophic terrorist attack from succeeding, as well as torture of military prisoners to gain information of military importance.

Torture consists of inflicting suffering in the form of intense physical pain, unbearably frightening or disgusting experiences, or other emotional and psychological trauma designed to destroy any vestiges of self-possession. It is now universally repudiated, though far from universally abandoned.

The abolition of judicial torture was no doubt influenced to some considerable extent by the writings of such eminent critics as Montesquieu, Voltaire, and Beccaria. Raw compassion for every human being who fell into the clutches of the law was too much to expect at that time, and there was also widespread concern that hardened criminals would be further emboldened by the abolition of torture. But the argument that endurance, not veracity, was being tested by torture, did have great force, as did the argument that torture inflicts suffering on those who are innocent but are tortured when initial appearances happen to tell against them. A fear that the general deterrent effect of torture would be lost provided the strongest argument against its abolition, and with that in mind abolition took place quietly through confidential directives sent to the courts by enlightened rulers. Perhaps most important of all was a marked increase in judicial self-confidence, with judges willing to rely on their own objective evaluation of the available evidence, and so no longer in need of confessions to impart an air of certainty to their judgments.

The wholesale condemnation of torture that is now enshrined in universal declarations is beset by many exceptions at the retail level. According to Amnesty International, more than half of the member states of the United Nations routinely practice torture. Much of it takes place in the course of ordinary law enforcement; much of it is political violence. In what is perhaps the only setting in which torture still has any respectable defenders, it is used (or proposed for use) by security services to extract information about imminent terrorist attacks. This last vestige of respectability rests, however, on very shaky foundations.

It is not, as is usually assumed, a matter of weighing one evil against another, the evil of inflicting pain against the evil of lives to be lost. Information given under torture may well be unreliable, and especially when a fanatic is the source, or when the hapless victim makes up a story but does not in fact have the information he is thought to have, as will often be the case once the power to torture is freely available and freely used by those who have the awesome responsibility of acting in desperate circumstances to prevent acts of terrorism. What is at stake is human dignity at a most basic level, not only for the victim, but for the torturer, who must either be gifted with psychopathic indifference to the suffering of others or must derive sadistic pleasure from it, if not when he takes up his grisly occupation, then very soon after as a consequence of it. Those who have not had experience of what goes on—preferably first-hand as observers or participants, or else vicariously through depictions and written accounts—are at a serious disadvantage in their appreciation of what really matters in arriving at sound judgments about the practice. It would undoubtedly be a salubrious moral experience for those who advocate such torture if they were required to prescribe in detail exactly what the torture should consist of and exactly what procedures should be followed in applying it.

War is hell, and never more so than now. There has never before been the means for killing and maiming vast numbers so quickly and so horribly. The armaments industry, with the many parts of other industries that depend on it, comprises the world's largest industrial complex, in recent times exceeding in the total value of its product the products of any industry devoted to satisfying basic human needs. Moreover, national markets for the means of killing and maiming are proportionally greater in countries in which the satisfaction of basic human needs is most retarded. Being armed to the teeth and keeping up as best they can with the latest developments in warfare is an obsession in many countries that have no reason to believe they are threatened by others, but where the power and prestige of the regime is enhanced by its ostensible ability to wage war.

At the same time, the modern world exhibits an unprecedented abhorrence of war. War is universally recognized as among the greatest of evils, the one generally accepted justification for it being self-defense, either in response to being attacked, or when acting pre-emptively in the face of an unmistakable and immediate threat of attack, and with an allowance made for others to join the victim in defending itself. This marks a moral advance from earlier times, when conquest for glory or enrichment was acceptable so long as some grievance could be found to provide a cosmetic pretext for aggression; or when conquest was justified as a means of spreading a religious faith or remaking a conquered society in the conqueror's image. It is also a moral advance over wars of national liberation, though the case can be a very close one when a war of liberation is directed to freeing people from oppression, and particularly when an ethnic minority is brutally oppressed by a government of the majority. In the contemporary world, the very term "war" proves something of an embarrassment in official circles. In the United Nations Charter, for example, the word "war" does not appear, but such terms as "aggression", "self-defense", and "international enforcement" are the terms used to designate various activities that constitute the waging of war.

There is also a heightened moral sensitivity to how wars may be fought—the issue of *jus in bello* that was contrasted by medieval writers with *jus ad bellum*, the justly fought war contrasted with the justness of the war itself. Concern is embodied in treaties, conventions, declarations, and resolutions that seek to curtail the use of the most appalling forms of modern military technology and to ensure the safety of the civilian population. These limitations are not as easy either to formulate or to enforce as are the conditions that must be met to legitimate a war. Even conventionally accepted means of waging war produce unspeakable horrors, and in the midst of the carnage of war it is often too much to expect that combatants will exercise restraint and run serious risks to themselves in the face of what they believe may be a deadly threat from the enemy.

War, then, is an institution riven by acute moral paradox. It is abhorrent to everyone, but possession of the means for carrying it on is a matter of national pride, and the production and sale of armaments is now cheerfully accepted as a hugely important element in world commerce. And though unqualified aspirations for peace are regarded as morally impeccable, a unilateral and unconditional abandonment of war by those who have responsibility for maintaining peace would be a reckless and morally indefensible act since survival then depends on the benign dispositions and universal goodwill of others in a world in which dangerous adversaries pose a threat and are willing to resort to force if need be in order to prevail.

Capital punishment is killing someone as punishment, and it involves killing someone quite deliberately. But deliberately killing someone is so momentous an event that it can pass muster morally only when it is a matter of dire necessity, as in combat or self-defense, where it is part of a plausible story of kill or be killed; or when, as with genuinely compassionate euthanasia, the particular circumstances make the taking of a life an event that really is not, after all, momentous in that way. Murder, in other words, and capital punishment for it have a *moral* equivalence and are terrible for the same reason. This thought was famously captured by JF Stephen in his *A History of the Criminal Law of England* when he observed that hundreds of thousands abstain from murder because they regard it with horror, and one great reason why they regard it with horror is that murderers are hanged. Murder and capital punishment are equally dreadful because in both personal existence—the very possibility of everything of value in life—is ended for all time then and there.

Defenders of capital punishment may suggest that justice is ill-served if those who deserve to die for what they have done are allowed to live. But even if the justice that resides in executing a murderer has more to it than the gratification of vengeful feelings, nothing that can be said for that justice makes it more important than the personal existence that is being extinguished in its name. Even those who deserve to die ought therefore not to be put to death. There are moral considerations that are superior to giving a person his just deserts, and the value of life is one of them. Having said this, I confess that I am not entirely comfortable when I think of people whose lives have been dedicated to inflicting wanton suffering and to slaughtering the innocent, and wonder if some of these people might meet the test of a life of such little worth that the taking of it is not the moral equivalent of murder that otherwise it would be. If, but only if, we were able to state the concrete circumstances that devalue the continuation of such a person's life with the same persuasive particularity that we do for benign euthanasia, perhaps a good argument might be made for the death penalty in these very exceptional cases.

Most European countries have abolished the death penalty for all crimes. Human rights has been the principal source of opposition in the European context even though the Universal Declaration of Human Rights of 1948 allows for the legal prescription of the death penalty. The right to life which it recognizes has, however, been the seminal idea in successive moves toward abolition, through the United Nations and the Council of Europe, with a 1994 protocol to the Convention on Human Rights and a decision of the European Court of Human Rights nailing down total abolition. In their reliance on a basic right enjoyed simply by virtue of being human, the Europeans reflect the sort of fundamental position I have suggested, which pre-empts arguments about justice by making its price morally unacceptable.

In the United States, where capital punishment remains well-entrenched, the arguments tend to be of a different sort. It is true that kindred arguments pointing to the sheer indecency of the practice have been mounted in futile attempts to persuade the Supreme Court that capital punishment is a cruel and unusual punishment. But for the most part arguments in the United States implicitly reject the European premise that there is a universal and inalienable right to life that cannot be amended to provide an exception for murderers. Rather, there is an initial acceptance that in principle the death penalty could remain on the books if there were some way to be sure that only those who were truly worthy of death were sentenced to death. Deathworthiness is not rejected; but there is doubt about the practical possibility of correctly certifying it in each case, or perhaps in any case at all. Because death is so momentous a penalty, it cannot be countenanced so long as such doubts exist. And in fact there are very good reasons to doubt that many of those who are found guilty deserve to die.

Mistakes about guilt are notorious, and when the penalty is death, the mistake cannot be corrected. Why such mistakes occur was made clear in the earlier discussion of the *élan* with which convictions are obtained, and when a crime is the sort that attracts the death penalty, there is an added measure of enthusiasm in seeking to gain a conviction, with even less regard to matters that tend to support a suspect's claim of innocence. The glaring inequality of resources between prosecution and defense that is commonplace in criminal courts becomes a matter of life and death when a guilty verdict may lead to execution.

Then there are the standards of deathworthiness. Recognizing that historically death sentences have been infected with arbitrariness and racial prejudice, the Supreme Court mandated that objective standards be set to take account of mitigating and aggravating factors in each case. But the task of setting necessary and sufficient conditions for killing a convicted person can be accomplished only by the use of very general terms whose significance will be understood in crucially different ways by different judges and jurors. Moreover, when there is an attempt to apply these standards in a particular case, different aspects of the facts will seem more important to one juror, or one judge, than another, and this will also introduce a strong subjective influence into a process that must be objective to be legally sound.

Beyond the issue of deathworthiness, there are the more mundane issues of deterrence and incapacitation. Does the law's threat of death deter more effectively than the threat of prison for life? Is the ultimate incapacitation that only death can achieve necessary to protect others from those criminals who are exceptionally dangerous? Only by killing such guilty persons now, to eliminate them or to frighten others, can innocent lives be saved later, so the arguments run. But in fact these controversial points rest on an even more controversial foundation. Not only do they require acceptance of the proposition that certain conduct makes a person worthy of death, but also acceptance of the further proposition that a person's being worthy of death creates a right to kill him. The basic human right to life stands in opposition to a purported right to kill someone who is worthy of death, and only if such killing can be shown conclusively to be a matter of dire necessity can it be justified.

★ ★ ★

Criminal punishment looks quite different when viewed in the company of those other social institutions with which it shares some of its most important features. All of these institutions are in themselves morally vicious, which is to say that, without the practical purposes they serve, they not only lack moral worth, but are also a moral disgrace. Yet all of them seemed, and some may still seem, indispensable.

Slavery in the southern United States was not simply a self-indulgent luxury, but the irreplaceable foundation of a society's way of life and a *sine qua non* of the economy that supported it. In many cases of serious crime, without the availability of judicial torture in those countries in which it flourished, the law would be trapped in a desperate quandary and could not be enforced. Judicial torture was no longer needed only when the gathering of evidence to place before the court became possible in communities with more developed structures of authority. War is still the indispensable last resort to defend oneself when a conflict is not resolved by peaceful means and the other side adopts the use of force to get its way. Capital punishment is clearly in a state of transition from being the seemingly indispensable ultimate penalty for the ultimate crime to being a penalty that is wholly unacceptable for any crime, with ever more rigorous conditions to be met marking the way. And finally there is criminal punishment, the institution that a fiercely compelling necessity makes most difficult to abolish, yet in a constant process of modification so that its immoderate and even savage exactions are eliminated by reforms that progressively recognize the evils that are inherent in the institution, reforms that are spurred on largely by a desire to punish more cheaply within humane constraints.

Justifications for all of these institutions have always been contrived with considerable ingenuity so that those who have a decent regard for the plight of victims can accept what practical necessities are thought to require. But the justifications aim at more than simply establishing permissibility, which would leave the practice with only a reluctant endorsement. They seek rather to infuse the institution with a positive moral worth, like saving the souls of heathen savages, giving one's life for the greater glory of God and country, or ensuring that justice is done. When justifications are mounted on the grand scale that social institutions require, they aim higher than mere palatability and applaud something that is supposed to be of great moral value—generally the more horrific the practice being justified, and the greater the perceived need for its continuation, the louder the applause.

No institution exhibits this more clearly than criminal punishment. The essentials of the long and obsessive history of attempts to justify it have been discussed earlier in the book, and the flow continues unabated, particularly with recent theories that emphasize the supposed virtues of punishment as a way of regaining good moral health and peace of mind on all sides—for victims and perpetrators of crime, as well as the community at large. A more fruitful enterprise, I suggest, would be to reassess criminal punishment as a social institution in moral evolution to which we must remain committed just as long as it continues to be needed, with a view to making sure that it is not employed promiscuously and that its practices fully reflect its moral evolution.

At various points in the book I have discussed the way the institution ought to be operated. Avoidance of the opportunities for injustice in sentencing is particularly important, but so is avoidance of the misconceived notions in criminal jurisprudence that affect guilt or innocence at an earlier stage. These are concerns with the status quo. But the institution has a dynamic of change in which a more civilized response to crime grows out of changing attitudes and replaces the callous indifference and studied impositions of misery that mark the path behind us.

New modes of disposition that shift the emphasis from punitive satisfaction to social engagements of a more optimistic and encouraging sort are proposed and are tried, and in time become established. Alternatives to imprisonment do not raise the specter of impunity so long as they can be justified as a response to crime that is shown to be no less meritorious than imprisonment. These civilized advances must not undermine the forbidding aspect of the law and they must not offer any encouragement to predators. Neither should they leave victims with a sense of injustice when all is said and done. With regard to those who might be inclined to ignore the policies of government that the law is meant to uphold, there is no reason to believe that in general only the certain terrors of prison can prevent them from pursuing their own selfish ends heedless of the law. What I suggest is that nothing more is needed than the existence of the institution itself, functioning robustly as part of a credible system of enforceable laws, in order to prevent the collapse into social chaos that justifies the institution's existence in the first place, but with opportunities for the continuing elimination of punitive elements at the top of its moral agenda. Political morality requires us to recognize that the practices that decent people are ashamed of are never an enduring necessity, and it requires us to work as best we can to bring about their abandonment.

Postscript: Reconceiving Response to Crime

Throughout the book imprisonment has served as the paradigm of criminal punishment, with putting people in prison for their crimes the practice needing to be justified. This is hardly surprising. Imprisonment, after all, is foremost in everyone's mind as punishment for crime. Throughout the world incarceration is the standard response to those crimes that make us sit up and take notice, with time in prison serving as the standard measure of punishment in penal legislation and in the sentences passed on those who are convicted of crime. Though doing time for a crime is a commonplace notion of what justice requires, even a superficial acquaintance with what is then being inflicted on fellow human beings can leave one in no doubt about the need for its justification.

There are of course alternatives to prison that avoid the worst of its evils and can even confer genuine benefits. Many of these alternatives do not violate basic human rights, or do so to an extent far less disturbing than imprisonment. Even within the strange world of prisons, there are many different varieties. In some of them people serving their time are encouraged to live as normal a life as their limited autonomy will permit, with punitive elements banished from normal prison life and significant periods of time allowed outside of prison to limit the damage that prison normally produces.

Alternatives to prison are many and varied. They include community service, which makes clear that the perpetrator is not getting away with his crime, while at the same time sparing the public purse a considerable expense, and in addition often consists of work that is of genuine public benefit. Monitored confinement at home or monitored activity elsewhere is another possibility. A considerable literature and some experimentation

has explored the feasibility of what is known as restorative justice, consist-
ing of negotiated arrangements between perpetrator and victim to provide
victim satisfaction, which makes normal criminal proceedings unnecessary or provides a private means of disposition after such proceedings.
There is also the possibility of court-ordered acts of reparation or, where
the law allows it, public humiliation, as when the perpetrator is required to
stand in a public place with a sign announcing his offense. Monetary penalties in the form of fines have a pedigree at least as venerable as imprisonment, and there are various other sorts of deprivation, such as confiscation
of property, loss of voting rights, or loss of the right to have a driver's license. Court orders can be made requiring attendance at a clinic or partici-
pation in some other sort of program designed to deal with a problem
thought to be a cause of criminal behavior. And of course there may be
sentences of imprisonment that are suspended pending good behavior.

Each of these alternatives to imprisonment has the forbidding authority of the law backing it up. The perpetrator of a crime has landed in the
clutches of the law, and a failure to cooperate when cooperation is required can still mean going to prison.

But which of these alternatives are punishments? The question will
seem important to anyone who believes that crimes must be punished. If
a response turns out not to be punishment, then the crime has been left
unpunished, which will not be acceptable. Even for the more modest
position I wish to defend, unpunished crime might seem to raise a dis-
quieting specter of impunity. The quest is for a touchstone of the punitive element that might or might not exist in any practice.

The infliction of pain or unpleasantness seems at first sight a perfectly
serviceable description of what is both necessary and sufficient. The term
"hard treatment" has come into vogue and has been identified with dep-
rivations rather than the exertions suggested by "hard labor". This too
seems at first sight a perfectly plausible description. The trouble is that
both descriptions tend to undermine the aims of enlightened penology,
which accepts that crimes are to be punished, but which seeks to allow
for the introduction of alternatives to imprisonment that minimize the
punitive element, and encourages largely non-punitive prison regimes
when imprisonment is necessary.

I want to suggest a radical reorientation in understanding our response
to crime. It calls for placing emphasis on the feelings we have in response

to crime. I have spoken earlier about the fear, anger, resentment, and indignation that in very broad terms suggest the complex emotional state that a crime produces not only in victims but in all those who allow themselves to react to it emotionally. This is not a passive state. We are disposed to move inexorably in vengeful, vindictive, and punitive directions in our thoughts and feelings. The suffering of unrequited love pales by comparison with the torment of unrequited crime, and so we must have the institution of criminal punishment in order to frustrate the unacceptable consequences of impunity. But of course not all crimes of the same sort produce the same feelings when the full circumstances are brought to light. A response that may seem to be virtual impunity for one crime may seem not at all an unreasonable response for a similar crime when all of its circumstances are considered.

In deciding on how to respond to a crime, as in much else, reason is indeed the slave of the passions.* But reason is the kind of slave that was not uncommon in the ancient world, a mentor that enlightens its master and produces those thoughts and feelings that reflect one's better self. Among the various options that are available in deciding how to deal with someone who has committed a crime there are some that are frankly punitive. Their distinctive mark is their ability to forestall the turbulent emotions that impunity would produce. Other options might be described as quasi-punitive or even pseudo-punitive, depending on the sort of balance that is struck between the daunting prospect of impunity and the countervailing considerations that political morality in a decent society must weigh in the balance. When the circumstances of the crime are such that impunity seems irrelevant, options are available that are starkly non-punitive. There is then an opportunity for the state to require a person who has come into its clutches through his crime to do or to undergo what is best for that person in any case, or perhaps an opportunity for the state simply to issue a suitable warning.

Reconceived in this way, our response to crime must take its full circumstances into consideration and then decide how great a defection from a punitive response is possible without exciting the demons of impunity. Indeed, it is *the justification of punitivity in each case*, rather than the justification of the institution of punishment, that is the overriding moral challenge, and a challenge to be met not by theorists, but by those who dispose of the lives of others in response to a crime.

Notes

PREFACE

p vii   *The concept of morality*

The elucidation of the concept of morality seems especially important to prevent impostors from assuming the paramount position occupied by moral principles. Whatever their origins may be, authentic moral propositions have by general agreement a loftier standing than other kinds of normative propositions. What is needed is a way of distinguishing the genuine article from other sorts of principles that guide us in deciding what we ought to do and in judging what is right and what is wrong. These other principles guide us when, for example, health or safety is an issue, when we exercise vocational skills, or play games, or need guidance in the etiquette of personal relations, the arts of war, or the techniques of law enforcement—and indeed in all of the many other departments of life in which there is a right way and a wrong way of doing things. There is also the matter of understanding *why* the moral position seems always entitled to speak *de haut en bas* when decisions must be made that threaten a collision between the moral position and some other perfectly respectable position based on principles of another sort.

p viii   *St Augustine's dilemma about time*

The quoted passage is in the *Confessions*, Book xi.

CHAPTER 1

p 2   *Impunity on such a grand scale means that life as we know it in civilized society cannot exist, or so we have very good reason to believe*

I know of no credible argument that contradicts what I suggest would be the consequences of universal impunity. AC Ewing expressed a view that is widely shared by many who would like to see an end to punishment if only that were possible. "It seems strange that a kind of action which under ordinary circumstances would be regarded as the very extreme of moral depravity, should become a virtue in the case of punishment" (*The Morality of Punishment* (1929) 29). Yet the many proposals for dispensing with punishment in special circumstances where this seems possible all stop short of advocating total abolition, which, I believe, is a silent acknowledgement of the unacceptable consequences that would follow. There are, of course, utopian proposals for the abolition of punishment which assume the existence of social conditions and attitudes radically different from our own, and are therefore outside the field of present concerns. An impressive abolitionist argument strictly on moral grounds is David Boonin's *The Problem of Punishment* (2008). But even Boonin by implication concedes a right to punish in extreme circumstances. "Many people will agree that if the stakes are high enough, this [imprisonment of an innocent person] can be permissible" (p 48).

p 6   *The total abolition of punishment*

The dilemma presented by the institution of punishment in many ways resembles the dilemma about the institution of slavery that exercised Thomas Jefferson when he said the South had "the wolf by the ears". It could neither safely hold it, nor let it go (Letter from Thomas Jefferson to John Holmes, 22 April 1820, in Thomas Jefferson, *Writings*, Library of America edn (1984) 1434).

CHAPTER 2

p 7   *Punishing crime is a moral imperative of the greatest importance*

Perhaps the most striking statement of this position is the famous passage in Kant's *Philosophy of Law* (W Hastie trans, 1887) 198: "Even if a Civil Society decided to dissolve itself with the consent of all its members... the last murderer lying in the prison ought to be executed before the resolution was carried out. This ought to be done in order that everyone may realize the desert of his deeds, and that blood-guiltlessness may not remain upon the people".

p 8   *The more extreme and less extreme versions of retributivism*

An example of the version that sees no need for justification of punishment because it is morally inseparable from crime is Bousanquet's view: "The violation of right within a moral community has called forth a shudder of repudiation which is at the same time a reflex stroke and shock directed against the guilty person" (Bernard Bousanquet, *Some Suggestions in Ethics* (1918) 193). Inseparability on metaphysical grounds is represented by Hegel's notion that "crime, as the product of a negative will, carries with it its own negation or punishment" (*Philosophy of Right*, (SW Dyde trans, 1896) s 101. A logical argument for inseparability is contained in Kant's assertion that "No one undergoes punishment because he has willed to be punished, but because he has willed a punishable action" (ibid 201). The less extreme forms of retributivism are discussed in Chapter 5.

p 9   *Justice Brennan's statement regarding proof beyond a reasonable doubt*

In Re Winship 397 US 358, 363 (1970).

p 11   *Strict scrutiny and compelling governmental interest*

This doctrine had its origins in a famous footnote in *United States v Carolene Products Co* 304 US 144, 152 n 4 (1938). For a fuller discussion of this doctrine, see LH Tribe, *American Constitutional Law* (2nd edn, 1988) 1451–66. For an illuminating discussion of the possible application of strict scrutiny to laws prescribing imprisonment, see SF Colb, "Freedom from Incarceration: Why is This Right Different from All Other Rights?" 69 NYU L Rev 781 (1994).

p 12   *A lower standard of equal protection for prisoners*

A full discussion of the more restrictive position taken by the courts and created by Congressional legislation can be found in "The Law of Prisons" (2002) 115 Harv L Rev 1838; "The Least among Us: Unconstitutional Changes in Prisoner Litigation under the Prison Litigation Reform Act of 1995" (1997) 47 Duke LJ 117; R S Jeffrey, "Restricting Prisoners' Equal Access to the Federal Courts: The Three Strikes Provision of the Prison Litigation Reform Act and Substantive Equal Protection" (2001) 49 Buff L Rev 1099.

p 12   *Evolving standards of decency and challenges based on higher standards*

Chief Justice Warren's oft-quoted statement appears in *Trop v Dulles* 356 US 86, 101 (1958).

p 13   *Unacceptable conditions of confinement*

The passive smoking case is *Helling v McKinney* 509 US 25 (1993).

p 13   *Eighth Amendment objection to disproportionately great punishment*

The Supreme Court has recognized that the cruel and unusual punishment clause encompassed a proportionality principle. See eg *Weens v United States* 217 US 349 (1910); *Rummel v Estelle* 445 US 263, 271–4 and n 11 (1979); *Hutto v Davis* 454 US 370, 374 and n 3 (1982); *Solem v Helm* 463 US 277 (1983). Whatever the purpose of punishment might be, there is implicit recognition that excessive punishment is the key to its being disproportionate, and being more than necessary to serve its purpose is the key to its being excessive. In *Harmelin v Michigan* 501 US 957 (1991), the Court's opinion, written by Justice Scalia, on an historical interpretation of the text, rejected the argument that in non-capital cases there was a proportionality principle under the Eighth Amendment. Three of the Justices were of the view that only "grossly disproportionate" sentences were prohibited under the Eighth Amendment. The minority dissenting opinion pointed out that since the Eighth Amendment provides that "excessive bail shall not be required, nor excessive fines imposed, nor cruel and unusual punishment inflicted", there is an implicit ban on excessive punishment, which again clearly means more than is necessary for the purposes at hand. In *Harmelin*, the defendant had been convicted of possession of 672 grams of cocaine under a Michigan law imposing a mandatory life sentence without parole for possession of more than 670 grams. (It is hard to imagine how a jury in a properly defended case could be convinced beyond a reasonable doubt that the defendant was two grams over the limit.)

For further discussion of proportionality see Steven Grossman "Proportionality in Non-Capital Sentencing: The Supreme Court's Tortured Approach to Cruel and Unusual Punishment", (1995) 84 KY LJ 107; Nancy J King, "Portioning Punishment: Constitutional Limits on Successive and Excessive Penalties" (1995) 144 U Pa L Rev 101, which broadens the issues to include successive punishments achieved by fragmenting conduct and then having proceedings under a number of different legal provisions of different sorts.

p 13   *Capital Punishment cases as a basis for objection to unnecessary punishment*

Capital punishment was determined to be cruel and unusual punishment by *Furman v Georgia* 408 US 238 (1972), and was resurrected subject to certain conditions being met by *Gregg v Georgia* 428 US 153 (1976). The excerpt from Justice Brennan's opinion in Furman appears at 272–3.

p 15   *The requirements for the defense of self-defense*

The statement that appears here is a considerable oversimplification since there are different requirements in different jurisdictions, and most especially with reference to the question of whether, and under what circumstances, retreat is required. But the taking of an aggressor's life, like the infliction of criminal punishment, needs justification by a showing of dire necessity because of the value of life in the one case, and the value of what basic human rights protect, in the other. For an excellent survey of the law in various jurisdictions and a careful analysis of the underlying jurisprudence, see Fiona Leverick, *Killing in Self-Defence* (2006). The European Convention on Human Rights, Article 2(2), provides that "Deprivation of life shall not be regarded as inflicted in contravention of this Article when it results from the use of force *which is no more than absolutely necessary*: (a) in defence of any person from unlawful violence..." (emphasis added).

p 15   *The rationale for allowing the defense of self-defense*

The issues that arise in connection with a right to life are discussed in Andrew Ashworth, "Self-Defence and the Right to Life" (1975) 34 Crim LJ 282.

CHAPTER 3

p 22   *Fundamental human rights*

Further illumination regarding the concept and its sources can be found in James W Nickel, *Making Sense of Human Rights* (1987); Carlos Santiago Nino, *The Ethics of Human Rights* (1991), Brian Orend, *Human Rights: Concept and Context* (2002); Michael J Perry, *Toward a Theory of Human Rights* (2007). It would be a mistake, however, to suppose that recognition of such basic human rights is a phenomenon of the modern era. Thomas Hobbes, for example, recognized them in these words:

And therefore there be some Rights, which no man can be understood by any words, or other signes, to have abandoned, or transferred. As first a man cannot lay down the right of resisting them, that assault him by force, to take away his life; because he cannot be understood to ayme thereby, at any Good to himselfe. The same may be sayd of Wounds, and Chayns, and Imprisonment...(Thomas Hobbes, *Leviathan* (1651), (CB Macpherson, ed, 1985) 192)

CHAPTER 4

p 29 *The uncertainty that disqualifies general deterrence*

An excellent selection from the vast literature discussing the evidence and the underlying issues appears in A von Hirsch and A Ashworth, *Principled Sentencing: Reading on Theory and Policy* (2nd edn, 1998) 86–7.

p 30 *Kant on the limits of punishment*

This statement appears in *Philosophy of Law* (W Hastie trans, 1887) 197.

p 30 *Kant on using a person to gain benefits through punishment*

"Legal punishment may never be inflicted on a criminal only as an instrument to achieve some good for the criminal himself or for civil society...for a man may never be used just as a means to the ends of another..." (ibid). But for Kant, it is not wrong to use a person as a means if he freely consents because he benefits from the ends for which he is used, or because his own ends require that he allow himself to be used by others. It is an interesting question whether punishment violates Kant's interdiction when it is to "annul the crime", or, in Kant's famous example, when the reason for it is "that blood-guiltlessness may not remain upon the people".

p 32 *Conclusions about dangerousness are at best speculative*

A comprehensive selection of references to the voluminous literature on incapacitation can be found in A von Hirsch and A Ashworth, *Principled Sentencing: Readings On Theory and Policy* (2nd edn, 1998) 138–40. Selections in that volume, at 88–136, illuminate the important issues in attempting to predict dangerousness and proceeding to act on such predictions.

p 32 *Objection to determinations of criminal dangerousness among the population at large*

Despite strenuous objections in principle, such statistical or pseudo-statistical generalizations silently insinuate themselves not only in sentencing decisions but in legislative decisions to criminalize certain activities that typically are carried on by persons of a certain age, race, social class, etc, where the activity criminalized is not itself dangerous but its criminalization is thought to be a means of thwarting the dangerous tendencies of members of the particular group that is being targeted. In addition to sentencing and criminal legislation, notions of supposed dangerousness of members of a particular group prompt laws that deprive members of that group of their freedom, as, for example, internment of Japanese American citizens during the Second World War.

p 33   *The expressive rationale for punishment*

Bentham's happy phrase for punishment that is explicitly expressive was "instructive ignominy". At one extreme, there is punishment that is obvious in its relation to the crime, such as the practice under Germanic law of removing the tongue of the false accuser or the right hand of the perjurer (see F Pollack and FW Maitland, *History of English Law*, vol 2, 1895). At the other extreme, what is expressed by punishment is an attitude toward crime, and in particular an attitude that passes moral judgment (see, for example, Andrew von Hirsch's discussions of censure in *Censure and Sanctions* (1993)). These extremes represent, respectively, the symbolic and non-symbolic forms that punishment may take in its expressive mode. A most illuminating work on the expressive aspect of punishment is Joel Feinberg's "The Expressive Function of Punishment" in his *Doing and Deserving* (1970.)

p 34   *Reformation and rehabilitation*

A comprehensive selection of items in the literature can be found in A von Hirsch and A Ashworth, *Principled Sentencing: Readings on Theory and Policy* (2nd edn, 1998) 42–3.

p 36   *Economic theories of crime and punishment*

The position amounting to a demurrer regarding the question of justification is exhibited in the work of the leading legal economic theorist, Richard Posner. See his "An Economic Theory of Criminal Law" (1985) 85 Colum L Rev 1193, and his *Economic Analysis of Law* (2nd edn, 1977) ch7, and *passim*.

CHAPTER 5

p 38   *Crime punishable as moral wrongdoing*

Among many modern writers who in various ways espouse such a position are Nicola Lacey, *State Punishment: Political Principles and Community Values* (1988) ch 8; Robert Nozick, *Philosophical Explanations* (1981) 374–80; Jean Hampton, "The Moral Education Theory of Punishment" (1984) 13 *Philosophy & Public Affairs* 208–38; Herbert Morris, "A Paternalistic Theory of Punishment" (1981)

18 *American Philosophical Quarterly* 263–71. Interesting points of criticism are made by Jeffrie G Murphy in "Retributivism, Moral Education, and the Liberal State" (1985) 4 Crim Justice Ethics 3–11 in n 17. Good critical discussion appears in David Boonin's *The Problem of Punishment* (2008) 180–92.

p 40 *Punishment as payment of a debt*

John Mackie discusses the "pay back" theory of punishment in "Retributivism: A Test Case for Ethical Objectivity" appearing in H Gross and J Feinberg (eds), *Philosophy of Law* (3rd edn, 1986) 622–9. John Cottingham, in a survey of the various uses to which the idea of retribution has been put, considers "paying back" to be the basic sense of retribution. He points out that Pauline doctrine had made the suffering of Christ a payment for the offenses of mankind, which perhaps points to the primal notion at the heart of retributivism. J Cottingham, "Varieties of Retribution" (1979) 29 *Philosophical Quarterly* 238–46.

p 41 *Punishment providing satisfaction for victims and for the public*

In recent times, prominence has been given to involvement of victims in decisions concerning prosecutions, appropriate sentence, and parole, with the aim of providing victim satisfaction. An illuminating critical discussion of the issues in the context of "victim impact statements" is A Ashworth's "Victim Impact Statements and Sentencing" (1993) Crim L Rev 498–509. More general discussion can be found in Paul Rock, *Constructing Victims' Rights* (2004).

p 41 *Punishment as a means of redressing unfairness*

This general view has been advanced by many writers, and perhaps most notably by H Morris in "Persons and Punishment" (1968) 52 *The Monist* 475–501; and G Sher, *Desert* (1987). An excellent critical survey is presented by D Boonin in *The Problem of Punishment* (2008) 120–43.

p 45 *Punishment as annulment*

It is Hegel who makes annulment explicitly the aim of punishment, declaring that to punish "is to annul the crime, which otherwise would have been held valid, and to restore the right". Hegel's *Philosophy of Right* (TM Knox trans, 1942) 69. Kant's most famous pronouncement concerning punishment stresses annulment when he says that a society that has decided to dissolve itself must execute the last murderer lying in prison before carrying out the dissolution "that blood-guiltlessness may not remain upon the people". Kant, *Philosophy of Law* (W Hastie trans, 1887) 198. But more generally, it is uncertain just what Kant's theory of punishment might be. See JG Murphy, "Does Kant Have a Theory of Punishment?"(1987) 87 Colum L Rev 509. However, arguing that Kant does have a complete and consistent theory of punishment, see BS Byrd, "Kant's Theory of Punishment: Deterrence in its Threat, Retribution in its Execution" (1989) 8 *Law and Philosophy* 151.

p 45   *A theory of lèse majesté*

Punishment justified as a response to the wrongdoer's lèse majesté appears in J Kleinig, "Punishment and Moral Seriousness" (1991) 25 Israel L Rev 401, 416–18. This same sort of theory, but emphasizing a humbling of the will, is to be found in H Fingarette, "Punishment and Suffering" (1977) 50 Proceedings and Addresses of the American Philosophical Association 499, 509–11. Kleinig draws support from Hegel's metaphysics, while Fingarette draws his inspiration from Kant. Another anti-defiance theory is to be found in J Hampton, "Mens Rea" (1990) 7 *Social Philosophy and Policy* 1–28; and a more explicitly lèse majesté version in "The Retributive Idea" in J Hampton and JG Murphy, *Forgiveness and Mercy* (1988) 111, 130–1.

p 46   *Justification of punishment by the cumulative force of everything that can be said in its favor*

The quoted passage is from John Gardner's essay "Crime in Proportion and in Perspective" in A Ashworth and M Wasik (eds), *Fundamentals of Sentencing Theory* (1998) 32. The same point is made by Gardner in "The Functions and Justifications of Criminal Law and Punishment" in his *Offences and Defences* (2007). My difference with Gardner on this point stands in marked contrast to the very large areas in which I find myself in general agreement with what he has to say.

CHAPTER 6

p 53   *The illusions of proportionality*

The ongoing struggle to make the punishment fit the crime, and to find ways of ensuring that this is done, occupies a vast literature that has been admirably collected in a bibliography that appears in A von Hirsch and A Ashworth, *Principled Sentencing: Readings on Theory and Policy* (2nd edn, 1998) 209–10.

p 53   *The problem of disparity*

Thoughtful works addressing this problem are ME Frankel, *Criminal Sentences: Law without Order* (1972); DA Thomas, *Principles of Sentencing* (2nd edn, 1979); A Ashworth, "Four Techniques for Reducing Sentencing Disparity" in A von Hirsch and A Ashworth, *Principled Sentencing: Readings on Theory and Policy* (2nd edn, 1998) 227–39.

CHAPTER 7

p 58   *Joel Feinberg's work*

His discussion of offenses is found in his *Offense to Others* (1985), the second volume of his four-volume study *The Moral Limits of the Criminal Law*, a monumental work exploring the concept of harm and related matters in criminal jurisprudence.

p 65   *The harm in rape*

For extended discussions, see J Gardner and S Shute, "The Wrongness of Rape" in J Horden (ed), *Oxford Essays in Jurisprudence* (4th series, 2000), reprinted in J Gardner, *Offences and Defences* (2000) 1–32; and also M Davis, "Setting Penalties: What Does Rape Deserve?" (1984) 3 Law and Philosophy 61–110.

p 69   *The morally binding undertaking of the good citizen*

An unfairness argument might be seen lurking in the wings here, to the effect that others who abide by these laws that confer no general benefit and afford no general protection suffer a disadvantage by virtue of their compliance, and that this is unfair. An argument of this sort has been dealt with in Chapter 5.

CHAPTER 8

p 72   *Claiming conduct was culpable denies that it was not blameworthy*

Interpreting an assertion of culpability in this rather odd way is really less strange that it may seem. It is meant to move the center of gravity from the assumption that conduct's culpability is something about the conduct over and above what appears on its face. Instead, I am locating the ascription of culpability at the point where (in one form or another) the response "But I'm not to blame" is commonly made in answer to an accusation.

p 74   *Proposed explanations for difference in punishment of attempts and completed crimes*

Michael Davis has suggested that the difference can be understood by analogy to an auction of licenses to commit crimes. A full discussion, with references to Davis's exposition, appears in R A Duff, "Auctions, Lotteries, and the Punishment of Attempts" (1990) 9 Law and Philosophy 1, 3–17. David Lewis has proposed the "penal lottery" explanation (D Lewis, "The Punishment that Leaves Something to Chance" (1989) 18 *Philosophy & Public Affairs* 53), which is also discussed critically in Duff's article at 17–30. In his article, at 30–37, Duff argues that the difference in punishment can be explained by the difference in the seriousness of the attempt and the completed crime because of the harmful consequences of the latter, the seriousness being an important part of what is to be communicated by punishment. Duff discusses his communicative theory of punishment and how it provides support for the more severe punishment of completed crimes in his *Criminal Attempts* (1996) 351–54.

p 74   *Plato regarding punishment for attempts*

Plato, *Laws,* Book ix, 877. Plato insists the perpetrator of an intended murder that did not succeed must submit to trial for murder, and does not deserve to be pitied. But out of respect for the divinely inspired good fortune of both perpetrator and victim, the perpetrator is not made to suffer the death penalty, but is instead only exiled for life, and is also liable for any injury he has caused the victim.

p 74   *Adam Smith regarding punishment for attempts*

Adam Smith, *Lectures on Jurisprudence* (RL Meek, DD Raphael, and PG Stein eds, 1978) 138. Smith recognizes the apparently universal practice of imposing a lesser punishment for the attempt, though he does not give his unqualified endorsement, saying "With regard to the guilt of the offender, there can be no difference", and goes on to say that the offender is equally dangerous whether successful or not.

p 75   *Being affected more by what has happened that by what has been done*

There is of course no suggestion here that feelings of grievance that arise in response to what has happened should determine the extent of punishment, but only that the difference between punishment for the completed crime and for the attempt is justifiable by reference to the effect upon feelings of what has or has not happened.

p 75   *Assessing the conduct must take into account all of its elements*

I am taking an objective view of the threat (not risk) of harm, since that must be the basis on which conduct is judged, and it is conduct that must be judged in determining criminal liability. If the perpetrator knows his gun is not loaded, his conduct is different because it threatens the less serious harm of simply frightening the victim. Confusion on this point is prompted by introducing the concept of risk, since the risk of harm is the same whether or not the perpetrator knows that the gun is unloaded. But it is not the likelihood of the harm occurring on a particular occasion—the risk—that matters. It is the character of the conduct (which comprehends what the actor believes) that interests the criminal law, and which is best expressed as the threat of harm (not the risk) it poses.

p 76   *Impossible attempts*

The many other issues that arise in cases of attempting the impossible and in the theoretical excursions that they encourage are explored with particular thoroughness in RA Duff, *Criminal Attempts* (1996) 76–115, 154–65, 206–33.

p 77   *The threshold of attempt liability*

An extended discussion of this topic is contained in RA Duff, *Criminal Attempts* (1996) 33–75.

p 79   *Model Penal Code degrees of culpability*

The four designations and their defining terms are found in the Model Penal Code (Official Draft and Revised Comments) (1985) sec 2.02.

CHAPTER 9

p 86   *The formula for culpability*

The formula proposed warrants blaming only prima facie. It might be the case that a person had a duty to exercise control to avoid or prevent the untoward occurrence, but was unaware that he had such a duty in circumstances in which it would be unreasonable to expect him to be aware of having such a duty. Or it might be that he failed to exercise that control in circumstances that justified his forbearance. It should also be noted that he still might be deemed culpable if he lacked the requisite ability as a result of acts of his that were themselves culpable in the circumstances.

It should also be noted that condition (1) provides in general terms the grounds of excuse when the condition is not satisfied; and condition (2) provides in general terms the grounds of justification when that condition is not satisfied.

p 90   *Choice of evils*

This general justification is recognized in the Model Penal Code (Official Draft and Revised Comments) (1985) sec 3.02.

p 91   *Homicide provisions in the Model Penal Code*

Murder is defined and discussed in sec 210.2; manslaughter in sec 210.3; and negligent homicide in sec 210.4. Model Penal Code and Commentaries (1980).

CHAPTER 10

p 105   *Tom Wicker's understanding of "with intent to cause acts of violence"*

New York Times (22 January 1970) 36.

p 107   *The Lady Eldon cases*

The original case appears in Wharton, *Criminal Law*, vol 1 (12th edn, 1932) 304 n 9. The variation appears in SH Kadish and MG Paulson, *Criminal Law and its Processes* (3rd edn, 1975) 365.

p 110   *Mrs Hyam's case*

This much discussed case is *Hyam v DPP* [1974] 2 WLR 607, HL.

CHAPTER 11

p 114   *Character providing a foundation for inculpation and exculpation*

Acting out of character as exculpatory is a corollary of the more general proposition that a criminal act is simply evidence of bad character, and it is the bad character that is the true basis of criminal liability. "Character theorists" abound in the literature (a representative selection appears in Some Further

References), some of them taking their inspiration from Hume's discussion of virtue and vice in *A Treatise of Human Nature* (1740), where actions have their moral significance only as "A sign of some quality or character" of the person.

p 114 *A more limited effect of character on judgments of inculpation and exculpation*

See DM Kahan and MC Nussbaum, "Two Conceptions of Emotion In Criminal Law" (1996) 96 Colum L Rev 269 for an illuminating discussion of the issues raised here.

p 120 *The impeachment of President Clinton*

For a comprehensive account of this affair, see M McLoughlin (ed), *The Impeachment and Trial of President Clinton* (1999).

p 121 *Justice Scalia's dissenting opinion*

Morrison v Olson 487 US 654, 697–734, especially 727–32. The excerpt from Attorney General Jackson's address is at 727–8, a powerful statement of how the vast discretion with which any prosecutor is endowed may easily be turned into an instrument of persecution directed against people who are unpopular or are considered in some way undesirable.

p 122 *Hate crimes*

In *Wisconsin v Mitchell* 508 US 476 (1993), the United States Supreme Court unanimously upheld a conviction under a Wisconsin statute providing for an enhanced penalty for an attack that was, in essence, a hate crime. In this high profile case, which attracted amicus submissions to the Court from dozens of states and many national organizations, a young white boy had been beaten unconscious by black youths because of his race. The court rejected the contention that it is the assailants' racial bias or animus that is being punished by the enhanced sentence, but said the statute

singles out for enhancement bias-inspired conduct because this conduct is thought to inflict greater individual and societal harm . . . bias-motivated crimes are more likely to provoke retaliatory crimes, inflict distinct emotional harms on their victims, and incite community unrest (at 487–8).

p 124 *Quoted passage explaining defense of mental abnormality*

RA Duff, "Choice, Character and Criminal Liability" (1993) 12 Law and Philosophy 345, 360.

p 127 *Capacity and fair opportunity to choose*

Capacity and fair opportunity are discussed with characteristic insight by HLA Hart in the essays appearing in his *Punishment and Responsibility* (1968) 21–4, 181–3, 227–30.

CHAPTER 12

p 131 *Considerations extraneous to the crime that has been committed*

The occasion of sentencing is regularly used by the sentencing judge to pass judgment on the offender rather than the crime. In the United States, even the Constitution is not allowed to stand in the way. It is common practice in both Federal and State courts to consider prior conduct for which the defendant has been previously tried and acquitted as grounds for enhancing his sentence, though plainly this flies in the face of the Fifth Amendment's protection against double jeopardy and the Sixth Amendment's guarantee of a jury trial. It is also common practice at the sentencing stage to enhance a sentence by counting against the offender certain items of conduct with which he had not been charged because it was felt there was insufficient evidence for a conviction, again clearly an affront to the Constitutional jury trial guarantee. The longer sentence that is regularly imposed as a penalty for choosing to go to trial instead of pleading guilty is another common practice that undermines the guarantee of a jury trial. Failure to express remorse, and utterances inconsistent with remorse, are regularly invoked to enhance a sentence, though this ignores the Fifth Amendment privilege against self-incrimination, as well as violating the First Amendment protection of free speech, which extends to not having to express oneself. Finally, the Due Process Clause stands as a challenge to the very common practice of enhancing sentences because of supposed future dangerousness, that is, imposing punishment for what it is supposed one might do in the future, not just for what one has already done. For a full discussion of these issues, see CB Hessick and FA Hessick, "Recognizing Constitutional Rights at Sentencing" (2011) 99 Cal L Rev 47.

p 136 *Sentencing guidelines*

The most ambitious of the American sentencing guidelines is the Federal Sentencing Guidelines, which went into effect in the Federal Courts in November 1987. Sentencing Guidelines have been recommended by the American Law Institute and the American Bar Association, and nearly half the states have their own guidelines for sentencing in state courts. The principal purpose is to eliminate arbitrariness and unwarranted disparity in sentences. This includes parole board decisions, which are eliminated by federal guidelines legislation. In *United States v Booker* 543 US 220 (2005), the requirement that Federal judges at the sentencing stage make Federal Guideline calculations regarding features of an offense that may increase the sentence beyond the statutory maximum for the crime was held to be unconstitutional as a violation of the Sixth Amendment's guarantee of trial by jury since these features had not been proved beyond a reasonable doubt nor had they been admitted by the defendant. The Guidelines, however, continue to have an advisory status. In invoking Constitutional objections, *Booker* applied Supreme Court decisions in previous cases concerned with state guidelines to the Federal Sentencing Guidelines. For a powerful critique of the Federal Sentencing Guidelines and an illuminating discussion of guideline problems generally, see K Stith and JA Cabranes, *Fear of Judging: Sentencing Guidelines in Federal Courts* (1998).

   p 138   *The multiple rape case*

Director of Public Prosecutions v Morgan [1975] 2 All ER 347, HL. The core issue was whether an honest belief in the woman's willingness to have intercourse was sufficient as a defense, or whether the belief had to be reasonable as well.

   p 139   *Pre-emptive self-defense*

The gist of the problem is how much credit to give to the state of mind of the actor in a situation whose dangers are ambiguous, and yet it is not unreasonable to say of the action taken "better safe than sorry". The dilemma presented itself in a much discussed New York case in which a white passenger on a New York City subway was confronted in a rather menacing setting by four black youths whom he summarily proceeded to shoot. The full range of issues in this case is discussed in GP Fletcher, *A Crime of Self-Defense: Bernhard Goetz and the Law on Trial* (1998).

   p 139   *Acts of self-preservation*

Cannibalism to stay alive in a lifeboat is the subject of the famous English case of *Dudley and Stephens* (1884) 14 QBD 273. Cannibalism to prevent death by starvation in a cave is the basis of a well-known fictional case, invented with considerable factual and jurisprudential embellishment by Professor Lon Fuller. LL Fuller, "The Case of the Speluncean Explorers" (1949) 62 Harv L Rev 616.

   p 141   *Hobbes on impossibility of abandoning right of self-defense*

Hobbes, *De Cive* (1651) (English version, H Warrender ed, 1983) 58–9.

   p 141   *Waldron's hypothetical case*

This appears in an article that discusses present issues in a most illuminating way, drawing on the work of Hobbes, Locke, and Sanford Kadish. J Waldron, "Self-Defense: Agent-Neutral and Agent-Relative Accounts" (2000) 88 Cal L Rev 711, 714, 729.

CHAPTER 13

   p 148   *Great majority of cases disposed of mainly through plea bargaining and other mechanisms*

Exact numbers are hard to determine, since it is often not clear what, precisely, influenced a guilty plea. Normally at least 90 per cent of cases are disposed of in this way at the pleading stage. The defendant's perceived likelihood of conviction is one factor determining his plea, as is anxiety about the trial itself. But most prominent at this stage is the "bargain" routinely on offer from the prosecution for reduced charges and/or reduced sentence in exchange for a guilty plea. Apart from the terms of the particular bargain, there is normally on general offer a reduced sentence for an early guilty plea, along with a standing threat of a longer sentence if convicted after trial. The sheer perversity of fulfilling this threat is obvious when one considers that it amounts to saying "Since you have put us to needless expense by insisting on a trial, we now choose to incur a great deal more needless expense by keeping you in prison for a longer time".

p 149 *Confessions are manifestly unreliable*

False confessions are not at all unusual, nor, as popularly imagined, are they mainly the result of some sort of brutality by the police. All of us know from our own experience the momentary feelings of irrational anxiety followed by an exaggerated complaisance when approached by the police. Many suspects are especially vulnerable psychologically, not least because the people targeted by the police in criminal investigations are often people who suffer some psychological disability not unconnected to the margins of society in which they live. Any of us, even the most robust personalities among us, are manipulable in a police interrogation, where the tactics employed derive their strength ultimately from our awareness of the awesome power that the police have over us. Of course we do have a right to remain silent, but our fear of remaining silent was nicely captured by Jeremy Bentham's observation, which applies to innocent and guilty alike. "Silence . . . on the part of the affrighted culprit, seems to his ear to call for vengeance; confession holds out a chance for indulgence" (J Bentham, *Rationale of Judicial Evidence*, vol 5 (1827) 134).

p 150 *Confessions preserved as knockout evidence*

A confession has an overwhelming effect on a jury, for what could be more convincing than the person who knows most about the crime declaring against his own deepest interest that he committed it, with any later retraction when the pressure is off being treated dismissively by the jury as "He would say that, wouldn't he!" Both the likelihood of false confession and its immense impact on a jury are recognized in the English requirement that to be admissible a challenged confession must be proved by the prosecution *beyond a reasonable doubt* not to have been obtained by oppression of the person who made it, and not obtained in consequence of anything likely to render it unreliable, such proof to be made before a judge in the absence of the jury. In the United States, where the need is greater, the law is far less diligent in affording protection.

Judicial concern is expressed about the need to balance the law enforcement interest in gaining convictions against the need to prevent abuse of police powers. The landmark Supreme Court decision in *Miranda v Arizona* 384 US 436 (1966), in an opinion written by Chief Justice Warren, held that custodial interrogation by the police is "inherently coercive", and extended the Fifth Amendment privilege against self-incrimination to create rights of silence and legal representation during interrogation, though exceptions recognized in subsequent Supreme Court cases, which most often adopt a balancing rationale, have whittled down these protections.

But neither the English nor the American legal systems have confronted the fundamental objections to confessions emanating from police interrogation while in custody. There are in fact three good reasons why such confessions should be summarily declared inadmissible if retracted by the defendant. First, and more generally, the privilege against self-incrimination makes it impossible for a defendant to be called as a witness and examined by the prosecution in court, even though the fact of open court and the rules that govern examination of witnesses protect them from all of the objectionable features of police interrogation. Even the Court itself may not conduct such an examination. Why, then, should a very broad license be given to the police to extract self-incriminating statements behind the closed doors of interrogation rooms in police stations when such an undertaking is deemed beyond the pale even if carried out with the ample protection afforded by court proceedings? Second, a confession is hearsay evidence, since it is a statement offered for its truth, yet not made by someone who is a witness in court and so subject to cross-examination. It is said to be admissible as an exception to the rule excluding hearsay evidence in accordance with a principle in the law of evidence which allows such exceptions if the evidence is deemed both necessary and reliable. But in fact, if the confession is retracted, it is neither necessary nor reliable: not necessary because it is the retraction that is the best evidence of what the defendant has to say about whether or not he is guilty; and not reliable because it has been retracted, not frivolously but presumably because of the notorious conditions under which it was made. A retracted confession therefore has the status of inadmissible hearsay. Third, a confession, like a plea, is in essence a performative act, not a disclosure of information. A retraction is similarly a performative act which has the effect of nullifying the confession, just as changing one's plea from guilty to not guilty has the effect of nullifying the guilty plea. A retracted confession, which is a nullity, has no probative value and will have a prejudicial effect upon a jury if it is introduced in evidence. There are of course further issues concerning when it is that an admission constitutes a confession and not simply a damaging disclosure, but these issues need not be pursued here.

p 150   *Eyewitness identification a notorious source of miscarriages of justice*

The most persuasive kind of testimonial evidence that can be presented to a jury is a disinterested witness who says "Yes, that's the man I saw doing it". There are two principal reasons why such evidence is notoriously unreliable. Numerous studies have established that people's memories of what they saw are amazingly unreliable, and furthermore, what they think they saw at the time is itself very often subject to misperception. The other reason is that, in seeking eyewitness identification of a suspect, the police will often lead witnesses in a show of helpfulness, with witnesses for their part anxious to help the forces of law and order in their fight against crime. Identification parades are discussed here, but more notorious forms of identification are witness-suspect confrontations (known as "showups"), usually employed when there is no opportunity for an ID parade (for example, when a witness is critically ill in hospital), or else at the scene of the crime in its immediate aftermath. Another identification procedure is photographic identification, in which the witness is shown an array of photos (or sometimes just one picture). Both the confrontation and the photo procedures provide greater opportunity for the witness to be directed in the desired directions by the police, either overtly or by the very fact of a suspect being identified as such when there is a confrontation. A fuller picture of all these matters is to be found in Some Further References on this topic that follows these Notes.

p 153   *Obtaining testimony of a reluctant witness by promises or threats*

It is standard practice for such witnesses to be asked in cross-examination whether they have been offered anything for the testimony they are giving, and for the witnesses to answer in the negative. A particularly absurd situation is presented when a "jailhouse informant", a person who is a fellow prisoner, testifies that the defendant has admitted to him that he committed the crime, and says that he is simply testifying because he thought it important to do so, even though it is a notorious fact that such a witness (a "jailhouse snitch" of the most despised sort) puts himself in danger of the most extreme retaliation. In all these cases of suspect witnesses giving evidence, it is within the court's power to require police and prosecution to state under oath that they have no knowledge of any attempt to procure the witness's testimony by promises or threats, but in fact judges regularly allow the testimony without any interference in spite of, or perhaps because of, the notoriety of the methods of obtaining it.

p 156   *A large number of people who are not guilty spend time in prison*

I speak here only of those who are wrongly convicted, though there are huge numbers of unconvicted persons languishing in prison on remand for unconscionable periods awaiting a trial date or other disposition of their cases. A comprehensive discussion of the many additional issues implicated in the problem of wrongful convictions appears in Daniel Givelber's "Meaningless Acquittals, Meaningful Convictions: Do We Reliably Acquit the Innocent?" (1997) 49 Rutgers L Rev 1317.

p 158   *Right to remain silent has been compromised in England*

The legislation is the Criminal Justice and Public Order Act 1994, secs 34–8. But this legislation delivers an even nastier shock to criminal jurisprudence. Under sec 35, the judge must ask defendant's counsel in open court whether the defendant has been informed of his right to testify, and informed of the adverse inferences that may be drawn from his failure to testify. This of course flies in the face of the fundamental principle of Anglo-American jurisprudence, which has the burden of proving the accusation resting entirely with those who make the accusation, a principle bolstered by the traditional requirement that a judge must caution a jury *not* to make the very inference that this legislation encourages the jury to make.

p 158   *Measures enacted in England in 2003*

The Criminal Justice Act 2003 is an egregious example of a law designed to facilitate convictability, and for that reason I have chosen to give it the critical examination it receives here, albeit hardly a comprehensive critique. In particular, I do not discuss the radical revision of the law regarding hearsay evidence, which has the baleful effect of allowing in prosecution evidence which cannot be challenged by cross-examination. Apart from evidence of a propensity to commit a crime of the sort at issue and a propensity to be untruthful, I also do not discuss the provisions for admitting evidence of bad character, a drastic revision of the law which opens the door to just the sort of speculative inferences about people and what they might do that previously the law has been careful to guard against because it is notoriously unreliable when judged by the standards of a proceeding that requires proof beyond a reasonable doubt, and because there is a clear possibility that it will excite prejudice in the minds of jurors, regardless of any cautionary instructions from the judge.

It is worth quoting from the inaugural speech of the Chairman of the Bar Council in which he addressed the pending Bill.

Indeed, as things stand with the Bill, the Government is neither tough on crime nor tough on the causes of crime, to borrow an expression. It is tough on people's basic rights. Tough on the right to a jury trial in a serious case. Tough on the right to a fair trial. And tough on the presumption of innocence. Tampering with the scales of justice will never solve the crime problem. It will make it easier to convict the wrong person for an offence. We are working closely with Justice, Liberty, the Legal Action Group and the Law Society in lobbying for changes to the Bill. We have already lined up a powerful coalition in the House of Commons against the Government's proposals. The All-party Home Affairs Select Committee. The Conservative and Liberal Democrat frontbenches.

There will be an intense battle in the Lords as well. And the Home Secretary should not waste his breath on lectures about it being his democratic duty to strip away people's rights. The public did not vote to abolish jury trial and to create miscarriages of justice. Democracy is a borrowed book in the hands of the politician. It is not the Home Secretary's right to tear out its pages.

The Bill survived with its controversial provisions intact despite strong opposition.

p 158   *Double jeopardy when there is compelling new evidence*

The legislation allowing this is the Criminal Justice Act 2003, Part 10. But the quite formidable conditions to be met for quashing a previous acquittal does not prevent police and prosecution from using the threat of a possible second trial as an intimidating tactic to extract guilty pleas from people they have targeted, as I suggest. This is where serious mischief is likely to occur and where greater concern should be directed. The formidable conditions to be met before an acquittal can be quashed are not likely to be part of the calculations of a suspect being pressured to plead guilty. All he knows is that acquittals are now unsafe; indeed, he may well think the weaker the prosecution case now, the greater the likelihood of an acquittal being quashed in the indefinite future when a stronger case can be put together. The vast majority of cases are in fact disposed of at the pleading stage, and it is the threat of one's acquittal being quashed in the future if one decides to stand trial now that is helpful in gaining convictions, which of course is the overriding objective.

p 158   *Jury trials curtailed by the 2003 Act*

Part 7 of the Criminal Justice Act 2003 is the enabling legislation.

p 159   *Exploitation of deep-seated prejudices*

See sec 103 of the Criminal Justice Act 2003.

p 159   *Evidence of defendant's propensity to be untruthful*

This hardly believable amendment of English criminal jurisprudence would, of course, seriously undermine any attempt by a defendant who has such evidence introduced against him to challenge any dubious evidence introduced against him by the prosecution.

The Law Commission had previously considered this provision and rejected it, stating:

We take the view, however, that the defendant's general propensity to be untruthful is not a matter which it would be fair to allow the prosecution to assert as part of its case against the defendant. Where the defendant simply denies the truth of some or all of the prosecution's evidence in relation to the offence charged, and makes no attempt to attack anyone else's credibility, we think it virtually inconceivable that evidence of the defendant's general untruthfulness could ever have sufficient probative value to outweigh the risk of prejudice.

See A Keogh, *Criminal Justice Act 2003* (2004) at 65–6.

The unfairness of this provision appears even more remarkable when one considers that evidence of a general propensity to be untruthful is made admissible in this legislation only against the defendant, while no corresponding provision is made under this reform of the common law for prosecution witnesses (for whom there is no issue of prejudice to concern the court) to be shown to be habitual liars.

POSTSCRIPT

p 176   *Reason is the slave of the passions*

This echoes Hume's famous dictum: "Reason is, and ought only to be the slave of the passions, and can never pretend to any other office than to serve and obey them". But I am suggesting service may include enlightened mentoring, and obedience may then be to the enlightened passions. The passage from Hume is in *A Treatise of Human Nature*, edited by LA Selby-Bigge (1958) at 415.

Some Further References

Readers may wish to become better acquainted with topics that were addressed in the book quite sparingly, just to meet the needs of particular arguments. The literature is vast and what follows is a selection of items not already mentioned in the Notes, intended to shed more light on the fascinating and troubling issues that crime and punishment comprehend. There is no pretense here of a comprehensive scholarly bibliography. I have limited in a somewhat arbitrary fashion the number of items listed for each topic, which has meant that a good deal of deserving work has not been included. The ambitious reader will of course find further references to such work in the works that have been included. I might add that innovative theoretical work is often heedless of topical boundaries, which means that readers may sometimes find themselves learning more than they had bargained for.

Attempts

Bayles, MD, 'Punishment for Attempts' (1982) 8 *Social Theory and Practice* 19.
Becker, LC, 'Criminal Attempts and the Theory of the Law of Crimes' (1974) 3 Philosophy & Public Affairs 262.
Brady, JB, 'Punishing Attempts' (1980) 63 *The Monist* 246.
Crocker, L, 'Justice in Criminal Liability: Decriminalizing Harmless Attempts' (1992) 53 Ohio St LJ 1057.
Davis, M, 'Why Attempts Deserve Less Punishment than Complete Crimes' in M Davis (ed), *To Make the Punishment Fit the Crime* (1992) 101.
Dennis, IH, 'Preliminary Crimes and Impossibility' (1978) 31 Current Legal Problems 31.
Duff, RA, 'Auctions, Lotteries, and the Punishments of Attempts' (1990) 9 Law and Philosophy 1.
—— 'Attempts and the Problem of the Missing Circumstance' (1991) 42 Northern Ireland L Quarterly 87.
—— *Criminal Attempts* (1996).
Elkind, J, 'Impossibility in Criminal Attempts: A Theorist's Headache' (1968) 54 Virginia LR 20.
Feinberg, J, 'Criminal Attempts: Equal Punishment for Failed Attempts' in J Feinberg, *Problems at the Roots of Law* (2003).
Fletcher, G, 'Constructing a Theory of Impossible Attempts' in P Fitzgerald (ed), *Crime, Justice and Codification* (1986) 87.
Glazebrook, PR, 'Should we have a Law of Attempted Crimes?' (1969) 85 L Quarterly Rev 28.

Hart, HLA, 'The House of Lords on Attempting the Impossible' in HLA Hart, *Essays in Jurisprudence and Philosophy* (1983) 367.

Hasnas, J, 'Once More unto the Breach: The Inherent Liberalism of the Criminal Law and Liability for Attempting the Impossible' (2002) 54 Hastings LJ 1.

Herman, B, 'Feinberg on Luck and Failed Attempts' (1995) 37 Arizona L Rev 143.

Hogan, B, 'The Criminal Attempts Act and Attempting the Impossible' (1984) Crim LR 584.

Horder, J, 'Varieties of Intention, Criminal Attempts and Endangerment' (1994) 14 Legal Studies 335.

Jareborg, N, 'Criminal Attempts and Moral Luck' (1993) 27 Israel L Rev 213.

Lewis, D, 'The Punishment that Leaves Something to Chance' (1989) 18 Philosophy & Public Affairs 53.

Skilton, RH, 'The Mental Element in a Criminal Attempt' (1937) 3 U of Pittsburgh L Rev 181.

Smith, JC, 'Two Problems in Criminal Attempts' (1957) 70 Harv L Rev 422.

Spjut, RJ, 'When is an Attempt to Commit an Impossible Crime a Criminal Act?' (1987) 29 Arizona L Rev 247.

Stannard, JE, 'Making Up for the Missing Element: A Sideways Look at Attempts' (1987) 7 Legal Studies 194.

Stuart, D, 'The Actus Reus in Attempts' (1970) Crim LR 505.

Westen, P, 'Impossibility Attempts: A Speculative Thesis' (2008) 5 Ohio State J of Crim L 523.

Williams, G, 'The Problem of Reckless Attempts' (1983) Crim LR 365.

—— 'Wrong Turnings in the Law of Attempts' (1991) Crim LR 416.

Crime

Ashworth, A, 'Defining Criminal Offences without Harm' in P Smith (ed), *Criminal Law: Essays in Honour of JC Smith* (1987) 7.

Clarkson, CMV, 'General Endangerment Offences: The Way Forward?' (2005) 32 U of Western Australia L Rev 1.

Dubber, MD, 'The Possession Paradigm: The Special Part and the Police Model of the Criminal Process' in RA Duff and SP Green (eds), *Defining Crimes: Essays on the Special Part of the Criminal Law* (2005) 91.

Duff, RA, 'Crime, Prohibition and Punishment' (2002) 19 J of Applied Philosophy 97.

—— 'Virtue, Vice and Criminal Liability: Do We Want an Aristotelian Criminal Law?' (2002) 6 Buff Crim L Rev 147.

—— 'Action, the Act Requirement and Criminal Liability' in J Hyman and H Steward (eds), *Agency and Action* (2004) 69.

—— 'Criminalizing Endangerment' (2005) 65 Louisiana L Rev 941.

—— and Marshall SE, 'How Offensive Can You Get?' in AP Simester and A von Hirsch (eds), *Incivilities: Regulating Offensive Behaviour* (2005) 57.

Feinberg, J, *Harm to Others* (1984).

—— *Offense to Others* (1985).

—— *Harm to Self* (1986).

—— *Harmless Wrongdoing* (1988).

Finkelstein, CO, 'Is Risk a Harm?' (2003) 151 U Pa L Rev 963.

Garvey, SP, 'What's Wrong with Involuntary Manslaughter?' (2006) 85 Tex L Rev 333.

Goldberg, SB, 'Morals-Based Justifications for Lawmaking: Before and After Lawrence v Texas' (2004) 88 Minnesota L Rev 1233.

Goldman, A, 'Action and Crime: A Fine-Grained Approach' (1994) 142 U Pa L Rev 1563.

Gray, RL, 'Eliminating the (Absurd) Distinction between Malum in Se and Malum Prohibitum Crimes' (1995) 73 Washington U L Quarterly 1369.

Green, SP, 'Why it's a Crime to Tear the Tag off a Mattress: Over-Criminalization and the Moral Content of Regulatory Offenses' (1997) 46 Emory Law J 1533.

—— 'Lying, Misleading and Falsely Denying: How Moral Concepts Inform the Law of Perjury, Fraud, and False Statements' (2001) 53 Hastings LJ 157.

—— *Lying, Cheating, and Stealing: A Moral Theory of White-Collar Crime* (2006).

Hall, J, 'Negligent Behavior Should be Excluded from Penal Liability' (1963) 63 Colum L Rev 632.

Harcourt, BE, 'The Collapse of the Harm Principle' (1999) 90 J of Crim L & Criminology 109.

Hart, HLA, 'Negligence, Mens Rea, and Criminal Responsibility', in HLA Hart, *Punishment and Responsibility* (1968) 136.

—— 'Punishment and the Elimination of Responsibility' in HLA Hart, *Punishment and Responsibility* (1968) 158.

—— 'Morality and Reality' (1979) 9 March, *New York Review of Books* 35.

Horder, J, 'The Classification of Crimes and the Special Part of the Criminal Law' in RA Duff and SP Green (eds), *Defining Crimes: Essays on the Special Part of the Criminal Law* (2005) 21.

Husak, DN, 'Crimes outside the Core' (2004) 39 Tulsa L Rev 755.

—— '*Malum Prohibitum* and Retributivism' in RA Duff and SP Green (eds), *Defining Crimes: Essays on the Special Part of the Criminal Law* (2005) 65.

—— *Overcriminalization: The Limits of the Criminal Law* (2008).

—— 'Does Criminal Liability Require an Act?' in D Husak, *The Philosophy of Criminal Law* (2010) 17.

Kahan, D, 'The Anatomy of Disgust in Criminal Law' (1998) 96 Mich L Rev 1651.

Kleinig, J, 'Crime and the Concept of Harm' (1978) 15 American Philosophical Quarterly 32.

Moore, MS, 'More on Act and Crime' (1994) 142 U Pa L Rev 1749.

Morris, H, 'Punishment for Thoughts' in H Morris, *Guilt and Innocence* (1976) 1.

Morse, SJ, 'Neither Desert nor Disease' (1999) 5 Legal Theory 265.

Pillsbury, SH, 'Evil and the Law of Murder' (1990) 24 UC Davis L Rev 437.
—— *Judging Evil: Rethinking the Law of Murder and Manslaughter* (1998).
Ripstein, A, 'Beyond the Harm Principle' (2006) 34 Philosophy & Public Affairs 215.
Robinson, PH, 'A Theory of Justification: Societal Harm as a Prerequisite for Criminal Liability' (1975) 23 UCLA L Rev 266.
Simester, AP, 'Rethinking the Offense Principle' (2002) 8 Legal Theory 269.
—— and von Hirsch, A (eds), *Incivilities: Regulating Offensive Behaviour* (2006).
Slobogin, C, 'A Jurisprudence of Dangerousness' (2003) 98 Northwestern U L Rev 1.
von Hirsch, A, 'Extending the Harm Principle: "Remote" Harms and Fair Imputations' in AP Simester and ATH Smith (eds), *Harm and Culpability* (1996) 259.
Wilson, W, 'What's Wrong with Murder?' (2007) 1 Crim L and Philosophy 157.

Culpability and Responsibility

Alexander, L, 'Crime and Culpability' (1994) 5 J of Contemporary Legal Issues 1.
—— 'Insufficient Concern: A Unified Conception of Criminal Culpability' (2000) 88 Cal L Rev 931.
—— and Ferzan, KK, *Crime and Culpability: A Theory of Criminal Law* (2009).
Arenella, P, 'Character, Choice, and Moral Agency' (1990) 7 Social Philosophy & Policy 59.
—— 'Convicting the Morally Blameless: Reassessing the Relationship between Legal and Moral Accountability' (1992) 39 UCLA L Rev 1511.
Bayles, M, 'Character, Purpose and Criminal Responsibility' (1982) 1 Law and Philosophy 5.
Brandt, RB, 'Traits of Character: A Conceptual Analysis' (1970) 7 American Philosophical Quarterly 23.
Cohen, E, 'Distinctions among Blame Concepts' (1977) 38 Philosophy and Phenomenological Research 151.
Costa, M, 'The Trolley Problem Revisited' in JM Fischer and M Ravizza (eds), *Ethics: Problems and Principles* (1992).
Denno, DW, 'Criminal Law in a Post-Freudian World' (2005) Illinois L Rev 601.
Dressler, J, 'Does One Mens Rea Fit All? Thoughts on Alexander's Unified Conception of Criminal Culpability' (2000) 88 Cal L Rev 955.
Duff, RA, 'Choice, Character, and Criminal Liability' (1993) 12 Law and Philosophy 345.
—— 'Character and Action' in RA Duff, *Criminal Attempts* (1996) ch 7, 173.
Eldredge, L, 'Culpable Intervention as Superseding Cause' (1938) 86 U Pa L Rev 121.

Fletcher, GP, 'On the Moral Irrelevance of Bodily Movements' (1994) 142 U
Pa L Rev 1443.

Hart, HLA, 'Intention and Punishment' in HLA Hart, *Punishment and
Responsibility* (1968) 113.

Helm, P, 'Hume on Exculpation' (1967) 42 Philosophy 265.

Horder, J, 'Criminal Culpability; The Possibility of A General Theory' (1993)
12 Law and Philosophy 193.

—— 'Crimes of Ulterior Intent' in AP Simester and ATH Smith (eds), *Harm
and Culpability* (1996) 153.

—— 'On the Irrelevance of Motive in Criminal Law' in J Horder (ed), *Oxford
Essays in Jurisprudence* (4th Series, 2000) 173.

Husak, DN, 'The Sequential Principle of Relative Culpability' (1995) 1 Legal
Theory 493.

—— 'Rethinking the Act Requirement' (2007) 28 Cardozo L Rev 2437.

Lacey, N, 'The Relevance of Responsibility' in N Lacey, *State Punishment*
(1988) ch 3.

Moore, MS, 'Choice, Character, and Excuse' (1990) 7 Social Philosophy & Policy 29.

—— 'Foreseeing Harm Opaquely' in J Gardner, J Horder, and S Shute (eds),
Action and Value in Criminal Law (1993), reprinted in MS Moore, *Placing
Blame: A General Theory of the Criminal Law* (1997) 363.

—— 'The Independent Moral Significance of Wrongdoing' (1994) 5 J of
Contemporary Legal Issues 1, reprinted in MS Moore, *Placing Blame: A
General Theory of the Criminal Law* (1997) 191.

—— 'Prima Facie Moral Culpability' (1996) 76 Boston U L Rev 319.

Morris, H, 'Nonmoral Guilt' in FD Schoeman (ed), *Responsibility, Character,
and Emotions: New Essays in Moral Psychology* (1987) Pt II 9.

Morse, SJ, 'Acts, Choices, and Coercion: Culpability and Control' (1994) 142
U Pa L Rev 1587.

—— 'Culpability and Control' (1994) 142 U Pa L Rev 1587.

Nourse, V, 'Hearts and Minds: Understanding the New Culpability' (2002) 6
Buff Crim L Rev 361.

Pincoffs, EL, 'Legal Responsibility and Moral Character' (1973) 19 Wayne State
L Rev 905.

Robinson, PH, 'A Brief History of Distinctions in Criminal Culpability' (1980)
31 Hastings LJ 815.

—— 'Should the Criminal Law Abandon the Actus Reus/Mens Rea
Distinction' in S Shute, J Gardner, and J Horder (eds), *Action and Value in
Criminal Law* (1993) 187.

Simester, AP, 'Moral Certainty, and the Boundaries of Intention' (1996) 16
Oxford J of Legal Studies 445.

—— 'Can Negligence be Culpable?' in J Horder (ed), *Oxford Essays in
Jurisprudence* (4th series, 2000) 85.

Simons, KW, 'Mistake and Impossibility, Law and Fact, and Culpability: A
Speculative Essay' (1990) 81 J Crim L & Criminology 447.

—— 'Does Punishment for "Culpable Indifference" Simply Punish for "Bad Character"? Examining the Requisite Connection between Mens Rea and Actus Reus' (2002) 6 Buff Crim L Rev 219.

Solomon, RC, *Not Passion's Slave: Emotions and Choice* (2003).

Strawson, G, 'The Impossibility of Moral Responsibility' (1994) 75 Philosophical Studies 5.

Sullivan, GR, 'Intent, Subjective Recklessness and Culpability' (1992) 12 Oxford J of Legal Studies 381.

Sverdlick, S, 'Crime and Moral Luck' (1988) 25 American Philosophical Quarterly 79.

Thomson, J, 'The Trolley Problem' (1985) 94 Yale LJ 1395.

Wallace, RJ, *Responsibility and the Moral Sentiments* (1994).

Wasik, M, 'Abandoning Criminal Intent' (1980) Crim LR 785.

Watson, G, 'Responsibility and the Limits of Evil' in F Schoeman (ed), *Responsibility, Character, and the Emotions: New Essays in Moral Psychology* (1987) 256.

Desert

Andre, J, 'Nagel, Williams and Moral Luck' (1983) 43 Analysis 202.

Burgh, RW, 'Do the Guilty Deserve Punishment?' (1982) 79 J of Philosophy 193.

Carcasole, J, 'Punishment: Self-Protection and Desert' (2000) 14 Public Affairs Quarterly 225.

Davis, LH, 'They Deserve to Suffer' (1972) 32 Analysis 136.

Davis, M, 'Using the Market to Measure Deserved Punishment: A Final Defense' in M Davis (ed), *To Make the Punishment Fit the Crime* (1992) 234.

—— 'Criminal Desert, Harm, and Fairness' in M Davis (ed), *To Make the Punishment Fit the Crime* (1992) 213.

—— 'Criminal Desert and Unfair Advantage: What's the Connection?' (1993) 12 Law and Philosophy 133.

Domsky, D, 'There is No Door: Finally Solving the Problem of Moral Luck' (2004) 101 J of Philosophy 445.

Enoch, D, and Marmor, A, 'The Case against Moral Luck' (2007) 26 Law and Philosophy 405.

Fischer, JM, 'Punishment and Desert: A Reply to Dolinko' (2006) 117 Ethics 109.

Garcia, JLA, 'Two Concepts of Desert' (1986) 5 Law and Philosophy 219.

Husak, D, 'Why Punish the Deserving?' in D Husak, *The Philosophy of Criminal Law* (2010) 393.

Kershnar, S, 'George Sher's Theory of Deserved Punishment and the Victimized Wrongdoer' (1997) 23 Social Theory and Practice 75.

Kessler, KD, Comment, 'The Role of Luck in the Criminal Law' (1994) 142 U Pa L Rev 2183.

Kleinig, J, *Punishment and Desert* (1973).

Levy, K, 'The Solution to the Problem of Outcome Luck: Why Harm is Just as Punishable as the Wrongful Action that Causes it' (2005) 24 Law and Philosophy 263.

Miller, D, 'Comparative and Noncomparative Desert' in S Olsaretti (ed), *Desert and Justice* (2003) 25.

Moriarty, J, 'Against the Asymmetry of Desert' (2003) 37 Nous 518.

—— 'Ross on Desert and Punishment' (2006) 87 Pacific Philosophical Quarterly 231.

Murphy, J, 'Review of George Sher, *Desert*' (1990) 99 Philosophical Review 280.

Olsaretti, S (ed), *Desert and Justice* (2003).

Pillsbury, SH, 'The Meaning of Deserved Punishment: An Essay on Choice, Character, and Responsibility' (1992) 67 Indiana LJ 719.

Richards, N, 'Luck and Desert' (1986) 95 Mind 198.

Robinson, PH, 'Competing Conceptions of Modern Desert: Vengeful, Deontological, and Empirical' (2008) 67 Cambridge LJ 145.

Schafer-Landau, R, 'Retributivism and Desert' (2000) 81 Pacific Philosophical Quarterly 189.

Sher, G, *Desert* (1987).

—— 'Deserved Punishment Revisited' in G Sher, *Approximate Justice: Studies in Non-Ideal Theory* (1997) 165.

Statman, D, 'The Time to Punish and the Problem of Moral Luck' (1997) 14 J of Applied Philosophy 129.

Stern, L, 'Deserved Punishment, Deserved Harm, Deserved Blame' (1970) 45 Philosophy 317.

von Hirsch, A, *Doing Justice: The Choice of Punishments* (1976).

Williams, B, 'Moral Luck' in B Williams, *Moral Luck* (1981) 20.

Zimmerman, M, 'Taking Moral Luck Seriously' (2002) 99 J of Philosophy 553.

Enforcement of the Law

Alschuler AW, 'The Prosecutor's Role in Plea Bargaining' (1968) 36 U Chi L Rev 50.

—— 'Implementing The Criminal Defendant's Right To Trial: Alternatives to The Plea Bargaining System' (1983) 50 U Chi L Rev 931.

Andrews, JA, 'Uses and Misuses of the Jury' in PR Glazebrook (ed), *Reshaping the Criminal Law* (1978) 37.

Ashworth, AJ, 'Should the Police be Allowed to Use Deceptive Practices?' (1998) 114 L Quarterly Rev 108.

—— 'Article 6 and the Fairness of Trials' (1999) Crim LR 261.

—— 'Criminal Justice Act 2003, (2) Criminal Justice Reform: Principles, Human Rights and Public Protection' (2004) Crim LR 516.

—— and Blake, M, 'The Presumption of Innocence in English Criminal Law' (1996) Crim LR 306.

Baldwin, J, and McConville, M, *Negotiated Justice* (1977).

Bibas, S, 'Plea Bargaining Outside the Shadow of Trial' (2004) 117 Harv L Rev 2463.

Borchard, EM, *Convicting the Innocent: Errors of Criminal Justice* (1932).

Burns, RP, *A Theory of the Trial* (1999).

Clark, SJ, '"Who Do You Think You Are?": The Criminal Trial and Community Character' in RA Duff et al (eds), *The Trial on Trial II: Judgement and Calling to Account* (2006) 83.

Dewar, EN, Note: 'A Fair Trial Remedy for *Brady* Violations' (2006) 115 Yale LJ 1450.

Domsky, D, 'Double Jeopardy' (2006) 35 Georgetown LJ Annual Review of Criminal Procedure 422.

Driver, ED, 'Confessions and the Social Psychology of Coercion' (1968) 82 Harv L Rev 42.

Duff, RA, The Defendant's Right to Trial by Jury' (2000) Crim LR 85.

Fenwick, H, 'Procedural Rights of Victims of Crime' (1997) 60 Modern L Rev 317.

Fisher, G, 'Plea Bargaining's Triumph' (2000) 109 Yale LJ 857.

Friedland, M, *Double Jeopardy* (1969).

Garrett, BL, *Convicting the Innocent* (2011).

Grano, JD, 'Voluntariness, Free Will and the Law of Confessions' (1979) 65 Va L Rev 859.

Gross, S, 'Loss of Innocence: Eyewitness Identification and Proof of Guilt' (1987) 16 J of Legal Studies 395.

Hamer, D, 'The Expectation of Incorrect Acquittals and the "New and Compelling Evidence" Exception to Double Jeopardy' (2009) Crim LJ 63.

Innocence Project, The, 'Reevaluating Lineups: Why Witnesses Make Mistakes and How to Reduce the Chance of Misidentification' (2009). <http://www.innocenceproject.org>

Langbein, JH, 'Torture and Plea Bargaining' (1978) 46 U Chi L Rev 3.

Loftus, EF, 'Eyewitness Testimony: Psychological Research and Legal Thought' (1981) 3 Crime and Justice 105.

McConville, M, 'Videotaping Interrogations: Police Behaviour On and Off Camera' (1992) Crim LR 532.

—— 'Plea Bargaining' in M McConville and G Wilson (eds), *The Handbook of the Criminal Justice Process* (2002) 353.

—— Sanders, A, and Leng, R, *The Case for the Prosecution: Police Suspects and the Construction of Criminality* (1991).

McEwan, J, 'Ritual, Fairness and Truth: The Adversarial and Inquisitorial Models of Criminal Trial' in RA Duff et al (eds), *The Trial on Trial I: Truth and Due Process* (2004) 51.

Michaels, A, 'Constitutional Innocence' (1999) 112 Harv L Rev 828.

Mnookin, JL, 'Uncertain Bargains: The Rise of Plea Bargaining in America' (2005) 57 Stanford L Rev 1721.

Mollen Commission Report, *Report of the Commission to Investigate Allegations of Police Corruption and the Anti-Corruption Procedures of the Police Department* (1994).

Note, 'Did Your Eyes Deceive You? Expert Psychological Testimony on the Reliability of Eyewitness Identification' (1977) 29 Stan L Rev 969.

Note, 'Should We Really "Ban" Plea Bargaining?: The Core Concerns of Plea Bargaining Critics' (1998) 47 Emory LJ 773.

Phillips, M, 'The Inevitability of Punishing the Innocent' (1985) 48 Philosophical Studies 389.

Read, FT, 'Lawyers at Lineups: Constitutional Necessity or Avoidable Extravagance?' (1969) 17 UCLA L Rev 339.

Reiner, R, *The Politics of the Police* (3rd edn, 2000).

Roberts, A, and Clover, S, 'Managerialism and Myopia: The Government's Consultation Draft on PACE-Code D' (2002) Crim LR 873.

Roberts, P, 'Double Jeopardy Law Reform: A Criminal Justice Commentary' (2002) 65 MLR 393.

—— and Zuckerman, A, *Criminal Evidence* (2nd edn, 2010) ch 12, 'Confessions'; ch 13, 'The Accused's Privilege against Self-Incrimination'; ch 14 'The Accused's Character and Extraneous Misconduct'.

Rock, P, *Constructing Victims' Rights* (2004).

Rosenberg, I, and Rosenberg, Y, 'A Modest Proposal for the Abolition of Custodial Interrogation' (1989) 68 N Car L Rev 69.

Rosenthal, K, 'Prosecutor Misconduct, Convictions, and Double Jeopardy: Case Studies in an Emerging Jurisprudence' (1998) 71 Temple L Rev 887.

Ross, JE, 'The Entrenched Position of Plea Bargaining in United States Legal Practice' (2006) 54 American J of Comparative L 717.

Sanchirico, CW, 'Character Evidence and the Object of Trial' (2001) 101 Colum L Rev 1227.

Sanders, A, Young, R, and Burton, M, *Criminal Justice* (4th edn, 2010) ch 4 'Detention in the police station' 195, and ch 5 'Police questioning of suspects' 255.

—— Young, R and Burton, M, *Criminal Justice* (4th edn, 2010) ch 8, 'The mass production of guilty pleas', 438.

Schulhofer, SJ, 'Plea Bargaining as Disaster' (1992) 101 Yale LJ 1979.

Scott, RE, and Stuntz, WJ, 'Plea Bargaining as Contract' (1992) 101 Yale LJ 1909.

—— and Stuntz, WJ, 'A Reply: Imperfect Bargains, Imperfect Trials, and Innocent Defendants' (1992) 101 Yale LJ 2011.

Solan, LM, 'Refocusing the Burden of Proof in Criminal Cases: Some Doubt about Reasonable Doubt' (1999) 78 Texas L Rev 105.

Stuntz, WJ, 'Plea Bargaining and Criminal Law's Disappearing Shadow' (2004) 117 Harv L Rev 2548.

Tadros, V, and Tierney, S, 'The Presumption of Innocence and the Human Rights Act' (2004) 67 Modern L Rev 402.

Uviller, RH, 'Evidence from the Mind of the Criminal Suspect' (1987) 87 Colum L Rev 1137.

Vamos, N, 'Please Don't Call it "Plea Bargaining"' (2009) Crim LR 617.

White, WS, 'Police Trickery in Inducing Confessions' (1979) 127 U Pa L Rev 581.

Wright, RF, 'Parity of Resources for Defense Counsel and the Reach of Public Choice Theory' (2004) 90 Iowa L Rev 219.

Human Rights

Feinberg, J, 'Voluntary Euthanasia and the Inalienable Right to Life' (1978) 7 Philosophy & Public Affairs 93.

Frankena, WK, 'Natural and Inalienable Rights' (1955) 64 Philosophical Review 212.

Ignatieff, M, 'Human Rights: The Midlife Crisis' (20 May 1999) The New York Review of Books 58.

McConnell, T, 'The Nature and Basis of Inalienable Rights' (1984) 3 Law and Philosophy 25.

Melden, AI, *Human Rights* (1970).

Morsink, J, *Inherent Human Rights: Philosophical Roots of the Universal Declaration* (2009).

Nino, CS, *The Ethics of Human Rights* (1991).

Richards, DAJ, 'Human Rights and the Moral Foundations of the Substantive Criminal Law' (1979) 13 Georgia L Rev 1395.

Schauer, F, 'A Comment on the Structure of Rights' (1993) 27 Georgia L Rev 415.

Waldron, J (ed), *Theories of Rights* (1984).

Justification and Excuse

Austin, JL, 'A Plea for Excuses' in J Austin, *Philosophical Papers* (1961) 123.

Berman, M, 'Justification and Excuse, Law and Morality' (2003) 53 Duke LJ 1.

Dressler, J, 'New Thoughts About the Concept of Justification in Criminal Law' (1984) 32 UCLA L Rev 61.

—— 'Justifications and Excuses: A Brief Review of the Concepts and the Literature' (1987) 33 Wayne L Rev 1155.

—— 'Battered Women Who Kill Their Sleeping Tormentors: Reflections on Maintaining Respect for Human Life while Killing Moral Monsters' in S Shute and AP Simester (eds), *Criminal Law Theory: Doctrines of the General Part* (2002) 259.

Duff, RA, 'Rethinking Justifications' (2004) 39 Tulsa L Rev 829.

Fletcher, GP, 'Should Intolerable Prison Conditions Generate a Justification or an Excuse for Escape?' (1979) 26 UCLA L Rev 1355.

—— 'The Nature of Justifications', in S Shute, S Gardner, and J Horder (eds), *Action and Value in Criminal Law* (1993) 179.

Gardner, J, 'Justifications and Reasons' in A Simester and ATH Smith (eds), *Harm and Culpability* (1996) 103.

—— 'The Gist of Excuses' (1998) 1 Buff Crim L Rev 575.

Greenawalt, K, 'The Perplexing Borders of Justification and Excuse' (1984) 84 Colum L Rev 1897.

Hart, HLA, 'Legal Responsibility and Excuses' in HLA Hart, *Punishment and Responsibility* (1968) 28.

Hurd, HM, 'Justifiably Punishing the Justified' (1992) 90 Mich L Rev 2203.

—— 'Justification and Excuse, Wrongdoing and Culpability' (1999) 74 Notre Dame L Rev 1551.

Husak, DN, 'Conflicts of Justifications' (1999) 18 Law and Philosophy 41.

Kadish, SH, 'Excusing Crime' in S Kadish, *Blame and Punishment* (1987) 81.

Mison, RB, 'Homophobia in Manslaughter: The Homosexual Advance as Insufficient Provocation' (1992) 80 Cal L Rev 133.

Robinson, PH, 'Competing Theories of Justification: Deeds vs Reasons' in AP Simester and ATH Smith (eds), *Harm and Culpability* (1996) 54.

Simmons, AJ, *Justification and Legitimacy: Essays on Rights and Obligations* (2001).

Sullivan, R, 'Making Excuses' in A Simester and ATH Smith (eds), *Harm and Culpability* (1996) 131.

Tadros, V, 'The Characters of Excuse' (2001) 21 Oxford J of Legal Studies 495.

Westen, P, 'An Attitudinal Theory of Excuse' (2006) 25 Law and Philosophy 289.

Wolheim, R, 'Crime, Punishment, and Pale Criminality' (1988) 8 Oxford J of Legal Studies 1.

Kindred Institutions

Bagaric, M, and Clarke J, 'Not Enough Torture in the World? The Circumstances in which Torture is Morally Justifiable' (2005) 39 U of San Francisco L Rev 581.

Banner, S, *The Death Penalty: An American History* (2002).

Bedau, HA, 'The Right to Life' (1968) 52 The Monist 569.

Card, C, 'Ticking Bombs and Interrogations' (2007) 2 Crim L and Philosophy 1.

Curtis, MK, 'The Curious History of Attempts to Suppress Antislavery Speech, Press, and Petition in 1835–37' (1995) 89 Northwestern U L Rev 785.

Donohue, JJ, and Wolfers J, 'Uses and Abuses of Empirical Evidence in the Death Penalty Debate' (2005) 58 Stan L Rev 791.

Ekland, AK, 'The Death Penalty in Montana: A Violation of the Right to Individual Dignity' (2004) 65 Montana L Rev 135.

Hood, R, 'Capital Punishment' in M Tonry (ed), *The Handbook of Crime and Punishment* (1998) 739.

Kamm, FM, 'Failure of Just War Theory: Terror, Harm, and Justice' (2004) 114 Ethics 650.

Kershnar, S, *Desert, Retribution and Torture* (2001).

Langbein, JH, *Torture and the Law of Proof* (1977).

McMahan, J, 'Innocence, Self-Defense, and Killing in War' (1994) 2 J of Political Philosophy 193.

—— 'The Ethics of Killing in War' (2004) 114 Ethics 693.

Moore, MS, 'Torture and the Balance of Evils' (1989) 23 Israel L Rev 280, reprinted in MS Moore, *Placing Blame: A General Theory of the Criminal Law* (1997) 669.

Morris, TD, *Southern Slavery and the Law, 1619–1860* (1996).

Nagel, T, 'War and Massacre' (1972) 1 Philosophy & Public Affairs 123.

Rodin, D, *War and Self-Defense* (2002).

Sellin, JT, *Slavery and the Penal System* (1976).

Steiker, C, 'No, Capital Punishment is Not Morally Required: Deterrence, Deontology, and the Death Penalty' (2005) 58 Stan L Rev 751.

Steinhoff, U, 'Torture—The Case for Dirty Harry and against Alan Dershowitz' (2006) 23 J of Applied Philosophy 337.

Sunstein, CR, and Vermeule, A, 'Is Capital Punishment Morally Required? Acts, Omissions, and Life-Life Tradeoffs' (2005) 58 Stan L Rev 703.

Sussman, D, 'What is Wrong with Torture?' (2005) 33 Philosophy & Public Affairs 1.

Symposium, 'How the Death Penalty Works: Empirical Studies of the Modern Capital Sentencing System' (1998) 83 Cornell L Rev 1431.

Mental Elements

Anscombe, GEM, *Intention* (2nd edn, 1963).

Ashworth, A, 'Belief, Intent and Criminal Liability' in J Eekelaar and J Bell (eds), *Oxford Essays in Jurisprudence* (3rd Series, 1987) 1.

Brand, M, *Intending and Acting* (1984).

Dan-Cohen, M, 'Harmful Thoughts' (1999) 18 Law and Philosophy 379.

Davidson, D, 'Intending' in D Davidson, *Essays on Actions and Events* (1980) 83.

—— 'Mental Events' in D Davidson, *Essays on Actions and Events* (1980) 207.

Duff, RA, 'Intention, Mens Rea and the Law Commission Report' (1980) Crim LR 147.

Gardner, J, and Jung, H, 'Making Sense of Mens Rea: Antony Duff's Account' (1991) 11 Oxford J of Legal Studies 559.

Hornsby, J, 'On What's Intentionally Done' in S Shute, J Gardner, and J Horder (eds), *Action and Value in Criminal Law* (1993) 55.

Ryle, G, *The Concept of Mind* (1949).

Simons, KW, 'Rethinking Mental States' (1992) 72 Boston U L Rev 463.

Smith, AM, 'Responsibility for Attitudes: Activity and Passivity in Mental Life' (2005) 115 Ethics 236.

Yaffe, G, 'Conditional Intent and *Mens Rea*' (2004) 10 Legal Theory 273.

Overviews

Ashworth, A, 'Is The Criminal Law A Lost Cause?' (2000) 116 L Quarterly Rev 225.

Bennett, J, *The Act Itself* (1995).

Dressler, J, *Understanding Criminal Law* (2nd edn, 1995).

Duff, RA, *Intention, Agency and Criminal Liability* (1990).

—— (ed), *Philosophy and the Criminal Law* (1998).

Ewing, AC, *The Morality of Punishment* (1929).

Fischer, JM and Ravizza, M, *Responsibility and Control: A Theory of Moral Responsibility* (1998).

Fletcher, GP, *Rethinking Criminal Law* (1978).

—— *With Justice for Some* (1995).

—— 'Rise and Fall of Criminal Law Theory' (1998) 1 Buff Crim L Rev 275.

Foot, P, 'Are Moral Considerations Overriding?' in P Foot, *Virtues and Vices* (1978).

Foot, P, 'Morality as a System of Hypothetical Imperatives' in P Foot, *Virtues and Vices* (1978).

Frankfurt, H, 'The Problem of Action' (1978) 15 American Philosophical Quarterly 157.

Gardner, J, *Offences and Defences* (2007).

Gay, P, *The Cultivation of Hatred* (1993).

Goldman, AI, 'The Individuation of Actions' (1971) 18 J of Philosophy 761.

Gross, H, *A Theory of Criminal Justice* (1979).

Harris, DA, *Profiles in Injustice; Why Racial Profiling Cannot Work* (2002).

Horder, J, *Provocation and Responsibility* (1992).

Hospers, J, *Human Conduct* (1961).

Kadish, SH, *Blame and Punishment: Essays in Criminal Law* (1987).

Katz, L, *Bad Acts and Guilty Minds: Conundrums of the Criminal Law* (1987).

Kupperman, J, *Character* (1991).

Morris, H, *On Guilt and Innocence* (1976).

Murphy, J, and Hampton J, *Forgiveness and Mercy* (1988).

Nagel, T, 'Moral Luck' in T Nagel, *Mortal Questions* (1979) 24.

Nourse, VF, 'Reconceptualizing Criminal Law Defenses' (2003) 151 U Pa L Rev 1691.

Packer, HL, *The Limits of the Criminal Sanction* (1968).

Robinson, PH, and Cahill, MT, *Law without Justice: Why Criminal Law doesn't Give People what they Deserve* (2006).

Scanlon, T, 'The Significance of Choice' in SM McMurrin (ed), *The Tanner Lectures on Human Values* (1988) viii, 149.

Sheffler, S, *Human Morality* (1992).

Smith, JC, 'The Element of Chance in Criminal Liability' (1971) Crim LR 63.

—— *Justification and Excuse in the Criminal Law* (1989).

Stuntz, WJ, 'The Pathological Politics of Criminal Law' (2001) 100 Mich L Rev 505.

Thomson, J, *Acts and Other Events* (1977).

Tonry, M, *Thinking about Crime* (2003).

Waldron, J, 'A Right to do Wrong' (1981) 92 Ethics 21.

Whitman, JQ, *Harsh Justice: Criminal Punishment and the Widening Divide between America and Europe* (2003).

—— *The Origins of Reasonable Doubt: Theological Roots of the Criminal Trial* (2008).

Williams, B, 'Morality and the Emotions' in B Williams, *Problems of the Self* (1973) 207.

—— 'The Actus Reus of Dr Caligari' (1994) 142 U Pa L Rev 1661.

Punishment and Alternatives

Acton, HB (ed), *The Philosophy of Punishment* (1969).

Adler, MD, 'Expressive Theories of Law: A Skeptical Overview'(2000) 148 U Pa L Rev 1364.

Alexander, L, 'Consent, Punishment, and Proportionality' (1986) 15 Philosophy & Public Affairs 178.

Allen, RJ, 'Retribution in a Modern Penal Law: The Principle of Aggravated Harm' (1975) 25 Buff L Rev 1.

Ashworth, A, 'Punishment and Compensation: Victims, Offenders and the State' (1986) 6 Oxford J of Legal Studies 86.

Avio, KL, 'Economic, Retributive and Contractarian Conceptions of Punishment' (1993) 12 Law and Philosophy 249.

Bagaric, M, 'New Criminal Sanctions—Inflicting Pain through the Denial of Employment and Education' (2001) Crim LR 184.

Barton, CKB, *Getting Even: Revenge as a Form of Justice* (1999).

Becker, GS, 'Crime and Punishment: An Economic Approach' (1968) 76 J Pol Econ 169.

Bedau, HA, 'Retribution and the Theory of Punishment' (1978) 75 J of Philosophy 601.

Bennett, C, 'Taking the Sincerity out of Saying Sorry: Restorative Justice as Ritual' (2006) 23 J of Applied Philosophy 127.

Beres, LS, and Griffith, TD, 'Do Three Strikes Laws Make Sense? Habitual Offender Statutes and Criminal Incapacitation' (1998) 87 Georgetown LJ 103.

Berns, W, *The Morality of Anger* (1979).

Blanshard, B, 'Retribution Revisited' in E Madden et al (eds), *Philosophical Perspectives on Punishment* (1968) 59.

Blume, R, and Blume, D, 'The Crime of Punishment' (1989) November/December, The Humanist 12.

Bowers, J, 'Punishing the Innocent' (2008) 156 U Pa L Rev 1117.

Braithwaite, J, *Crime, Shame and Reintegration* (1989).

—— and Pettit, P, *Not Just Deserts: A Republican Theory of Criminal Justice* (1990).

Charvet, J, 'Criticism and Punishment' (1966) 75 Mind 573.

Cragg, W, *The Practice of Punishment: Towards a Theory of Restorative Justice* (1992).

Davis, M, 'How to Make the Punishment Fit the Crime' (1983) 93 Ethics 726.

—— 'Harm and Retribution' (1986) 15 Philosophy & Public Affairs 236.

Dolinko, D, 'Some Thoughts about Retributivism' (1991) 101 Ethics 537.

—— 'Mismeasuring "Unfair Advantage": A Response to Michael Davis' (1994) 13 Law and Philosophy 493.

—— 'The Future of Punishment' (1999) 46 UCLA L Rev 1719.

Dripps, DA, 'Fundamental Retribution Error: Criminal Justice and the Social Psychology of Blame' (2003) 56 Vanderbilt L Rev 1383.

Duff, RA, 'Review of Jacob Adler, The Urgings of Conscience: A Theory of Punishment' (1993) 104 Ethics 1.

—— 'Penal Communications: Recent Work in the Philosophy of Punishment' (1995) 20 Crime and Justice 1.

—— *Punishment, Communication and Community* (2001).

—— and Garland, D, *A Reader on Punishment* (1994).

Dworkin, G, and Blumenfeld, D, 'Punishment for Intentions' (1996) 75 Mind 396.

Ellis, A, 'A Deterrence Theory of Punishment' (2003) 53 The Philosophical Quarterly 337.

Farrell, DM, 'The Justification of General Deterrence' (1985) 94 Philosophical Rev 367.

—— 'The Justification of Deterrent Violence' (1990) 100 Ethics 301.

Finnis, J, 'Retribution: Punishment's Formative Aim' (1999) 44 American J of Jurisprudence 91.

Garvey, S, 'Punishment as Atonement' (1999) 46 UCLA L Rev 1801.

—— 'Can Shaming Punishments Educate?' (1998) 65 U Chi L Rev 733.

Gert, HJ, Radzik, L, and Hand, M, 'Hampton on the Expressive Power of Punishment' (2004) 35 J of Social Philosophy 79.

Hampton, J, 'The Moral Education Theory of Punishment' (1984) 13 Philosophy & Public Affairs 208.

—— 'Correcting Harms versus Righting Wrongs: The Goal of Retribution' (1992) 39 UCLA L Rev 1659.

—— 'An Expressive Theory of Retribution' in W Cragg (ed), *Retributivism and its Critics* (1992) 1.

Hare, RM, 'Punishment and Retributive Justice' (1986) 14 Philosophical Topics 211.

Hart, HLA, 'Prolegomenon to the Principles of Punishment' in HLA Hart, *Punishment and Responsibility* (1968) 1.

Hawkins, G, 'Punishment as a Moral Educator' in RJ Gerber and PD McAnany (eds), *Contemporary Punishment* (1972) 120.

Hessick, CB, 'Motives Role in Criminal Punishment' (2006) 80 Southern Cal L Rev 89.

Hoekema, D, 'Trust and Obey: Toward a New Theory of Punishment' (1991) 25 Israel L Rev 332.

Honderich, T, *Punishment: The Supposed Justifications* (1969).

Huigens K, 'The Dead End of Deterrence and Beyond' (2000) 41 William and Mary L Rev 943.

Husak, D, 'Malum Prohibitum and Retributivism' in D Husak, *The Philosophy of Criminal Law* (2010) 410.

Johnstone, G, 'Restorative Justice, Shame and Forgiveness' (1999) 21 Liverpool L Rev 197.

Kang, Y-S, 'Alternatives to Incarceration' (1998) 111 Harv L Rev 1863.

Kahan, D, 'What Do Alternative Sanctions Mean?' (1996) 63 U Chi L Rev 591.

Kasachkoff, T, 'The Criteria of Punishment: Some Neglected Considerations' (1973) 2 Canadian J of Philosophy 363.

Katyal, NK, 'Deterrence's Difficulty' (1997) 95 Mich L Rev 2385.

Kidder, J, 'A Sketch of an Integrative Theory of Punishment' (1982) 19 American Philosophical Quarterly 197.

Knowles, D, 'Punishment and Rights' in M Matravers (ed), *Punishment and Political Theory* (1999) 28.

Laquer, T, 'Festival of Punishment' (5 October 2000) London Review of Books 17.

Lewis, CS, 'The Humanitarian Theory of Punishment' in S Grupp (ed), *Theories of Punishment* (1971) 301.

Lippke, RL, 'Arguing against Inhumane and Degrading Punishment' (1998) 17 Crim Justice Ethics 29.

—— 'Criminal Offenders and Right Forfeiture' (2001) 32 J of Social Philosophy 78.

—— 'No Easy Way out: Dangerous Offenders and Preventive Detention' (2008) 27 Law and Philosophy 383.

Locke, D, 'The Many Faces of Punishment' (1963) 72 Mind 568.

McCloskey, HJ, 'The Complexity of the Concepts of Punishment' (1954) 37 Philosophy 308.

McDermott, D, 'The Permissibility of Punishment' (2001) 20 Law and Philosophy 403.

Mackie, JL, 'Morality and the Retributive Emotions' (1982) 1 Crim Justice Ethics 3.

Marshall, JD, 'Punishment and Moral Education' (1984) 13 J of Moral Education 83.

Martin, R, 'On the Logic of Justifying Legal Punishment' (1970) 7 American Philosophical Quarterly 253.

Menniger, K, *The Crime of Punishment* (1969).

Metz, T, 'Censure Theory and Intuitions about Punishment' (2000) 19 Law and Philosophy 491.

Miller, WA, 'Mr Quinton on "An Odd Sort of Right"' (1966) 41 Philosophy 258.

Montague, P, 'Recent Approaches to Justifying Punishment' (2002) 31 Philosophia 1.

Moore, MS, 'The Moral Worth of Retribution' in J Murphy (ed), *Punishment and Rehabilitation* (3rd edn, 1987) 94.
—— 'Justifying Retributivism' (1993) 27 Israel L Rev 15.
Morris, CW, 'Punishment and Loss of Moral Standing' (1991) 21 Canadian J of Philosophy 53.
Morris, H, 'Persons and Punishment' (1968) 52 The Monist 475.
—— 'A Paternalistic Theory of Punishment' (1981) 18 American Philosophical Quarterly 263.
Murphy, J, 'The Retributive Emotions' in J Murphy and J Hampton, *Forgiveness and Mercy* (1988) 1.
—— 'Hatred: A Qualified Defense' in J Murphy and J Hampton, *Forgiveness and Mercy* (1988) 88.
—— 'Getting Even: The Role of the Victim' in J Murphy, *Retribution Reconsidered* (1992) 61
—— *Getting Even: Forgiveness and its Limits* (2003).
Nino, CS, 'Does Consent Override Proportionality? (1986) 15 Philosophy & Public Affairs 183.
Oldenquist, A, 'The Case for Revenge' (1986) 82 *The Public Interest* (1986) 72.
Pillsbury, SH, 'Emotional Justice: Moralizing the Passions of Criminal Punishment' (1989) 74 Cornell L Rev 655.
Primoratz, I, 'Punishment as Language' (1989) 64 Philosophy 187.
Quinn, W, 'The Right to Threaten and the Right to Punish' in AJ Simmons et al (eds), *Punishment* (1994) 47.
Reitan, E, 'Punishment and Community: The Reintegrative Theory of Punishment' (1996) 26 Canadian J of Philosophy 57.
Roberts, JV, *The Virtual Prison* (2004).
Robinson, PH, 'Punishing Dangerousness: Cloaking Preventive Detention as Criminal Justice' (2001) 114 Harv L Rev1429.
—— and Darley, JM, 'The Role of Deterrence in the Formulation of Criminal Law Rules: At its Worst when Doing its Best' (2003) 91 Georgetown LJ 949.
—— 'Does Criminal Law Deter? A Behavioural Science Investigation' (2004) 24 Oxford J of Legal Studies 173.
Roche, D (ed), *Accountability in Restorative Justice* (2004).
Schafer, S, *Compensation and Restitution to Victims of Crime* (2nd edn, 1970).
Scheid, D, 'Constructing a Theory of Punishment, Desert, and the Distribution of Punishments' (1997) 10 Canadian J of Law and Jurisprudence (1997) 441.
Schulhofer, SJ, 'Harm and Punishment: A Critique of Emphasis on the Results of Conduct in the Criminal Law'(1974) 122 U Pa L Rev 1497.
Sendor, BB, 'The Relevance of Conduct and Character to Guilt and Punishment' (1996) 10 Notre Dame J of L, Ethics and Public Policy 99.
Simmons, AJ, 'Locke and the Right to Punish' in AJ Simmons et al (eds), *Punishment* (1994) 219.
Smilansky, S, 'Two Apparent Paradoxes about Justice and the Severity of Punishment' (1992) 30 Southern J of Philosophy 123.

Solomon, RC, 'Justice v Vengeance: On Law and the Satisfaction of Emotion' in SA Bandes (ed), *The Passions of Law* (1999) 123.

Strang, H, *Repair or Revenge: Victims and Restorative Justice* (2002).

Tasioulas, J, 'Punishment and Repentance' (2006) 81 Philosophy 279.

Ten, CL, 'Positive Retributivism' (1990) 7 Social Philosophy and Policy 194.

Tunick, M, *Punishment: Theory and Practice* (1992).

von Hirsch A, *Censure and Sanctions* (1993).

—— Roberts, J, Bottoms, AE, Roach, K, and Schiff, M (eds), *Restorative Justice and Criminal Justice: Competing or Reconcilable Paradigms?* (2003).

Waldron, J, 'Lex Talionis' (1992) 34 Ariz L Rev 25.

Walker, N, *Why Punish? Theories of Punishment Reassessed* (1993).

—— 'Even More Varieties of Retribution' (1999) 74 Philosophy 595.

Wertheimer, A, 'Deterrence and Retribution' (1976) 86 Ethics 181.

Westen, P, 'Why Criminal Harms Matter: Plato's Abiding Insight in the Laws' (2007) 1 Crim Law and Philosophy 307.

Whitman, JQ, 'What is Wrong with Inflicting Shame Sanctions' (1998) 107 Yale LJ 1055.

—— 'Making Happy Punishers', a book review of MC Nussbaum, *Hiding From Humanity: Disgust, Shame, and the Law* (2004) in (2005) 118 Harv L Rev 2698, especially 2715–24.

Wolgast, EH, 'Intolerable Wrong and Punishment' (1985) 60 Philosophy 161.

Young, R, and Goold, B, 'Restorative Police Cautioning in Aylesbury—From Degrading to Reintegrative Shaming Ceremonies?' (1999) Crim LR 126.

Self-Defense

Beale, JH, 'Retreat from a Murderous Assault' (1903) 16 Harv L Rev 567.

Christopher, R, 'Self-Defense and Defense of Others' (1998) 27 Philosophy & Public Affairs 123.

Fletcher, GP, 'Proportionality and the Psychotic Aggressor: A Vignette in Comparative Criminal Theory' (1973) 8 Israel L Rev 367.

Thomson, JJ, 'Self-Defense' (1991) 20 Philosophy & Public Affairs 283.

Uniacke, S, *Permissible Killing: The Self-Defence Justification of Homicide* (1994).

Sentencing and Imprisonment

Ashworth, A, 'Victim Impact Statements and Sentencing' (1993) Crim LR 498.

—— *Sentencing and Criminal Justice* (2nd edn, 1995).

Bagaric, M, 'Double Punishment and Punishing Character: The Unfairness of Prior Convictions' (2000) 19 Crim Justice Ethics 10.

Cole, D, 'Can Our Shameful Prisons be Reformed?' (19 November 2009) The New York Review of Books 41.

Collins, J, 'Preemptive Prevention' (2000) 97 J of Philosophy 223.

Comment, 'The Prison Litigation Reform Act: Striking the Balance between Law and Order' (1999) 44 Villanova L Rev 981.

Cross, R, 'Paradoxes in Prison Sentences' (1965) 81 L Quarterly Rev 205.

Deparle, J, 'The American Prison Nightmare' (12 April 2007) The New York Review of Books 33.

Fox, RG, 'When Justice Sheds a Tear: The Place of Mercy in Sentencing' (1999) 25 Monash U L Rev 1.

Frankel, ME, *Criminal Sentences: Law without Order* (1973).

Harding, R, 'Private Prisons' in M Tonry (ed), *The Handbook of Crime and Punishment* (1998) 626.

Leader, 'Rough Justice' in The Economist (24 July 2010) 9 and Briefing, 'Rough Justice in America' in The Economist (same issue) 23.

Lynch, M, 'Waste Managers? The New Penology, Crime Fighting, and Parole Agent Identity' (1998) 32 Law and Society Rev, especially references at 867–9.

Mears, DP, 'The Sociology of Sentencing: Reconceptualizing Decision-making Processes and Outcomes' (1998) 32 Law and Society Rev 667.

Note, 'The Constitutionality of Statutes Permitting Increased Sentences for Habitual or Dangerous Criminals' (1975) 89 Harv L Rev 356.

Note, 'The Least Among Us: Unconstitutional Changes in Prisoner Litigation under The Prison Litigation Reform Act of 1995' (1997) 47 Duke LJ 117.

Note, 'Awaiting the Mikado: Limiting Legislative Discretion to Define Criminal Elements and Sentencing Factors' (1999) 112 Harv L Rev 1349.

Nussbaum, MC, 'Equity and Mercy' (1993) 22 Philosophy & Public Affairs 83.

Ogletree, CJ, Jr, 'The Death of Discretion? Reflections on the Federal Sentencing Guidelines' (1988) 101 Harv L Rev 1938.

Shaw, GB, *The Crime of Imprisonment* (1946).

Thomas, DA, *Principles of Sentencing* (2nd edn, 1979).

Volokh, A, 'The Law of Prisons' (2002) 115 Harv L Rev 1838.

von Hirsch, A, *Past or Future Crimes* (1985).

—— and Jareborg, N, 'Gauging Criminal Harm: A Living-Standard Analysis' (1991) 11 Oxford J of Legal Studies 1.

Walker, N, *Sentencing in a Rational Society* (1969).

Zimring, FE, 'Sentencing Reform in the States: Lessons from the 1970s' in M Tonry and FE Zimring (eds), *Reform and Punishment* (1983) 101.

—— and Hawkins, G, *Incapacitation: Penal Confinement and Restraint of Crime* (1995).

Index